REDRAWING THE MAP OF EUROPE

SEVEN DAY LOAN

This book is to be returned on
or before the date stamped below

PLYMOUTH LIBRARY

Tel: (01752) 232323
This book is subject to recall if required by another reader
Books may be renewed by phone
CHARGES WILL BE MADE FOR OVERDUE BOOKS

Redrawing the Map of Europe

Michael Emerson
Centre for Economic Performance
London School of Economics and Political Science

First published in Great Britain 1998 by
MACMILLAN PRESS LTD
Houndmills, Basingstoke, Hampshire RG21 6XS and London
Companies and representatives throughout the world

A catalogue record for this book is available from the British Library.

ISBN 0–333–73446–7 hardcover
ISBN 0–333–73447–5 paperback

 First published in the United States of America 1998 by
ST. MARTIN'S PRESS, INC.,
Scholarly and Reference Division,
175 Fifth Avenue, New York, N.Y. 10010

ISBN 0–312–21697–1

Library of Congress Cataloging-in-Publication Data
Emerson, Michael.
Redrawing the map of Europe / Michael Emerson.
p.   cm.
Includes bibliographical references and index.
ISBN 0–312–21697–1 (cloth)
1. Europe—Politics and government—1989–   I. Title.
D2009.E49   1998
940.55'9—dc21

98–21461
CIP

for Elena

Contents

Contents

List of Tables, Figures and Appendix

xii

List of maps

Glossary

CIS	Commonwealth of Independent States, Minsk and Moscow
CFSP	Common Foreign and Security Policy of the EU
CJTF	Combined Joint Task Forces (of NATO)
Council of Europe	
	40 European member states, Strasbourg
CSCE (now OSCE)	
	Conference on Security and Cooperation in Europe, Vienna
EBRD	European Bank for Reconstruction and Development, London
ECHR	European Court of Human Rights, Strasbourg
EC	European Community, Brussels, Luxembourg and Strasbourg
ECB	European Central Bank, Frankfurt
ECOFIN	EU Council of ministers of economics and finance
EEA	European Economic Area
EEC	European Economic Community
EFTA	European Free Trade Association, Geneva
EMS	European Monetary System
ESDI	European Security and Defence Identity (of NATO)
EU	European Union, Brussels, Luxembourg and Strasbourg
European Council	
	Summit meetings of heads of state or government of the EU
EUROPOL	European Police Office (of EU), Amsterdam

GATT (now WTO)
                General Agreement on Trade and Tariffs, Geneva
HCNM   High Commissioner for National Minorities (of
                OSCE)
NATO   North Atlantic Treaty Organisation, Brussels
ODIHR   Office for Democratic Institutions and Human Rights
                of OSCE, Warsaw
OECD   Organisation for Economic Cooperation and
                Development, Paris
OEEC (now OECD)
                Organisation for European Economic Cooperation,
                Paris
OSCE   Organisation for Security and Cooperation in Europe,
                Vienna
WEU   West European Union, Brussels
WTO   World Trade Organisation, Geneva

Acknowledgments

I am indebted to Professor Richard Layard, Director of the Centre for Economic Performance of the London School of Economics for his invitation to work in the Centre and for his constant encouragement. Richard is one of those remarkable people, who, with one short sentence, can set one off on a big personal venture. In my case it went something like this: "Michael, why not come to the Centre and write a book about the future of Europe?"

The Centre and the LSE are a wonderful environment to undertake such a project, because of the School's extraordinary strength in all the social sciences, crammed into one tiny corner of London town. Typical of the architectural heritage of the London School of Economics and Political Science, the Centre for Economic Performance inhabits a modest space in the attic on top of the library. But that doesn't matter, because the atmosphere of friendly interest and stimulation is all that you notice.

I also benefitted from the support of many colleagues and would like to mention specially Adam Lubanski, Lucie Mathews and Anita Bardham-Roy for IT help; Marion O'Brien, who is the guardian angel of the Centre; and Jane Pugh of the Cartographic Unit of the LSE, who prepared all the maps.

I am indebted to correspondents, friends and colleagues who read the draft, spotted errors and gave me useful advice, notably: Alison Bayles, Jorge Braga de Macedo, Laurence-Jan Brinkhorst, Stanley Crossick, Sir Roy Denman, Andrew Duff, Daniel Gros, Markus Haaker, Nigel Haig, Martin Harvey, David Held, Irene Heidelberger-Leonard, Anthony Giddens, Richard Layard, Peter Ludlow, Mathias Mors, Thomas Ouchterlony, Diego Puga, Max van der Stoel and

Daniel Tarchys.

Thanks are due to the following for kind permission to reproduce published material: G.Brunner and the Bertelsmann Foundation Publishers, *"Nationality Problems and Minority Conflict in Eastern Europe"* [1996], R.Sivard and World Priorities Inc, *"World Military and Social Expenditures, 1996"* [1996]; J.Kay and Oxford University Press, *"Foundations of Corporate Success"* [1993], and D. Held and Polity Press, *"Democracy and the Global Order"* [1995].

Finally, I much appreciated the friendly help of Sunder Katwala and Lesley Steward of Macmillan.

But the story of Europe never stops, of course. Nowadays every month seems to produce events that will leave some mark, big or small, on "Redrawing the Map of Europe". In closing this book , the events of the last month have for example included, in the West, the decision to start the euro with 11 initial participating countries and peace in Northern Ireland; to the East, less happily, virtually civil war in Kosovo, a Turkey manifesting its bitterness over exclusion from EU accession negotiations and a Russia whose democracy shows itself to be still all too fragile. Deepening and widening proceed apace in the West but there is as yet no sign of a deepening of the widest Europe. This warns of trouble in due course.

London and Brussels, May 1998

The Main Argument

1. The questions

What is the map of Europe going to look like in the first decades of the 21st century? What does it really mean to be talking about the future map of Europe? Are our political leaders leading the process adequately? Indeed, do our political leaders really direct the process or are there stronger underlying forces shaping the trend?

2. The underlying forces

There are two underlying forces: integration and conflict. Europe, it seems, has a unique capacity not only for integration processes that can achieve the highest level of multi-cultural civilisation, but also for relapses into episodes of the bloodiest savagery that world history ever saw. So it has been in the 20th century, as it was also in medieval times. The underlying dynamics of integration, which stem from history mingled in with contemporary politics and economics, are very strong as the millennium closes. For the moment, across most of Europe, integration is progressively dominating and gradually extinguishing tendencies towards violent conflict. But this triumph is neither complete nor secure.

3. Maps and rules

We are concerned with the practical business of the governance of Europe, and the definition of the new order for the greater Europe of 800 million people, not just the European Union whose prospective enlargement will carry its population to around 500 million. Our redrawing of the map of Europe is based on the areas of jurisdiction of the political and economic rules that are essential for a civilised, secure and prosperous Europe. More precisely, we focus attention on eight sets of rules, four political and four economic, which may be regarded as the key components of the constitution of Europe:

Political	*- rules of democracy*
	- human rights
	- rights of ethnic minorities
	- rules of inter-state behaviour
Economic	*- rules for open markets*
	- rules for macroeconomic stability
	- rules of the social model
	- rules of corporate governance

5. Organisations

Most of these rules have been codified by the European Union and/or the Council of Europe, the OSCE, and other agencies. One can discuss the improvement of some of these codes, for example the social model, but taken as a whole they are already a capital investment in the infrastructure of modern European civilisation.

However the organisation and management of Europe's rules have grown up in a haphazard way, each innovation being the product of particular historical circumstances. Diversity and even competition among Europe's organisations offer some advantages. But this *ad hoc* development has created a system which now finds itself with two serious problems of inconsistency and incompleteness, and which Europe will neglect at its peril.

Alternative paradigms of federalism and cosmopolitan democracy struggle to hold sway over the emerging organisation of the system of rules of the new Europe, largely displacing old-fashioned nationalism, which has no future. Compromises are possible between these paradigms, indeed they are evident. But still the system has yet to face up to two major, concrete problems, which are obstacles in the way of a successful entry by Europe civilisation into the new century.

6. Problem No 1 - the euro and the inconsistent quartet

The euro will doubtless keep inflation away. It will also surely transform European geo-politics. But for the euro system to function well over a long period it will have to find a sound balance between its four policy components (monetary, budgetary, labour market and regional redistribution policies), so as to assure an adequate capacity for adjustment as well as stabilisation. This is especially critical in the core countries, which start out with high unemployment, such as France and Germany. Since the monetary and budgetary rules are being addressed first of all to stabilisation, and the redistribution instruments will remain modest by the standards of existing federations, then the labour market is going to have to acquire a greater adjustment capacity than exists in most of the core Europe. The Rhineland model has to be reformed accordingly, as has been seen already in the Netherlands but not yet in Belgium, France and Germany. Without such reform the quality and wider appeal of the euro system will be seriously at risk.

This problem is not impossibly far away from solution. At least it is much debated and now subject of a considerable degree of consensus among economists.

7. Problem No 2 - the order for the wider Europe

The maps of jurisdictions of the rules, beyond the European Union, are heterogeneous and incomplete, to the point that Europe's big outsiders (Russia, Ukraine and Turkey) do not know where they are going as a matter of national and societal destiny. Are they to be really part of Europe and its civilisation or not? This hiatus amounts to a grave fault in the European system. It is a danger for European stability and security, as well as for the countries concerned.

This problem is especially serious because the European Union does not presently find time and energy to think seriously beyond its euro and enlargement agenda, while the three "big outsiders" are preoccupied either with the travails of their transitions in the case of Russia and the Ukraine, or, in the case of Turkey, by the Islamic challenge to the secular state. We therefore advance a proposal ourselves for a new political initiative, under which all European democracies (i.e. members of the Council of Europe) would act to give coherence and synergetic strength to a set of rules for the wider European order. We give this proposed initiative a name, the "European Civil Society", and its mechanisms are set out below in Chapters 6 and 7.

8. What will become the main map of Europe?

There are four alternatives currently jockeying for position:

- *Two-block Europe*, with a European Union and associates, including the Euro-Med area on the one hand, and a Russian-led CIS including Central Asia on the other.

- *Brussels Europe*. Beyond the EU there is no other, wider European map of real coherence. Non-EU countries are a geo-political no-man's land.

- *Security Europe*, with the widest map of the OSCE, including the US and all the former USSR, and with a strong NATO core.

- *Civil Europe*, with the wide European map of the Council of Europe and a strong EU core.

At the present time the weakest of these contenders is the last, but this is the most desirable one for the long-run future of Europe, which is why the proposal for the "European Civil Society" is made.

9. Widening the deep Europe and deepening the wide

It is neither necessary nor desirable for Europe to agonise over the future frontiers of the European Union, which unfortunately is the only kind of map many people inside and outside the EU seem interested in at present. Better, for the first decades of the 21st century, envisage both a widening of the deep Europe and a deepening of the wide Europe, with the two processes deliberately converging. Whether the two would ultimately merge together into one would remain a mystery for the future to reveal. But at least those who want to go in that direction should have an idea and a structure to work with.

Maps

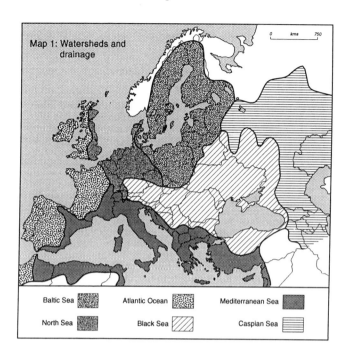

Map 1: Watersheds and drainage

Baltic Sea		Atlantic Ocean		Mediterranean Sea	
North Sea		Black Sea		Caspian Sea	

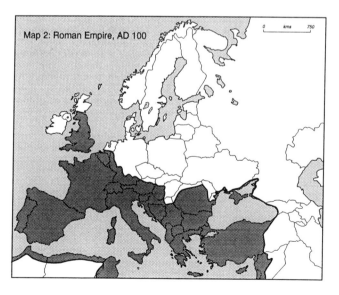

Map 2: Roman Empire, AD 100

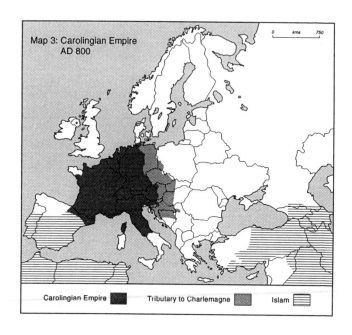

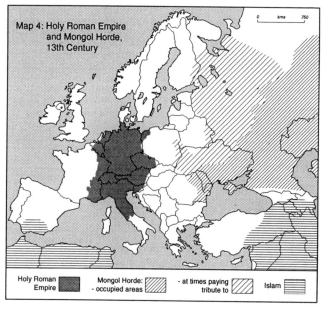

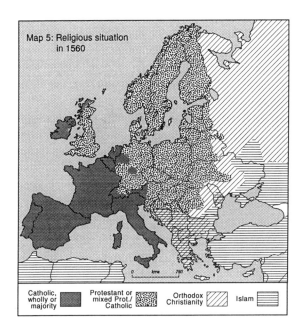

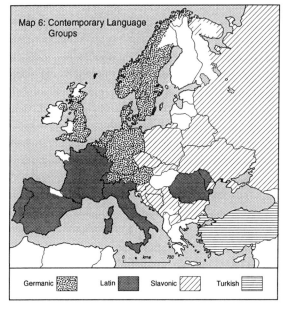

xxvi   *Maps*

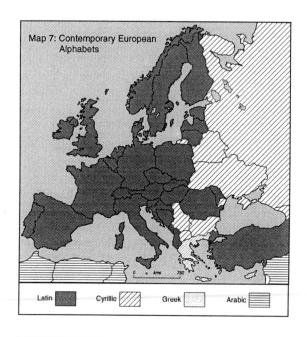

Map 7: Contemporary European Alphabets

Latin   Cyrillic   Greek   Arabic

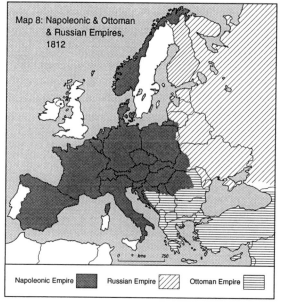

Map 8: Napoleonic & Ottoman & Russian Empires, 1812

Napoleonic Empire   Russian Empire   Ottoman Empire

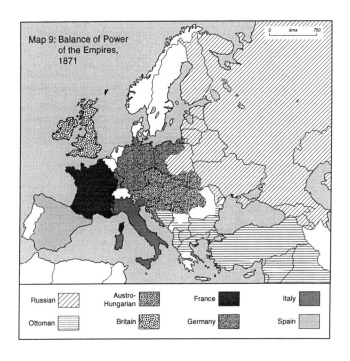

Map 9: Balance of Power of the Empires, 1871

Russian | Austro-Hungarian | France | Italy
Ottoman | Britain | Germany | Spain

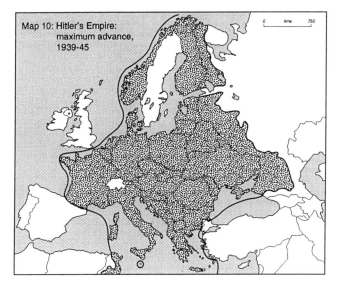

Map 10: Hitler's Empire: maximum advance, 1939-45

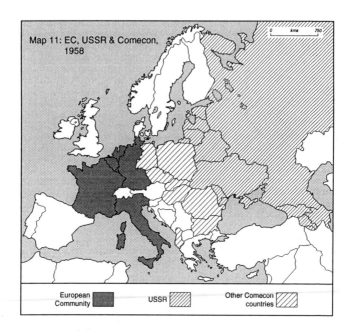

Map 11: EC, USSR & Comecon, 1958

European Community | USSR | Other Comecon countries

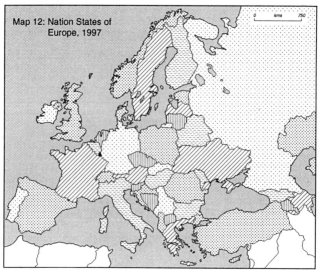

Map 12: Nation States of Europe, 1997

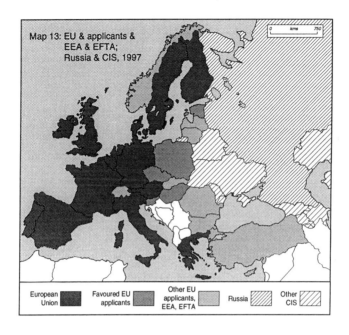

Map 13: EU & applicants & EEA & EFTA; Russia & CIS, 1997

European Union | Favoured EU applicants | Other EU applicants, EEA, EFTA | Russia | Other CIS

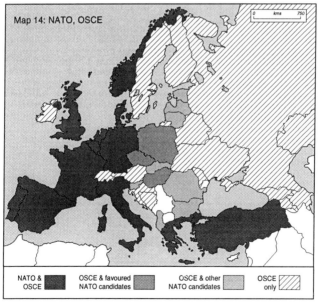

Map 14: NATO, OSCE

NATO & OSCE | OSCE & favoured NATO candidates | OSCE & other NATO candidates | OSCE only

Maps

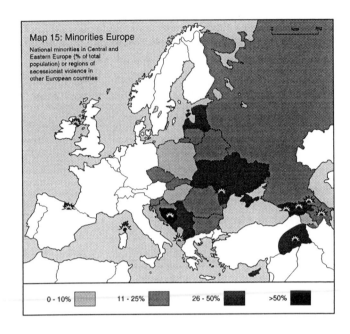

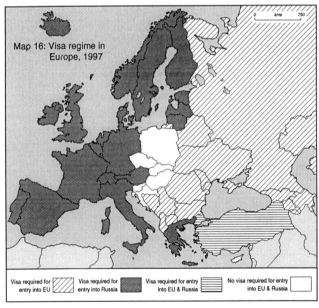

1. Introduction

*From Stettin in the Baltic to Trieste in the Adriatic, an iron
curtain has descended across the Continent.*

Winston Churchill, 5 March 1946, Fulton, Missouri.

*Oui, c'est l'Europe, depuis l'Atlantique jusqu'à l'Oural c'est
l'Europe, toute l'Europe, qui décidera du destin du monde.*

Charles de Gaulle, 23 November 1959, Strasbourg.

This book is about the future of the political and economic map of
Europe. There are many maps of Europe, some of which are illustrated
above: maps of geography, historical epochs, languages, religions,
alphabets and of economic and political organisation. Maps are a
medium for our analysis, but this book is no atlas. We are concerned
with the rules of governance of Europe. The contemporary maps show
the jurisdictions of these rules. The substance of the rules and the maps
of their application define our Europe.

The argument of the book is that a good setting of these rules and
maps, now at a time when so much is fluid, could virtually set Europe
on a path to a new golden age in the early decades of the 21st century.
These rules and maps are so fundamental that, if well set, our
economies and polities will be heading down this path as if on
automatic pilot.

The drama of Europe is also that when these rules and maps are
poorly set, then the continent can degenerate into savage conflict.

The time horizon is mainly about the next twenty years, up to around the year 2020 by when the major changes now in the pipeline may have settled down. These major changes have been programmed in the late 1990s to include EU and NATO enlargements, the introduction of the euro single currency and continuing institutional reforms in the EU; even bigger changes are under way in Russia, which is hastening down a rocky road to normalisation and modernisation in its own inimitable way.

But the time horizon also extends in places to consider questions of European organisation that may mature more likely between 2020 and 2050. For today's student this means no more than thinking ahead for roughly the span of his or her own working life. And for people closer to the end of their careers this time frame is an invitation to think back on the magnitude of changes that the map of Europe saw in their life-time, and so keep the mind open to the scale of possible changes that may lie ahead over a comparable period.

Analytically we have to draw on all the social sciences - history, politics, economics, law, international relations and sociology. The map of Europe begins with geography, later becomes economic geography but in the end is a matter of political philosophy.

Organisationally we have to deal with the alphabet soup of institutions in the glossary, which is a terrible ordeal for the reader. And where the institutions are so noble that they have no acronym they are perfectly confusing: the European Council and the Council of Europe.

But the book is no encyclopaedia. Its special task is to be overarching, to try and see the wood for the trees. It tries to offer a compact aid to the many people who ask these days with an air of desperation "where on earth is Europe going?" There is also the second question "where should Europe be going?", to which we also give our answer.

The core of the book is two couplets: one couplet on *integration* and *conflict*, and another on *economics* and *security*. This leads on to questions of *institutions*. At the end there are questions of strategic choice - about *rules and maps*.

The first couplet reflects the European drama. It is the story of a continent that manages by way of integration to achieve the highest level of multi-cultural civilisation, only alternating with episodes of the bloodiest savagery that world history ever saw.

Chapter 2 on *integration* tries to put together the main elements that explain this continuous process. It illustrates how the map of Europe has been changing over the centuries. It makes a contribution to the theory of integration, trying to give balanced weights to the three big factors: history, economics and politics. It identifies some of the dynamic factors that drive the integration process.

Chapter 3 on *conflict* surveys the European landscape for its actual or latent conflicts, since we know from bitter experience that the first objective of European integration has to be to avert conflict, and that in the social behaviour of European nationalities the mode can switch with alarming facility between civilized integration and savage conflict. We review all the apparent categories of violent conflict on the European stage, noting that nationalist-ethnic species is the most widespread and dangerous still.

Economists do many calculations over the costs and benefits of integration. We report these, but also stress the costs of conflict which are often overlooked. The human costs of conflict in Europe's 20th century experience were so colossal that they dwarf the pay-off from all conceivable refinements to west Europe's further integration. It supports what the founding fathers of post-world war integration felt: we need integration above all to avoid conflict.

The second couplet is about the rules of economic and political organisation at the European level, and examines whether these are well designed and whether the institutions are well placed to enforce them. We return here to the map question: what should be the coverage geographically of these rules and institutions?

In Chapter 4 we see *the economic system in terms of four sets of rules*. First and foremost are two well structured issues - the extent and depth of market and monetary integration, and then how to manage the market and money. *"One Market, One Money"* is a slogan of the European Union. Whether the slogan is right or not is an issue one can discuss. But at least we know what we are talking about, namely what the frontiers are or should be, if any, for trade, the movement of people and the monetary area. But there are two other sets of rules of great concern: the European *social model*, whose definition is still controversial; and the rules of *corporate governance* which are vital for the integration of the new Wild East of Europe with the West. Both these last two sets of rules are the joint responsibilities of business, government and civil society. The focus is on two overarching questions, first whether the euro area is set to get off to an auspicious start or not and, second, how far or fast the whole of Europe might be brought together under these four sets of rules.

In Chapter 5 *the security system is seen also in terms of four sets of rules:* the principles of *democracy, human rights, the rights of national minorities* and *inter-state behaviour*. All of these rules are rather well specified, but they are governed by complicated and overlapping institutional arrangements. The incentives for compliance are now very strong for all the countries of central and eastern Europe which aspire to EU and NATO membership in order to secure strategic economic and security advantages, as well as "rejoin Europe" as a matter of societal destiny. But further to the east this is not so clear.

In Chapter 6 we turn to Europe's *institutions*. One can discuss the future map of the European Union. But this cannot go very far without clarifying the more fundamental question what kind of political animal the European Union is to become, and what political substance is to be put behind the map of the wider Europe. For this we need some main concepts first. Political scientists have not been entirely asleep. They try to identify the alternative paradigms for Europe's polity. The debate now switches its focus, in academia as well as political circles. It used to be a struggle between the nation state and federal Europe. At its worst this has seemed to be a war of religion between *neo-nationalists* and *unreconstructed federalists*. Fortunately this war of religion seems to be on the wane.

New paradigms for Europe's political structure seems to be emerging. It is still a competition between two models, on the one hand a *reconstructed Euro-federalism* and, on the other hand - and here is the problem of naming the new animal - maybe *cosmopolitan democracy*.

Euro-federalists have refined their thinking. They have acknowledged the principle of subsidiarity. They have given respectability to flexibility. But still the idea is to achieve the essential coincidence of powers at the level of one main map, that of the EU or at least its core group. The powers concern the economy, money, security and citizens' rights, which is most of what is important for top level governance. When the system is mature it becomes a Euro-superpower, but this would still be better described as a *sub-federal* Europe, if there remained only a limited integration of the defence function. Being democratic, of course, it would still have to clarify how to give adequate democratic legitimacy to its political institutions. This question will not be resolved in the period to the year 2020, but might be in the period to 2050. For the time being the issue is not forced for several practical reasons. First, the euro has not only to be introduced but shown to work well, which is not a foregone conclusion. Second, the Brussels institutions have to show they are capable of de-congesting themselves in their decision-making and management performance, rather than grind into grid-lock. This also is not a foregone conclusion. Third, the American presence in NATO is sufficiently valuable, in spite of its awkward aspects, that a rapid and deep Europeanisation of defence is not presently on the agenda.

The alternative model of *cosmopolitan democracy* focuses on the rules of a European civil order, and on how best to put them into effect as extensively and efficiently as possible in the entire European space. This contrasts with the federalist approach which focuses on a given territory with several tiers of government, and then discusses how to distribute functions rationally between them. With *cosmopolitan democracy* the approach is therefore turned upside down. The substance of the rules are those already mentioned: four economic (markets, money, the social model, and corporate governance) and four political (democracy, human rights, minority rights, inter-state behaviour). Organisationally *cosmopolitan democracy* consists of multiple and overlapping networks of groups and associations which set the rules for given purposes. The actors include both governments and other associations. Also central to this thinking is the distinction between the *"modern"*, and the *"post-modern"* order. The "modern" state gave all sovereignty, law and morality to the nation and left international relations to the tender mercies of *Realpolitik.* The post-modern state dismisses the distinction between the morality of internal affairs and the immorality of international affairs. The post-modern order allows many of the main functions of government to be diffused through the responsibilities and rules of clusters of international networks.

Maybe the outcome is going to become a combination of a reconstructed *Euro-federal* order in the EU and a wider European cosmopolitan democracy. Both models, happily, can offer civilised futures for Europe. But the European Union has to show that it can perform institutionally sufficiently well, in terms of policy and management effectiveness and democratic accountability, to justify maturing towards sub-federal status. And then there is the question of how the EU relates to the wider Europe. The looser *cosmopolitan democracy* would have still to show it was not too weak in terms of coherence and backbone.

As the concluding Chapter 7 argues in more detail, Europe contains in outline four alternative maps - *Two-block Europe, Brussels Europe, Security Europe and Civil Europe*. The Two-block Europe is divided between the enlarged EU and the Russian sphere of influence (CIS). It has its historical foundations but if reinforced would be a retrograde step. Brussels Europe is alone, in the sense that there is no wider Europe of substance which the non-EU countries fit into. Security Europe is the residual inheritance of the Cold War, with the US still standing by to keep the peace, and Russia excluded from the enlarged NATO. This map should wither away. Civil Europe has the EU as its core, but it also sees a critical mass of civil functions clustered at the level of the all-European map, which we propose to call the *European Civil Society*.

This fourth map would be the key to resolving the dangerous hiatus in Europe's political geography, namely whether the countries on Europe's periphery - the very large Russia, the large Ukraine and Turkey are "part of Europe" or not. The wider Europe should deepen and the deeper Europe should widen. The maps and the rules become more and more convergent as the distinction between the deep and the wide Europes fades. Such is the process that we try to sketch.

2. Integration

*Rivers to the geographer are the bearers of sediment and trade.
To the historian they are the bearers of culture, ideas, and
sometimes conflict. They are like life itself.*
Norman Davies, *Europe - a History*, 1996.

2.1 Principles of integration

For contemporary Europe integration has several aspects, as in
different branches of the social sciences. Sociologists since Durkheim
stress integration of society as the first principle of social behaviour
[Giddens, 1993]. Social structures and specialised institutions have to
mesh together, work in harmony and cooperate, implying consensus
over basic values. For scholars of national identity the hallmarks of
integration are the sharing of a home-land, language and elements of
culture, as well as commonly known history and myths [Smith, 1991].
In economics the processes of trade, monetary integration and
economic convergence are the main ideas [Molle, 1990]. Calculations
are made of which countries form natural clusters for advantageous
trade and monetary integration [Gros and Steinherr, 1995, and Artis
and Zhang, 1997]. In political theory and international relations the
focus for integrating nations is on the mechanisms of cosmopolitan
democracy and a rule-based international community [Held, 1995]. In
political economy the focus is on the actors driving the process. Thus
the population, governmental elites and economic interest groups may
gradually switch their loyalties between regional, national, European

and global levels as integration proceeds [O'Neill, 1996, Schmitter, 1996].

An underlying argument of this book is that it is necessary in thinking about Europe's future to give more attention to an *integrated view of the integration process,* thus spanning these academic divides [Rosamund, 1995]. One way to begin is to use the principal categories of political economy analysis, and consider the interests and behaviour of the three actors: people, producers and government.

For *people* the first factors of integration are proximity and ease of movement. Across Europe affinities of culture and ethnicity formed over the last two thousand years. Contemporary affinities can only be developed further if the personal freedoms exist, such that family structures, professional acquaintances and friendships will form over a certain area. Today there are the rules of freedom (or restrictions) of movement across frontiers, places of work and residence.

For *producers* the analogous factors are also proximity and the freedoms of movement of goods, services and capital, and freedom of establishment. Integration is then deepened when market and monetary systems are given a common legal base or common money. As with people, the changing technologies of transport and communications are increasing effective proximity for business.

For *governments* integration turns on the chosen structures of international law, treaties and institutions. Governments may either lead or lag behind the integration of people and business. The mechanisms run the range from federalism to minimalist international cooperation.

Why do peoples, producers and governments want to integrate more or less strongly with their neighbours? Why are these wishes not always reciprocal, as between he who wants to enter a club and he who controls the entry door? These basic questions are too often buried in rhetoric about being pro- or anti-European. A more careful approach to these critical questions is called for. A schema is suggested in Table 2.1, with three broad categories: *history, economics and politics.* But each of these breaks down into three more precise arguments, before they can be usefully applied. Nine determinants of integration may seem an inconveniently large number. But the actual European

Table 2.1: Factors determining integration tendencies

Demand - *country X' s wish to integrate with Y, or with core group Z*
Supply - *willingness of country Y, or core group Z to admit country X*

Explanatory variables

I. Historical integration
1 Geography - watersheds, mountains, river basins
2 Culture - language, religion, alphabet
3 Perceptions - of citizenship, trust, destiny

II. Economic integration
4 Markets - benefits and costs
5 Money - benefits and costs
6 Redistribution - benefits and costs

III. Political integration
7 Values - commonality or otherwise
8 Power - gains or losses
9 Security - gains or losses

---

structure is full of complexities that are really important. It is better to start with a reasonably complete view.

The notion of *core group* is also indispensable, in a Europe of 800 million people and 50 sovereign states. A core group is where a *cluster* of integration factors reinforce each other for a certain group of populations or states, making for a leadership role in the integration process. Usually a core will be geographically central, in relation to others on the periphery. In practice core groups are more or less clearly evident in western and eastern Europe, with or without formal legal status, with the initial six member states of the EU and Russia. The importance of the core group is that it affects the demand for, and supply of integration regarding other countries outside the core. It highlights the issue of *exclusion*.

The core-periphery distinction is also important because it affects the dynamics of the integration process (to which we return at the end of this chapter). One may think of business interest groups and national governments having various preferences for the most desirable degree of integration with all or parts of Europe. These preferences might first be defined, at least in theory, without knowing or discussing the preferences and intentions of the others. But if there were a powerful core group that intended to pursue a given integration strategy in any case, then the periphery has to take that as given and decide as a second preference whether they wish to include themselves or be excluded. The core itself will also consider whether it wishes to include or exclude the periphery, with its known differences of preference. This calculation has to bring into account, in a further logical step, judgement over how the periphery will behave in the event of exclusion. Such judgements will typically involve a difficult synthesis of the economic, the political and even sociological. The practical relevance of this will be discussed below, having obvious applications with the enlargements of the EU and NATO.

2.2 Historical integration

- *Geography*
Geography was the first, primeval factor responsible for the European race and cultures. Geography is still fundamental if there is any sense to discussing European integration. For otherwise the New World is full of European countries.

Europe's primary zones are marked out by the geography of watersheds and rivers. The Alps became the central and dividing point of three of the main watersheds (Map 1). As the ice ages receded the great river basins of Europe started to function. The Rhine, Rhone and Danube are very close at their origins, but then go their different ways - south-west, north-west, south-east - into the Mediterranean, Atlantic and Black Sea.

Further to the east there are no large mountainous barriers between the basins of the Dniester, Dniepr and Don flowing into the Black Sea and the Volga flowing into the Caspian. But still the smallest gradients make all the difference for waterways. This makes the Volga the only one of these rivers that flows a long way north-east, before forced down to the Caspian Sea by the Urals, the geographer's frontier of Europe.

For Europe the four points of the compass, N-W, S-W, N-E, and S-E have some real geographic meaning. At the heart of these four zones flow the Rhine, Rhone, Danube and Volga, all in their different directions. There is a near-fit with the four sea basins - the Atlantic Ocean, Mediterranean and Black/Caspian Seas. We have to await the division of Christendom between Rome and Byzantium, thus between the western and eastern Mediterranean, to obtain cultural zones that fit more perfectly with the four points of the compass.

- *Culture*

These watersheds were highly relevant to the formation of the four main *language* groups of Europe: Latin, Germanic, Slavonic, Turkic (Map 6). Already here we have one of the deepest factors of integration at the personal level. But politics redrew somewhat the map compared to the watershed zones, notably through the exceptional strength of the Roman Empire which left its mark in Latin France north of the Alps, and Latin Romania north of the Danube (Map 2).

Equally fundamental is the four-way division of Europe by *religion:* Catholic, Protestant and Orthodox Christianity and Islam (Map 5). It leaves the Balkans as the tragic intersection point of all the main religious divides. Religion crucially made for the divide of the western and eastern Slavs, following Poland's decision to recognize Rome in the year 996. The Catholic-Protestant divide very roughly reflected and reinforced the Latin-Germanic divide.

The *alphabet* map is at times a political compromise between language and religion, and provides just a three-way split between the Latin, Cyrillic/Greek and Arabic (Map 7), following in fact the map of religions more closely than that of language groups. While much easier to change than language or religion, the alphabet carries strong symbolism of affinity or division. It allows for peoples and governments to signal their destinies. Thus the western Slavs symbolise their western inclinations with the Latin script, as well as religion. In the Balkans the Slavs of the former Austrian-Hungarian empire (Slovenia, Croatia) and of course the Romanians use the Latin script, whereas the Orthodox Slavs of Serbia, Bulgaria and Macedonia have retained Cyrillic. Scripts can be changed relatively easily by political initiative. Turkey only dropped the Arabic script for Latin in 1935, as part of Ataturk's programme for a lay Islamic and western oriented state. Moldova dropped the Cyrilic script for Latin in 1991 in breaking with the Soviet Union and reasserting its Latin (Romanian) culture.

These four layers of maps of Europe so far - *geography, language, alphabet and religion* - offer substantially overlapping but partly different variants of Europe's fault lines. They identify four cultural zones, tending broadly to fit with the geographic: the North-West, predominantly Germanic and Protestant, the South-West, predominantly Latin and Catholic, the North-East, predominantly Slavonic and Orthodox, and the South-East with its incursions of Turkic-Arabic cultures and Islamic religion. The overarching question of European integration is how far history has conditioned the loyalties of populations, such as to facilitate or impede integration across these four cultural zones. Issues of relations between nations and regions within these primary cultural zones are mostly at a more secondary level. Many of the sharpest local tensions, to which we return in the next chapter, are in fact at points on the major fault lines. The best chance to overcome these lower level conflicts is to succeed at the higher level integration.

Given their exceptional importance, let us review a little more carefully these four major frontiers and fault-lines within Europe, those between NW and SW, between NW and NE, between SW and SE, and between NE and SE.

The only one of the four major frontiers already largely overcome by integration is that between Germanic-Protestant NW and the Latin-Catholic SW. The Alpine-Pyrenean divide was breached first when the Romans established a province in southern Gaul in 120 BC, with a Latin tongue taking root in due course later. In the year 800 the Empire of Charlemagne, in the name of the Holy Roman Empire, assembled almost exactly what became the EEC of the Six of 1958 (Maps 3, 11).

Table 2.2: Principal affinities and divides of language and religion

NORTH-WEST	NORTH-EAST
GERMANIC, Latin *PROTESTANT, Catholic*	*SLAVONIC, Turkic* *ORTHODOX, Islamic*
SOUTH-WEST	*SOUTH-EAST*
LATIN *CATHOLIC*	*TURKIC, Slavonic, Latin* *ISLAMIC,Orthodox,Catholic*

Note: Each box indicates language group and religion, with capital letters given to the predominant categories.

NW and SW were already rather deeply integrated, but were then set back by the Great Schism between the papacies of Rome and Avignon at the end of the 14th century, and then more durably with the Reformation, starting with Luther's protests in 1517 followed by the Calvinists and Anglicans (Map 5). The ensuing wars of religion culminated in the Thirty Years War, and were concluded by the Peace of Westphalia of 1648, which settled the issue in favour of religious pluralism. Only Northern Ireland sees still a small residue of war of religion, and maybe that now heads towards resolution at long last.

Today the integration of the Germanic and the Latin peoples hinges around the German-French relationship. The whole area has known devastating attempts at hegemonic control by both sides, most recently with Napoleon and Hitler. Napoleon's empire took in almost all of western Christendom, in a clear three-way split of Europe with the Russian and Ottoman empires (Map 8). Napoleon bequeathed an early progress for European legal harmonisation. Hitler's short-lived empire made less plausible incursions into the Orthodox Slavonic world (Map 10). Hitler provided such a horrific experience for all that the basis for deep reconciliation was finally reached. Hence this divide is now the subject of continuous symbolic acts of unity, starting with De Gaulle and Adenauer, continued by Giscard d'Estaing and Schmidt using Aachen to prepare their European monetary initiative in 1978, and by all leaders since. The NW - SW partnership also works with a recognisable degree of symmetry and mutual respect, as shown by their respective priorities for southern and northern enlargements of the EU, each taking place in turn.

Yet tensions between the two cultures still exist, as the road to monetary union in the late 1990s has shown, with the apparent nervousness of German public opinion over sharing their monetary union with Italy. The NW - SW fault line has also its regional zones of tension. Belgium is split fairly cleanly in half between its Latin and Germanic areas, and maintains the peace with some strains. South Tyrol, left by the world wars on the wrong side of the cultural frontier, only recently became peaceful.

The NW - NE frontier was seriously shifted west when Miezsko, the first ruler of Poland, opted in 966 for Roman Christianity, followed by others in central Europe, including the Magyars whose King Stephen was crowned in the name of Rome in 1001. The western Slavs thus affirmed their principle leanings towards Germanic Europe, in spite of their linguistic heritage. The Orthodox Slavs became further cut off from the west when they succumbed to the Mongol Horde, which captured Kiev in 1240. The Mongols ravaged much of Russia from the 13th to 15th centuries, which thus missed out on the Renaissance (Map 4). After a period of very partial westernisation from Peter the Great to the 1917 Revolution, the cultural gap between NE and NW was deepened again by the period of Soviet domination. After World War II, moreover, Stalin moved the frontier west (Map 11), to the point of re-uniting the eastern and western Slavonic world in an attempt to undo a thousand years of history since Miezsko and Stephen. But the brutality of this domination over the western Slavs and the Baltic states only confirmed the determination to reunite with the west as soon as Communism collapsed at the end of the 1980s.

The SW - SE zones are where history has seen the most drastic changes of regime between Christianity and Islam. The struggle over this frontier has been interpreted by Pirenne as the first defining act of the European identity. "....Charlemagne without Mahomet would have been inconceivable" [quoted in Davies, 1996, p. 258]. From the death of Mohammed in the year 632 it took only until 738 for Islam to reach up through Spain deep into France. Europe was "saved" at the battle of Poitiers in 732, but Islam nonetheless held most of Spain for 700 years, and was only finally ejected from Granada in 1492. But meanwhile the Ottoman empire was beginning its great expansion, taking Constantinople in 1483 and reaching Vienna in 1683. Europe had to be "saved" again. Metternich, once asked where Europe ended and Asia began, said just outside his Viennese office window.

Following the collapse of the Ottoman empire, Turkey embarked upon a course of radical westernisation. Under Ataturk Turkey became a lay state in 1928, with its switch of alphabets already mentioned and other basic reforms. In 1987 Turkey applied for EU membership. Nonetheless Islamic political parties have grown in strength. The Christian Democrat parties of the EU in early 1997 notoriously declared that the EU was for Christian nations, prompting official protests from Turkey and non-confessional politicians in the EU.

The NE - SE frontier is no less deep in historical resonance, Orthodox Russia being confronted successively with the Mongol Horde, whose army was largely manned by the original Turks from Siberia, east of Lake Baikal, and later the Ottoman Turks. Muslim expansion had already reached out from Arabia up to the Caucasus by the mid-7th century and then to the Central Asia of Samarkand and Bukhara (now in Uzbekistan) in 710. The Turks from Siberia, who later settled in Central Asia and Anatolia, became converted to Islam, and passed the religion on to the centres of the Mongol empire, notably Kazan in today's Tatarstan. Islam thus became the main resistance to Russian imperial expansion in both the Caucasus and Central Asia in the 18th and 19th centuries, as well as remaining the religion of the Tatars west of the Urals. Already in 1493 when Constantinople fell to the Ottoman empire, Moscow took up the mantle of leadership of the Orthodox church.

Russia found itself again at war with Islam, indeed with Islamic fanaticism in Chechnya in 1995. Hardly surprisingly it views modern Turkey with suspicion as a broader threat to its assumed sphere of influence in the Caspian and Central Asian zones. The Turkish businessman makes himself understood in his mother tongue in Tatarstan, Azerbaijan and most of Central Asia. The President of Azerbaijan says in 1997 that he favours exporting his country's oil through Turkey. The Mongols of Mongolia hardly represent a geo-political worry for modern Russia, but modern Turkey can serve as the contemporary representative of the old Mongol Horde deep down in the Russian psyche.

Thus only the NW - SW fault-line has been overlaid with rather deep integration. In fact their obvious complementarity of cultures seems now to be considered mutually beneficial, to add a touch of Latin style to the NW and a touch of Germanic order to the SW. The other frontiers are still tense or worse.

Worst of all is the unique place of intersection of the four quadrants NW, NE, SW, SE: in the former Yugoslavia. There the tensions of two millennia of history have proved too much for the fragile institutions of the newly independent states to contain, and to this worst of contemporary conflicts we must return in the next chapter.

In addition to the four quadrants, there is a further point to be made about Europe's core and the periphery. The only core Europe that manifested itself at the beginning and end of the present millennium is that which started with Charlemagne and later became the EEC Six, both representing enlightened episodes of history. In between time this core saw successive attempts to establish vast hegemonic empires, most recently under Napoleon and Hitler. There were just a few large countries on the geographic periphery who managed to avoid or resist the invaders. These are Britain, Turkey and Russia (of course Russia was invaded and Moscow reached on both occasions, but it also repulsed the invaders). This combination of geographic peripherality and avoidance of total occupation seems still to condition attitudes to post-war integration. The invading and occupied countries of the core seem to have been more inclined to draw the conclusion that profound integration is the recipe for avoiding a repetition of history.

The periphery is more inclined to say "we stood alone" and can afford a more distant position on integration questions. Also the UK, Russia and Turkey all look away from Europe with their windows out across the Atlantic or to Asia, where they wish to keep their options and interests open. The periphery seems more receptive still to notions of balance of power diplomacy in Europe, which is a 19th century concept (Map 12), epitomised by Lord Palmerston's phrase "we have no permanent friends, only interests".

- Perceptions

How is it possible to read the political inclinations of European governments over the shape of the future map of Europe, in advance of the outcome of long and tortuous negotiations over EU and NATO enlargements for example? One of the most revealing of contemporary European maps is that of the visa regime (Map 16). The interest of the visa map is that it surely reveals judgements about which peoples of Europe can or cannot be liberally admitted into one's family without problems or worries. It is also a policy instrument that can be disconnected from other major negotiations, such as over trade policy. It is also the most personal of personal instruments, the most relevant for the integration of peoples. It may be an advance indicator of how other more political maps of integration could eventually turn out.

The European Union's visa-free zone includes all of the western Europe of the pre-Cold War period, plus the three Baltic States and the central Europe of the western Slavs (Poland, Czech Republic, Slovakia, Slovenia and Croatia) and Hungary. Western Christendom passes. The rest of the Balkans, Turkey, North Africa and the former Soviet Union do not.

Russia's visa-free zone includes all of the former Soviet Union (except the three Baltic states), all the former Comecon countries and all the Balkan states including the former Yugoslavia. Basically all the Slavs pass. The European Union and Turkey do not.

This means that only the western Slavs of central Europe enjoy the privilege of being welcome visa-free in both the European Union and Russia. Central Europe turns out to be the heart of Europe indeed. Of European countries only the Turks need visas for both the European

Table 2.3: Feelings of citizenship towards EU, nation, region (%)

	European Union	Nation	Region
Italy	30	53	16
Luxemburg	25	62	12
France	16	61	23
Ireland	16	77	7
Netherlands	16	67	15
EU average	16	61	22
Belgium	15	51	32
UK	15	71	14
Germany	14	59	27
Austria	11	71	18
Spain	10	51	38
Greece	10	74	16
Portugal	9	64	25
Denmark	7	79	13
Sweden	6	69	25
Finland	4	78	18

Source: Eurobarometer No 45, spring 1996 [Commission of the EU, 1997a]

Union and Russia. The three big blocks - The European Union, Russia and Turkey - seem still today to be acting out the parody of a Europe divided between Western Christiandom, the Orthodox Slavs and Islam. NW + SW are together, NE and SE are apart and outside.

Some insight into what people, rather than just their governments think about these questions is offered in the *Eurobarometer* opinion polls. Within the European Union polls are conducted to test feelings of multiple citizenship as between the nation, the region and the EU. In a 1995 survey respondents were invited to indicate their first, second and third preferences in terms of multiple identification: the nation was rated highest as a first preference (61%), the region as a second preference (22%) and the EU as the third preference (16%). Alternatively in 1996 it was found that 46% of the population identified with both nation and the EU, whereas another 46% identified with the nation only (Table 2.3). The nation ranks strongest, but multiple loyalties do develop within the EU.

A further *Eurobarometer* question asks EU citizens about the extent of their trust for other EU nationalities and some non-EU nationalities (Table 2.4). The highest degree of trust is earned by the small nationalities of northern Europe, including the Swiss and Norwegians as well as EU nationalities. Interpreting this result, these small and very open economies, long dependent on international dealings for their prosperity, have deeply learned the importance of conduct justifying trust. The comparison would be with larger countries, of comparable levels of economic development, which have at times been sufficiently powerful to be tempted by more arrogant behaviour internationally, or by a fluctuating mix of *Realpolitik* and rule-based behaviour. Only Germany from among the large countries is ranked together with these very highly trusted small countries, which says something important and extremely positive about Germany's post-war culture.

A second category includes almost all the other large EU countries, as well as Americans and Japanese. A third category groups the Greeks and central European nationalities. Finally, in the lowest category of trust, come the Russians and Turks, close together (the visa map has some popular basis).

The opinions of individual EU nationalities (shown in the detailed source to Table 2.4) show remarkably little variations. On might have imagined that the Latins or Germanic peoples or other closer groups trust each other within these groups more than between them. Such is only mildly the case, if at all.

For the rest of Europe the poll asks the question "where does the future of your country lie ?" - as between the EU, US, Russia and other countries (such as Germany and Turkey).

For most of the central and east European countries which are applicants to join the EU, the predominant result is to favour the EU,

Table 2.4: Trust of EU citizens in EU and other nationalities (% indicating a lot of, or some trust)

EU nationalities		Other nationalities	
		Swiss	69
Swedes	67		
Dutch	65		
Danes	64	Norwegians	64
Germans	64		
Luxemburgers	63		
Austrians	61		
Belgians	61		
Finns	59	Americans	59
French	59		
Spanish	58		
British	53		
Portuguese	51		
Italians	50	Japanese	50
Greeks	43		
		Hungarians	37
		Poles	36
		Czechs	34
		Slovaks	30
		Russians	24
		Turks	21

Source: Eurobarometer, No 46, May 1997 [Commission of the EU, 1997b]

with much less weight in favour of the US. With respect to Russia, however, the results are more differentiated, with those favouring Russia in the Baltic states numbering about half those favouring the EU, reflecting the substantial Russian national minorities and territorial proximity. Bulgaria is exceptional in giving nearly equal weights to the EU and Russia, reflecting profound cultural and historical associations. Bulgaria, alone of the EU applicants, retains the Cyrillic script, and Russia was Bulgaria's protector against Turkey at the end of the last century. In the former Yugoslavia (Croatia and Macedonia) and Albania, however, the US is favoured roughly on a par with the EU, no doubt reflecting the perceived value of the US as enforcer of peace.

In Belarus and the Ukraine opinion differs categorically from that in neighbouring Poland or former Czechoslovakia. Russia is favoured with a large majority over the EU and US. Similar results are observed in Armenia and Kazakhstan. Public opinion is ratifying the significance of historical maps. The division between the Western and Eastern Slavs, for reasons seemingly blending religion and Soviet politics, is confirmed. Only Georgia among the former Soviet Union states, which is neither Slavonic nor Orthodox, takes a roughly balanced view as between West (EU and US) and Russia.

Russia itself gives the largest weight to the other CIS countries (35%), then to the US (25%) and then to the EU (12%). One may suspect that Russia feels comfortable with a leading role in the CIS, that at least they know what they are dealing with in super-power US, but are rather unclear about the EU.

The overall picture confirms that the distinction between NW and SW has largely been eroded. But in central and east Europe there is a very sharp divide between those countries which look west to the EU and those which look east to Russia of the CIS. Levels of trust of both Russians and Turks are still very low for EU citizens. Popular attitudes give grounding to a three-block Europe: the EU (NW + SW), NE and SE.

Table 2.5: "Where does the future of your country (of central or eastern Europe) lie ?"

	EU	*US*	*Russia*
Poland	*40*	*14*	*8*
Czech Rep.	*37*	*9*	*1*
Slovakia	*32*	*13*	*6*
Hungary	*26*	*15*	*3*
Bulgaria	*27*	*6*	*23*
Romania	*30*	*32*	*8*
Slovenia	*44*	*44*	*0*
Estonia	*45*	*5*	*17*
Latvia	*33*	*8*	*24*
Lithuania	*30*	*7*	*16*
Albania	*44*	*39*	*4*
Macedonia	*34*	*39*	*1*
Croatia	*20*	*39*	*0*
Belarus	*7*	*5*	*68*
Russia	*12*	*25*	*35(CIS)*
Ukraine	*14*	*10*	*54*
Armenia	*3*	*11*	*76*
Georgia	*15*	*14*	*34*
Kazakhstan	*3*	*4*	*53*

Source: Eurobarometer No 45, Spring 1996

2.3 Economic integration

- *Market integration*

Whether the reader likes it or not, the language must now turn to that of economics. Trade has been the traditional engine of international integration, and the least discriminating. Traders want to do business wherever it is profitable. They are not so interested in the preferences of politicians, or cultural differences of types important for social and political integration. Trade openness will always be beneficial to consumers, minimising prices and maximising choice and competition. Governments may lose tariff revenue, but will gain compensating revenue from other taxes if the economy is more productive and grows. Producers may suffer loss of protected incomes, but their long-term growth will not be favoured by protection. While trade openness between advanced economics is rather a non-controversial proposition, especially in recent years of globalizing technology, it has also become increasingly evident that for developing and emerging economies the costs of protection to medium-term growth performance will usually be severe [Sachs and Warner, 1996].

More controversial are the merits of regionalism and preferential trade openness, compared to non-discriminatory global openness. Theory shows that regional trade preferences may be welfare-reducing at the world level, by directing trade away from the most efficient suppliers. The World Trade Organisation supplies a framework for reciprocal trade openness at the global level. Gains from trade based on different comparative advantage thrive on the dissimilarity, rather than similarity of trade partners. Hong Kong has thrived on a policy of unilateral free trade with the world.

For these reasons there needs to be a strong set of specific reasons to justify regional trade integration in Europe, as for other regions. In fact there is a long and important list of such reasons [Fernandez, 1997]. These come in two categories relevant to the European situation, first, why a west European core group should have formed and, second, why there are special reasons for the core's market to be extended now to the periphery to the east.

The so-called *gravity model* represents the first and foremost rationale for the European common market, becoming later the EU's single market. The theory is that the major explanation of trade structures is the proximity and economic size of markets. This is the case, *par excellence,* for western Europe due to its compact space and great density of economic production and wealth. This proposition has been examined empirically with the aid of the gravity models, for Europe by Gros and Steinherr [1995]. Such calculations enable estimates to be made of the trade potential between different groups of countries, even where there are trade barriers at present. They show the EU market to be by far the heaviest centre of gravity for trade within Europe, and Germany to be its epicentre. It is natural therefore that EU countries should have wanted to give priority to securing the major trade opportunities on their door-steps. Sapir [1997] also tests a gravity model and finds that language is to be added as a significant explanatory factor.

So geography and economic culture (required for generating high levels of income) are both important for trade structures, while other cultural factors such as language are also significant.

The calculations by Gros and Steinherr [1995] go on to estimate the potential for trade in central and eastern Europe. They investigate these questions in relation to three regional groups: the EU, the accession candidates of central Europe and the former USSR countries. For the accession candidates they calculate the relative trade potential in the EU versus the former USSR markets. The EU offers about ten times the potential of the former USSR, showing that the former Comecon had little economic justification. Similarly for the former USSR countries the Comecon block offered rather minor trade potential, compared to entering into an all-European trade block whose potential is ten to twenty times as great. For the EU itself trade expansion to the east could be useful, but on a more modest scale proportionately.

The message of the gravity model is reinforced by a further series of arguments.

Within the EU it has been observed that the huge growth of intra-EU trade since 1958 consisted not so much of the comparative advantage type (e.g. bananas exchanged for machines), but so-called *intra-industry* in manufactured goods. This concerns trade in only slightly differentiated products (German Volkswagens, French Peugeots, Italian Fiats), offering none the less the key advantages of both improved economies of scale and increased consumer choice and competition. For this type of trade to flourish it is important that there be a virtually *complete opening of markets*, as in the single market of the EU, and virtual certainty that this openness can be guaranteed for the future [Emerson et al, 1988]. Such advantages, moreover, are particularly important for small countries, of which there are many in Europe. However a single market requires extensive common market regulations, of types that require sophisticated joint decision-making institutions, which in turn depends on factors permitting political integration, which links to issues of culture.

None the less for the advance market economies the gains from measures for perfecting trade liberalisation show only rather small amounts. The largest estimates were those made *ex ante* in 1987, in anticipation of the EU's single market programme of 1992. This suggested gains in a range of 4 to 6% of GDP [Emerson et al, 1988]. By 1996 official studies *ex-post* were able to detect gains so far of only 1% compared to what otherwise would have been the case [Commission of the EU, 1996]. This study had the admittedly difficult task of trying to separate the influence of the cyclical downturn from 1991 to 1994. The very long negotiations over the GATT Uruguay Round resulted in anticipated gains in economic welfare for western Europe mounting after 10 years to about 0.5% [Anderson et al., 1997]. Similar results were obtained by Francois, Macdonald and Nordstrom [1996], with gains in real income of 0.48% for the EU and 0.42% for the transition economies.

For the purpose of global negotiations, a large, cohesive trade block will also have greater *bargaining power* and thus chances of negotiating successfully for its interests world-wide. There are now so many small member states in the World Trade Organisation (WTO) that only the biggest members can have a major influence on world trade policy and have the weight to defend their interests against the major players.

A further argument driving the EU to complete its single market in 1992 was the concern growing in the 1970s that Europe was losing industrial *competitivity* in high value-added industries against the fast-growing Asian economies. It was judged that the stimulus of complete market integration within the EU would improve this situation. An argument especially important for neighbouring countries which might stay outside the EU market is that they would do badly in the competition to attract mobile international investment aimed at supplying the EU market.

Two arguments now relate more particularly to the interest for central and eastern European countries to tie themselves into commitments with the EU as the regional core. Tying trade policy into a deep regional integration system greatly reduces the prospect of subsequent policy reversal, since the economic and political costs of so doing would become extremely high. This is important in enhancing the *long-run credibility of commitment* to the policy and so enhances the confidence of the investor. Then there is the further argument that this trade policy commitment links deeply to the programme of domestic economic policy reform, especially with EU membership meaning legal obligations to limit subsidies and distortions of competition. The trade policy can thus amount to a clear and credible signal of overall economic policy strategy.

For the EU accession candidates there have been some attempts to assess the economic effects of enlargement. A recent study by Baldwin, Francois and Portes [1997] assumes that accession would reduce the costs of trade transactions by 10% and that the associated reduction of the borrowing risk premiums for the financing of investment might amount to 45 basis points (i.e. almost half a percentage point). The cumulative effect is simulated to raise the capital stock in the accession countries by 68% over a period of years, and thence raise real income levels by 18%. By contrast the impact on the EU itself would be very small (0.2% gain in real incomes). While these estimates have to be considered heroic methodologically, they are none the less suggesting very substantial orders of magnitude for the accession countries. This is not implausible, given that the question is all about how accession to the EU helps bring about a basic transformation of these economies, not a mere fine-tuning as in the case of trade liberalisation measures among the advanced industrialised economies.

Finally, a fundamental motive of the founding fathers of the EEC was to build up mutual economic interests so deeply as to guarantee against any renewed slide of politics towards nationalist hostilities. This strategy has, of course, been extraordinarily successful, in notable contrast to the experience after the first world war. The same argument could now become valid also for the post-Communist transition. The quicker a massive development of trade between west, central and eastern Europe the more remote will become the chances that aggressively nationalist politicians in the east will be listened to. This argument strongly supports the case for trade openness between close neighbours, especially where the frontiers in question are vulnerable to ethnic frictions, such as in the case of the Baltic-Russian frontiers, where trade barriers are now in fact quite high. (The costs of conflict will be discussed in the next chapter).

- Monetary integration
With the euro to be introduced on 1st January 1999 in a first group of 11 countries, this section discusses briefly the benefits and costs of forming a monetary union in Europe. Questions of management of the euro area and of the qualifications of individual countries are deferred until Chapter 4. Here we place monetary union in the strategic context.

Monetary union is one of those issues where politicians and economists have different perspectives. Economists are rather circumspect, weighing complex pros and cons, without being able to quantify the net balance. Politicians seem more inclined to take stronger positions, either positive or negative.

We can begin with a bridge to the historical-cultural factors already discussed. This bridge relates to the strictness of the Protestant ethic of the Germanic north-west, which embraces sound money and prudent house-keeping. The Latin south-west has an aura of loose financial management, not entirely without reason in recent times, and not even to mention the Ottoman south-east, or the new Wild East. The primary economic reasoning for monetary union for the Germanic north-west is to consolidate the realm of hard, stable money; and for the Latin south-west, having recently concluded that they too want to join this virtuous circle once and for all, to espouse complete and irreversible monetary union as easily the most plausible way to secure this.

The politicians also bring frankly political arguments to weigh heavily in the balancing of preferences (these belonging in principle to the next section of this chapter). Chancellor Kohl is given to saying that the euro is needed to secure integration so deep that war in Europe never happens again. France wants monetary union also so as to tie in Germany. Sceptical UK leaders of the recent past mixed up serious economic arguments with questions even of national regalia (monarchy, flag etc.).

The detailed work of economists is all the more important because of these tendencies of politicians to bring in extraneous arguments. The strictly economic arguments also lend themselves to questions of maps. The key concept is that of *optimal currency area,* the seminal contribution being that of Mundell [1961], with an up to date review applied to Europe coming from Gros and Thygesen [1997]. In this theory it is argued that structural economic factors determine what the map of an advantageous currency area should be. Monetary union has more risks attached to it than market integration. In particular there are the risks inherent on not being able to change the exchange rate. Broadly speaking these risks are low if economic structures and behaviour of the states or regions are similar, or if there is a high willingness of labour as well as capital to move between regions of the monetary union.

The title of a comprehensive, official study for the EU Commission *"One Market, One Money"* [Emerson et al, 1990] presented five major economic arguments as making up the case for or against monetary union.

Price stability. With the European Central Bank given institutional independence and the priority duty to maintain monetary stability there is every reason to expect that this objective will be achieved. Moreover the starting condition in the economies likely to be the initial members of the euro area is already one of virtual price stability. The culture of stability-oriented policy of the Bundesbank only has to be transported a short distance into the nearby building of the European Central Bank in Frankfurt. For countries not already enjoying price stability this is a great benefit. For such countries to establish a new credibility and reputation for monetary stability is usually a difficult and costly process, for example through demonstrating the political will to maintain strict monetary policy through several political and economic cycles. This argument has already shown its appeal to the Latin south-west, with Italy, Spain and Portugal making enormous efforts to qualify for the euro. Similarly in due course for Greece, and for central and eastern European countries, a stable euro and independent European Central Bank have much to offer. By contrast, for the UK this argument is not so appealing, especially after the Bank of England was granted effective independence under existing conditions of virtual monetary stability in 1997.

Interest rates. A closely related effect of joining the euro area will be elimination of interest rate premiums reflecting inflation expectations. This argument is especially important for countries with high public debts and inflationary track records, notably Italy which at last sees the possibility to escape the vicious circle of high deficits, debt and interest rate burdens. Also the real rate of interest may be reduced, where currencies were previously subject to perceived risks of monetary instability. This risk premium argument joins that already mentioned above in the context of trade integration, especially in central and eastern Europe, where political institutions are still fragile and lacking in credibility.

Microeconomic efficiency. Monetary union eliminates exchange transaction costs, but this is not a major argument for currencies with well-developed exchange markets. It is the only benefit of monetary union that stands straightforward quantification, which was estimated to amount to 0.4% of GDP in an official EU study [Emerson et al., 1990]. A more recent study by Gros and Thygesen [1997] reports an upward revision of this estimate to nearly 1% of GDP. An additional argument is that the single currency will give improved transparency in price comparisons, conducive to efficient investment and purchasing decisions, but this has proved difficult for economists to quantify.

International monetary affairs. The euro may well come to gain market share from the dollar as an international currency, by comparison with the sum of the prior national currencies. In central and eastern Europe in particular it is likely to gain ground as a parallel currency, until these countries become candidates to join the euro area officially. To the extent that this involves replacing the dollar notes in circulation this will be a pure profit for the European Central Bank and thence the governments which share in the distribution of its surplus. Alternatively one can think of foreign holdings of banknotes as public debt on which no interest has to be paid. However the scale of this gain is not going to make the EU significantly richer. It is estimated by Alegoskoufis, Portes and Rey [1997] that the US gains an annual 0.1% of GDP through these interest rate savings. They estimate also that the size, depth and depth of the dollar's securities markets, due to its international role, allows another 0.1% of GDP to be saved through interest rates being about 25-50 basis points lower than for AAA borrowers in narrower financial markets, even those of Germany, France and the UK. The same authors also suggest that an international portfolio shift in favour of the euro could result in further interest rate reductions, intended to prevent an unwanted appreciation of the euro's exchange rate. The coordination of international monetary policy will be affected, and policy and institutional questions are discussed further in Chapters 4 and 6. The EU's bargaining power will be more concentrated and therefore make for a more symmetrical situation in relation to the US.

Loss of exchange rate instrument. This is the essential argument in the optimal currency area theory. The loss of the possibility to change the exchange rate in response to a problem of fundamental misalignment of costs is a disadvantage, whereas elimination of pure exchange rate instability is an advantage. The question is one of evaluation of the net balance of this minus and plus, and its amplitude. The minus is somewhat attenuated by the fact that exchange rate changes are normally ephemeral in real impact, and are dissipated over a period of years by price and nominal wage adjustments. None the less this is the critical issue in determining which countries are placed to become a sufficiently beneficial, if not optimal currency area. As discussed in more detail in chapter 4, studies of these risks in relation to the euro area tend to show that Germany, France, Benelux and Austria are the most well-suited members of a core European monetary union. After that various arguments intervene to show that the risks in losing exchange rate independence are more substantial [Gros and Thygesen, 1997, and Pisani-Ferry, 1997].

In short, it is natural for a highly integrated market to tend towards monetary integration also. However the preconditions for a beneficial monetary union are more demanding than for market integration. It can be a question of time for these preconditions to mature adequately, maybe over many years. Countries with weak political institutions and poor reputations for sound finance will get a big bonus in importing a strong and stable money, but these countries are also quite likely (for example in central and eastern Europe) to have other structural economic differences making a hasty accession to a monetary union more problematic in other respects.

- Regional redistribution

Financial redistribution between rich and poor regions of nations and states of federations has invariably tended to be a critical factor glueing together parties to deep integration. This may be either directly by way of financial transfers through public budgets, or indirectly through preferential prices for trade. Federations often maintain their territorial integrity by paying large subsidies to peripheral, relatively poor regions which might otherwise secede. Within the EU redistributive arguments have been important at every stage of the EU's founding, enlargement and major systemic developments. Within the CIS a factor limiting its integration has been the contrary example of Russia deciding to withdraw from the previous redistributive policies of the USSR.

A study for the EU Commission [MacDougall,1977] analysed these redistributive mechanisms in modern federations and found them to be typically very powerful. In the short-term a region suffering losses of income, for example through a loss in demand for a region's main product, are compensated to the extent of two-thirds, whereas regions or states suffering from long-term economic weaknesses will receive transfers of the order of 40% of income differentials. Such transfers can also serve to keep a monetary union together, even when some of the states are not structurally well suited to being part of the monetary area.

While the EU budget is nowhere near on this scale, satisfaction or dissatisfaction with redistributive mechanisms in the EU has been a significant factor in the integration process.

The initial founding of the EEC in 1958 was based on a political understanding between France and Germany on the setting up of a Common Agricultural Policy (CAP) alongside a customs union and free trade for industrial goods. The CAP subsequently became a very large redistributive mechanism both through the EU budget and through support from price levels above world market prices. Other member states found themselves automatic beneficiaries from this Franco-German deal. This initially concerned the Netherlands and subsequently benefited Denmark and Ireland. The UK found itself the big loser on this account, which has been a major argument on the side of those opposing EU membership. These losses became so important that a series of special compensatory mechanisms had to be devised from 1976 onwards.

With the successive enlargements of the EU the pressure for expanded regional funds for the least prosperous regions and member states became also an important factor influencing support for EU membership. When further major integration initiatives were promoted by the EU core member states - the 1992 single market initiative and the single currency - countries with the weakest peripheral regions demanded increases in the size of the regional funds, which they obtained, such that by 1997 these funds had risen to a size comparable to that of the agricultural fund.

With the next prospective enlargement of the EU to the east the same issues arise, the existing Mediterranean member states fearing dilution of their present financial advantages. At the same time the net contributors, Germany in the first place, resist further expansion of the total size of these redistributive mechanisms.

The nature of these redistributive mechanisms may in a rosy view be seen as an efficient insurance mechanism to ensure a situation of "Pareto-optimality" for all members of an integrated area, i.e. to allow the economic gains of wider market and monetary integration to be achieved without any party becoming worse off. According to the insurance idea, the economically weak and peripheral regions run a risk of losing out in the rationalisation of production resulting from increased market integration. The transfers help the government responsible for the weak region overcome resistance to the increased competition.

A less rosy view observes tendencies towards welfare-dependency in the supported regions. The unemployed or poor of the region receiving transfers may lack incentives to work for reform of economic structures in the region, or to solve personal difficulties by migrating to more prosperous regions. Certainly such tendencies can be observed in some EU regions, for example the southern parts of Italy and Spain, which receive large transfers from their national budgets as well as from the EU. The transfer mechanisms may have served as glue to keep the nation or union together, but they may also have made the subsidised economic structures more sticky and resistant to adjustment as well.

In the former Soviet Union, in the early life of the CIS in 1991 and 1992, redistributive mechanisms continued to operate in a rough way. For example President of Kazakhstan is reported to have appealed to the President of Russia for money; the Central Bank of Russia then received instructions to send some plane loads of bank notes. In the case of the Ukraine the central bank was able to run up substantial debts to the Central Bank of Russia automatically. Cessation of these arrangements went with effective monetary disintegration between Russia and most other CIS states. Russia's caution over accepting the current desire of the President of Belarus for integration with Russia has been influenced by the wish to avoid commitments to redistributive transfers.

2.4 Political integration

- *Values*
Political integration means devolving power to common institutions. The prerequisite for this is a sufficient convergence of political values and ideology.

In fact this convergence has now been achieved within Europe with astonishing speed since the collapse of Communism in 1989-91. On this score the way is now wide open for all-European integration.

Cautious people in the west may wonder whether such fundamental changes can be made so quickly and irreversibly. But scepticism on this point would be a misreading of the facts. The collapse of Communism was preceded by a long erosion of Marxist-Leninist ideology, even in Russia (Layard and Parker, 1997). Intellectual leaders of the reform process in Russia, such as Yegor Gaidar or Anatoly Chubais, were students at the end of the nineteen-seventies. They recount that the intellectual credibility of the Communist ideology was already zero by then. In most of central and eastern Europe it never had broadly based credibility. The sudden collapse was that of an ideological house of cards.

It takes time however to develop deep democratic culture and civil society institutions, no less so than for restructuring the economy (actual trends in this regard are discussed in more detail in Chapter 5). In Europe only in Belarus and parts of the former Yugoslavia and Caucasus are there leaderships whose political ideologies are completely out of tune with normal democratic practice, with some problems still also in Slovakia. Other countries with weak democracies are none the less trying to adapt to the norms of the Council of Europe, as is expected by the EU and NATO of its accession candidates.

By contrast different rules apply to the CIS. The qualification for membership is to have been part of the former USSR, itself non-democratic. No serious evaluation of the functioning of democratic institutions in Central Asia, for example, is considered appropriate in the CIS. This places Russia, as the dominant power in the CIS, in a potentially ambiguous position. A Russia wishing to integrate progressively with western Europe will always have its democracy under scrutiny, as is normal for member states of the Council of Europe. Russia can also pursue a strategy of re-integration with other CIS countries, most of whom have less commitment to democracy for the time being.

Also fundamental is the relationship between state and church. Within western Europe the principle of religious tolerance and pluralism was fought over for centuries, but basically settled at the end of the Thirty Years War in 1648. Confessional political parties exist, indeed they are often ruling parties. Positions of religious doctrine enter into politics, most sharply on questions of family law on divorce and abortion. However there are no real obstacles to west European integration that derive from politico-religious divisions. Where there are politically difficult religious divides, such as in Northern Ireland, focus on European integration can be a help in diluting ancient but obsolete hostilities.

Nor is there any apparent political obstacle to integration between Western and Orthodox Christians. Commentators generally agree that the divisions between Catholics and Orthodox are less marked than between Catholics and Protestant.

Islam, though, is a different matter. In terms of contemporary politics the Islamic state threatens to impose rules that the western democratic state would either not want to exist (like restrictions on the place of women in society) or should be reserved for legislation by lay democratic institutions (such as in the nexus of law and punishment on matters of personal morality). The sovereignty of democratic institutions may be at stake.

This is why the question of Turkish accession to the EU is so sensitive. From a west European point of view it is an extraordinary chance, and a positive one, that a large Islamic state should have made itself a lay state. It helps break down the risks of a generalised tension or confrontation with Islam. On the other hand it is observed that within Turkey there is a real political struggle over maintenance of the legacy of Ataturk. This is a case where the dynamics of either integration on the one hand, or exclusion and ideological divergence on the other, could be strong.

- Power

The demand for political integration is influenced by (a) the relative satisfaction that a nation may have with the exercise of power by its own political institutions compared, and (b) expectations of the effective power and influence obtainable by its representatives through the European institutions.

Countries with notorious governmental instability, or with public administrations which are subject to particularly heavy criticism, look to the EU more positively. Belgium and Italy are cases in point. Countries with young democracies, including Spain, Portugal and Greece, are also warm to European political integration for support to their own democratic structures. Similarly the candidate countries from central and eastern Europe are looking also for consolidation of their democratic institutions, which integration into the EU seems likely to favour.

Germany has consistently in the post-war period viewed the development of European integration positively as an insurance against a repetition of history, i.e. relapse of its own political institutions into authoritarianism.

These are examples of "negative" demands for European political integration, motivated by perceived weaknesses in national institutions.

By contrast people in the Scandinavian countries and the UK feel rather confident that their own national institutions can function in many respects better than those of the EU. Switzerland and Norway, both having voted negatively on European integration in referenda, are even more acute examples.

Then there is the category of "positive" demand, where governments and their elites can see opportunities for enhancement of power and influence through the European institutions. These motivations are strongest in the core of the EU, especially in France and Germany acting individually or together as a special alliance, and the Benelux countries, anxious to have leverage on their two large neighbours.

The particularity of the French interest is an assumption almost of ownership of the European idea, invoking a range of personalities now attributed with almost mythical qualities (Schuman, Monnet). This combines with a strong unity of purpose and professionalism in the governmental elite, which has secured remarkable leverage on the workings of the EU institutions and policies (Jacques Delors was President of the Commission for 10 years, whereas four or now five years is generally considered to be the maximum). In France the European institutions are, to a higher degree than in other countries, perceived as extensions of national power, rather than competitors.

The particularity of German interest is that the EU structures are a congenial means of projecting German power in Europe and the world; congenial both for Germany and its partners because it allows German power to be deployed within constraints that exclude hegemony.

The French-German alliance builds further on these particularities. As long as that alliance remains credibly solid, with some doubts appearing in 1997, it is the pre-eminent informal power within the EU. Major initiatives such as the single market and single currency only happen with their advocacy. But their combined voting power is very far from a qualified majority (only 20 votes out of the 62 qualified majority of a total of 87, and even less with future enlargements). The alliance cannot impose initiatives that provoke widespread unease with other member states.

The Benelux countries are the traditional core of the small countries, which together number ten out of the fifteen member states of the EU. In total these countries command 39 of the weighted votes in the EU Council (we return to the question of reform of voting weights in chapter 6). With their proximity to France and Germany and centuries of experience in supplying the battlefields for the great powers of Europe, the Benelux value the EU as a large bonus to their power and influence. Ireland has effectively joined this group, deeper EU integration meaning a lesser political shadow from the UK. Austria has analogous interests in relation to Germany. All these countries see greater empowerment of the EU as a positive sum game.

By contrast the UK seems to have a chronic incapacity to play its diplomatic and political cards effectively in Europe, as analysed thoroughly by Denman [1996] in the perspective of the twentieth century as a whole, from the failed appeasement of Hitler to being constantly several laps behind the game in the post-war period.

- *Security*

Security against invasion, domination or civil war is the last but not least element in the calculus of benefits of European integration. Europe's twentieth century has been dominated by two security hazards: the German and Soviet hegemons.

The EU has from its beginning been viewed as the tool of

reconciliation between Germany and its neighbours. This has succeeded to the point that war within the EU is now generally considered virtually inconceivable. Nonetheless Chancellor Kohl still invokes the need to further secure Europe's political stability as a reason for to further deepen integration, through monetary union as well as security and defence policies. Germany's closest neighbours seem to agree.

The EU is judged relevant for strategic security especially by Finland in relation to Russia, notwithstanding the post-war history here of positive bilateral relations. Greece regards the EU as a major insurance in relation to its tensions with Turkey.

The central and eastern European countries are looking for security in relation to Russia. This does not have in mind Russia's present leadership, but others who in the future might conceivably be more old-fashioned. Certainly there are many members of the Russian Duma, whose speeches about re-constituting the former Soviet Union give grounds for apprehension by neighbouring countries, especially the Baltic states. Maybe such speeches have little chance of translating into any real political power. Yet the neighbouring countries will still want such manifestations to evaporate into insignificance before feeling beyond risk.

The Russian-led CIS seems in general to be valued by the countries of the Caucasus and Central Asia as providing security guarantees against perceived external threats or risks of internal secession or civil war (Georgia and Tajikistan already supplying examples). Armenia values its special relationship with Russia in view of long standing enmities with Turkey. Russia and the five Central Asian countries have signed the Tashkent Treaty providing mutual defence undertakings.

2.4 Dynamics

To summarise the factors that seem to drive the dynamics of the integration process, it is convenient to think in terms of two dimensions: first, how countries react to each other, which we call *domino dynamics*, and second, how different functional parts of the system react to each other, which we call *disequilibrium dynamics*.

Domino dynamics concern the case where a country may not initially want itself a certain integration step in the European system which nonetheless is being agreed upon by a core group. The periphery is then confronted with the second question, whether to stay outside an initiative that goes ahead in any case. Domino dynamics then see the periphery choose as a second best to join the core rather than be outsiders. Domino dynamics are observable in all the main fields of European integration: markets, money and security. They correspond to the *widening* aspect of integration, rather than the deepening aspect.

In the trade policy field domino dynamics have been analysed rather precisely [Baldwin, 1997 and Sapir, 1997], and shown to have been at work in the successive enlargements of the EU. The UK joined the EEC after its preference for just a European Free Trade Area failed to prevail. But the domino effect related to the demand for political influence as well as trade interests. The last enlargement with Austria, Finland and Sweden was a two-stage domino effect after the EU had decided upon its single market programme. First the EFTA countries negotiated the European Economic Area, giving full access to the single market, without membership of the policy and law-making institutions of the EU. They then judged this lack of representativity unsatisfactory and went ahead for full membership. The governments of the last EFTA enlargement even played a domino dynamics game among themselves, sequencing their referenda in 1995 in a very explicit way. They chose the order Austria-Finland-Sweden-Norway so as to create a positive band-wagon effect from the most likely "yes" results. This was achieved, with the Austrian and Finnish positive results just sufficient to carry a more sceptical Sweden along, leaving the resolutely negative Norwegians to the end [Baldwin, 1997].

The euro single currency also generates such domino effects, even among relatively sceptical countries. For example, already in the debate preceding the British general election in May 1997, apprehension developed whether exclusion of the UK from the euro might mean loss of favour as an investment location for industry and loss of market share in international finance. And the new government quickly turned to the argument that to remain outside would mean a loss of influence over European monetary policy, which would affect the British economy whether in or out.

In the security domain the domino effect has been seen over both NATO and EU enlargements. The Visegrad countries took the lead in accession requests. The Baltic states were left contemplating falling into a different category, without either of these explicit or implicit security guarantees, and feeling even more vulnerable as a result. They opted to join the accession queues of both NATO and EU.

By *disequilibrium dynamics* is meant the process whereby one step in systemic integration creates a new situation, in which a further step is now required if the system itself is not to become destabilised. An example was seen when the liberalisation of capital movements under the single market programme was found to be incompatible with the continued viability of the European Monetary System of pegged exchange rates. Padoa-Schioppa [1987 and 1994] called this problem the "inconsistent quartet". He argued : "... the Community will be seeking to achieve the impossible task of reconciling (i) free trade, (ii) full capital mobility, (iii) fixed, or at any rate managed exchange rates, and (iv) national autonomy in the conduct of monetary policy. These four elements form an inconsistent quartet: economic theory and historical experience show that they cannot co-exist, and at least one has to give way" (Padoa Schioppa, 1994, p.121). These predictions were borne out by the EMS crisis of 1992, when the exchange rate commitments gave way as the fluctuation margins widened to +/- 15 %, so wide to be practically meaningless. The system had either to abandon the quest for exchange rate stability, or jump ahead to monetary union. The EU in fact did both in turn, eventually concluding in favour of the jump to monetary union.

With the imminence of monetary union a new *disequilibrium dynamic* is developing, with calls for greater parallel responsibilities to be discharged by economic ministers to balance the powers of the European Central Bank. However this in turn will intensify calls for increased democratic accountability of the Economic and Monetary Union as a whole by the European Parliament to reduce the growing "democracy deficit" in the system. In addition there is the risk of a new "inconsistent quartet" within the set of policy instruments of the euro

Table 2.6: Evolution of loyalties in the EU (percentages)

Question: *"In the near future do you see yourself as....?"*

	Nationality only	Nationality and EU
Total	46	46
by age:		
15-24	38	53
25-29	40	52
40-54	45	47
55+	57	36
by educational level: (terminal age)		
16-	61	32
16-19	47	45
20+	31	60

Source: Eurobarometer, No 47, May 1997 [Commission of the EU, 1997a].

area as between its monetary, budgetary, social and regional elements (we return to this in Chapter 4).

These are all the dynamics of *deepening*. If the logic of the chain of integrative acts is denied, then the system risks breakdown, since it was not previously in a steady-state condition.

Within the EU opinion surveys reveal a third dynamic factor, and perhaps the most fundamental one - that of *changing attitudes* towards European integration. The most solid indicator of this is the difference between opinions by age, as shown in Table 2.6. It was already noted that on average the population is today evenly balanced between those who see themselves identifying only with their nationality and those recognizing dual loyalties, both national and European. But when

Table 2.7: Opinions on desirability of policy competences at the national or EU level. (Net majority of opinions favouring EU (+) versus national (-) competences)

External		Economic		Social, cultural	
Development aid	+54				
Foreign policy	+49				
Fight drugs	+49				
		Research	+45		
		Environment	+33		
		Regional aid	+31		
Asylum policies	+17	Monetary policy	+14		
		Unemployment	+10		
Immigration	+7	Value-added tax	+6		
Defence	+7	Agricultur. policy	+5		
				Media policy	-11
				Labour relations	-11
				Culture	-18
				Education	-22
				Health	-28

Source: Eurobarometer, No 47, May 1997 [Commission of the EU, 1997a].

the age structure of the population is examined the story is one of drastic changes. Older people over 55 retain a substantial majority of those only feeling a national identity versus a dual one (57 to 36). For young people the situation is reversed, with a substantial majority feeling inclined towards dual identity (53 to 38, for the under 24 year olds, with only slightly smaller majority for the 25-29 age bracket). In addition, those having received higher education show an even larger majority in favour of a dual identity (60 to 31).

As between countries, the extent of feelings of European citizenship in the most recently acceding countries is only about half that observed in the first nine member states (Table 2.3 above). This represents a difference of some twenty to thirty years in experience of the EU. In short, a sea-change in attitudes is observed within the time span of a generation, a span of around 30 to 40 years.

The population of the EU also have quite detailed and sophisticated views on what policy competencies should devolve to the EU level (as shown in Table 2.7). Opinions may be grouped as between three large groups of policy - external, economic and social/cultural. External policies should be most strongly Europeanised, economic policies to a substantial but lesser degree, and finally policies in the social, educational and cultural domain which should all remain national competences. Within these large categories there are some finer messages. The three most important policy functions - defence, unemployment and monetary policy - all receive majority support for Europeanisation (+7, +10, +4). This seems to reflect a degree of caution over how far such supremely political responsibilities should be devolved. Other policies of second level importance - development aid, R & D and others - get a far higher majority for Europeanisation. There seem to be less worries about the transfer of competencies here. However for two other policies of first importance - education and health - opinion is strongly against Europeanisation. This is hardly surprising for students of federalism. The important point is that the population in the EU seems to have quite precise and plausible opinions on how European governance should evolve by sector, and over time as the generations pass on.

3. Conflict

The twentieth century ended with the herding and murdering of nations in south-central-eastern Europe, where, in the early stages of the Balkan conflict, Bosnian Muslims - the Jews of the late twentieth century - were shot at, herded at gun-point from their burning houses or marched into columns to railway sidings, past rotting corpses, to be trucked off to concentration camps where they were raped or castrated and then made to wait, with bulging eyes and lanternous faces, for the arrival of their own death.

J. Keane, *Reflections on Violence*, 1996.

3.1 Why conflict ?

A well-known study of the causes of conflict and war focuses on three levels: the individual, the state and the international system [Waltz, 1959].

The individual, or human nature, has a capacity for violence that is traced to man's *discriminating sociability,* and his capacity to kill his own species. Europe's mosaic of ethnic divides, with its contemporary experiences of violent nationalism and ethnic cleansing, and its long history of wars of religion, tells us that the sociologist's antiseptic expression - discriminating sociability - is no benign condition. Man shows the unfortunate tendency of being able sometimes even to enjoy or be carried away with violence. Images of violence in the media are experienced for pleasure and excitement. For some, it seems that acts of violence provide fulfilment. Group violence has its own dynamics, as is seen in the behaviour of common gangs through to the groups of Serbian soldiers indulging recently in orgies of murder and brutality. Man also shows his capacity for rationally calculated violence, as with terrorist acts that have enormous leverage in terms of economic damage and political influence, and here it is an all-European experience, from Northern Ireland to Chechnya.

The state is an institution which is expected to go to war under certain circumstances. It is equipped for war. Aside from the romanticised notion of the *just war*, there is more frequently the complete tragedy of diabolic or just futile war. Europe has shown continuous evidence of how emotions of hatred, based on religious or ethnic divides, may connect with the mechanisms of the state for the pursuit of devastating war. Bosnia and Chechnya are just the two most recent examples from a Europe whose map is strewn with so many battlefields of religion, ethnicity or just the greedy ambition of leaders. Some are now no more than historical relics (Poitiers for example, battlefield of Christianity versus Islam in 732, and again of France versus England in 1356), but so many others stand for simmering hatreds, capable of re-ignition into conflict.

The state, like man, can exhibit a taste for violence out of macho nationalism. But here there is the vital distinction between the democratic and undemocratic state. It has been convincingly shown, for example by Rummel [1997], that real democracies practically never go to war with each other. Rummel's survey suggests that a necessary condition of inter-state violence is that at least one of the parties is partly or wholly non-libertarian. This argument is highly relevant to the Europe of the post-communist transition. The new democracies of east Europe have taken root with impressive speed, but they are often still imperfect and insecure. The practical question then is how the international system in Europe can consolidate democracy in the east and we return to this in Chapters 5 and 6.

But Europe has still to try to understand the two most gigantic episodes of violence in its history, the recent holocausts led by the tyrants Stalin and Hitler, and the wars - on the one hand with Germany and on the other hand the Cold War with Russia, standing behind the

Soviet Union. All other recent conflicts have been minor affairs by comparison. The political scientist's seemingly technical expression about *discriminating sociability* hardly grapples with the enormity of the holocausts and what they still mean, if anything, for the political organisation of Europe.

The raw facts on the costs of conflict are noted later. But first we have to register at least the questions that historians and political scientists have tried to discuss, however painfully, in relation to Stalin and Russia, and Hitler and Germany. The questions themselves are so clear and fundamental. Who was responsible? The tyrant or his people? Or maybe both, and if so with what degree of complicity?

Leo Tolstoy, maybe Europe's greatest writer but maybe not her greatest historical philosopher, wrote on this question in the 1860s in *War and Peace* in the context of the Napoleonic wars [Tolstoy, 1982, p. 719]. He took one extreme view: "In historical events great men - so-called - are but labels serving to give a name to the event, and like labels they have the least possible connexion with the event itself."

Tolstoy goes on to declare himself an even more extreme historical determinist: "Every action of theirs, that seems to be an act of their own free-will, is in the historical sense not free at all but is bound up with the whole course of history and preordained from all eternity".

An alternative extreme view, more comforting for the population, is that the tyrant was personally responsible, having mounted a machine of state terror that reached all the way down to the grass roots of society, forcing compliance at the risk of one's life.

Stalin became General Secretary of the Party in 1922, two years before Lenin's death, and he himself died in 1953. By 1956 Khrushchev was denouncing him at the 20th Party Congress. By the nineteen-eighties, with Gorbachev's liberalisation, the debate came out into the open, with important historical documentation, notably from Volkogonov [1991]. A succinct survey of the arguments and the literature is that edited by Nove [1993], entitled *The Stalin Phenomenon*.

A contribution going some of the way to Tolstoy's view summarises the essence as follows [Getty, in Nove 1993, pp. 132-136]: "At the end of the 1920s, we find almost all the necessary, long-term 'preconditions' for Stalinism, for repression and, eventually, for a major explosion. The gunpowder had been combined. Customary... social suspicion and violence, lack of a substantial legal tradition, bitter class hatred, a vicious, unrestrained, and recent civil war, hostile international encirclement, a messianic drive for development and modernization, and a contradictory, unstable political framework were the ingredients. ... Added to these preconditions, a series of 'precipitants' from the purely political realm touched off the repression, purging, and violence of the 1930s. They included a full-blown spy and war scare, short-term disputes over economic planning, treatment of the former opposition, and the relationship between the central and territorial party apparatus. ... Stalin's personality and personal role, then, were the 'triggers' which ignited the tinderbox. ..."

"Stalin had initiated a movement with vague instructions and ambiguous targets. As the process unfolded on the ground, though, it rapidly degenerated into chaotic and violent struggles based on local conditions. ... Things were out of control; everybody was arresting everybody. Of course, Stalin and his clique share ultimate responsibility for these 'excesses' ".

Nove [1993, p.35] tried to balance the judgement a bit more clearly on the side of Stalin: "While of course Stalin could not take all the decisions himself, and had to rely on proposals and suggestions from subordinates, all the evidence points to an astonishing degree of personal dominance."

But now the debate follows on about where de-Stalinised, post-Communist Russia is heading. Big options open up again, as well analysed by I. Neumann [1996], as between those wanting to fall back on the tradition of Russian nationalism and those wishing to bring Russia into civilised European society. Russian nationalism may have its romantic aspects, but translated into politics it is more likely to become a matter of self-definition in relation to a foreign enemy.

The analogous debate about Hitler, who rose to power in 1933 and killed himself in his bunker in 1945, developed also in the 1980s, with a 35 year delay for reflection. Of course many of the preconditions for the rise of Nazism were well established, like in the case of Russia. The immediate context was the humiliation of the end of the first world war and the Treaty of Versailles, the economic costs of reparations and the disastrous economic slump of the thirties, announced in Europe by the failure of the Austrian *Kreditanstalt* bank in 1931. The Nazi ideology then adopted "a brew of commonplace racism, German nationalism and vulgar socialism" [Davies, 1997, p.970].

But these basic facts hardly answered the big questions about the relationship between the German people and the Hitler phenomenon, or about conclusions for the future. The big questions were, however, debated within Germany in the 1980s, as represented in the collection of essays, many initially written for *Die Zeit*, and published by R. Augstein [1987] under the title *"Historikerstreit"* (historical quarrel). Two contributions, by J. Habermas and E. Nolte, can be taken as samples coming from opposite ends of the politico-philosophical spectrum, both representing none the less a certain strand of serious reflection among the contemporary German intelligentsia.

Habermas writes [in Piper, 1987, p.75] about the holocaust as a matter of collective guilt, but then also as purging a national fault and further leading to a new, viable concept of cosmopolitan patriotism for Germany: "The only patriotism, which will not alienate us from the west, is patriotism for the constitution. An adherence entered into with conviction about universal constitutional principles has unfortunately been able to establish itself in Germany only after - and through - Auschwitz. Whoever wants to chase away our blushing with a cliché like *obsessional guilt*, whoever wants Germany to return to a conventional form of national identity, they destroy the only reliable basis of our binding in with the west". This indeed could be a creed for Germany's specific participation in Europe.

But that was only one German philosopher. At the other end of the spectrum, Nolte writes [in Piper, 1987, p. 32-3] under the title *"Zwischen Geschichtslegende und Revisionismus"* (between historical legends and revisionism): "Auschwitz resulted not primarily from traditional anti-semitism and was not in its essence a clear *genocide*, but rather and above all the product of a fear-based reaction to the annihilation processes of the Russian Revolution. ... The demonisation of the Third Reich cannot be accepted". Lenin, and then Stalin, led to Hitler. The Russian and German questions had their domino dynamics as well, apparently.

In the 1990s the German debate moved on, with landmark books published under the names Ruth Kluger [1992], Victor Klemperer [1995] and Daniel Goldhagen [1996]. These three contributions are quite different, but have it in common that they mark a maturing of the debate about Germany and the holocaust. The enormous sales of these books show a willingness by Germans to look thoroughly at their recent past, and could be supporting the thesis that the German soul has been purged of its demons (if any). Goldhagen, an American-Jewish political scientist, writes 600 ardent pages under the self-explanatory title "Hitler's Willing Executioners - Ordinary Germans and the Holocaust". Kluger and Klemperer are meticulous diarists of the Hitler period, revealing at least that there was much common knowledge about what the Hitler regime was doing. These are not political diaries, just detailed personal chronicles, and they are read.

With apologies for these fragmentary remarks on such enormous subjects, we have felt it necessary so as to take position and mark some points for later. The German and Russian questions are Europe's biggest questions. These are Europe's most populous nationalities, and in recent times also the most powerful and politically erratic. If there is a secure, civilised order in Europe relating these two to the rest of Europe, then all other security problems are of a second order and can be sorted out. Crude historical determinism for these peoples or others is to be set aside, but so also both the complete personalisation of guilt (Stalin, Hitler) and the demonisation of peoples. In given economic, social, historical circumstances these two peoples have badly gone off the rails of civilisation, and still quite recently. On the other hand it seems blindingly obvious that contemporary, "ordinary Germans" and "ordinary Russians" (as Goldhagen would say) want ordinary, civilised lives. But they and the rest of complicated Europe need an adequate set of common structures of laws, rules, standards, institutions and commitments within which to live and work. A well functioning European Union is tailored for Germany with others of the west and centre, and also there needs to be something more weighty than already exists for Russia to share with the rest of Europe. To these practical issues we return later.

3.2 Human costs of conflict

Europe of the twentieth century was the world champion of conflict and violent death, despite priding itself as being the home and centre of civilisation. Europe of the twentieth century accounted for three quarters of the world's total war deaths, with no more than one-seventh of the world's population.

More precisely it is estimated [Sivard, 1996] that from 1900 to 1995 there were 31 million military deaths and 43 million civilian deaths in Europe, either on the battle-field or war-related. This total of 74 million Europeans compares with a world total of 110 million fatalities (see Annex D). These figures are just for wars. In addition there were the civilian deaths in the USSR under the Stalin regime which Davies [1996] reports as amounting to another 50 million between 1917 and 1953, excluding the war losses of 1939-45.

The scale of this disaster of the 20th century is measured also by the extent to which its 110 million fatalities world-wide exceeded the record of any other century. The 19th century saw only 19 million fatalities, the 18th century 7 million, the 17th century 6 million, the 16th century 2 million.

The losses of the 20th century were accounted for first and foremost through lives lost in the three great tragic theatres of operations, the two world wars, 1914-18 and 1939-45, and the Soviet regime between 1917 and 1953. The following data are taken from Davies [1996].

The First World War, the unnecessary war due to systemic failure of the balance of power regime, caused 8.4 million European military losses, rather equally shared by the great powers (1.8 million Germans, 1.7 million Russians, 1.4 million French, 1.2 million Austro-Hungarians, 0.9 million British, 0.7 million Italians).

The Second World War, due maybe to the disastrously conceived terms of peace imposed upon Germany after the First World War and the subsequent collapse of its democracy, resulted in 14.4 million European military deaths. This time the losses were heavily concentrated in the Soviet Union (8 to 9 million) and Germany (3.5 million). An even greater number of civilians lost their lives. The genocide of Jews by the Nazis totalled between 5 and 6 million lives, of which the majority were Poles and Soviet citizens. Other civilian losses during the Second World War are estimated at 27 million, of which there were 16 million Soviet citizens and 6 million Poles.

Almost as many civilians lost their lives in the Soviet Union during the period 1917-53 due to famines, political terrors and deportations as in the whole of Europe in the two world wars put together.

3.3 Economic costs of conflict

These are the shattering human costs which a reconstructed European political and economic system is in the first place intended to avoid. They make the economists' calculations about improvements in the functioning of economic and money markets in Europe a secondary matter by comparison.

However calculations of economic losses caused by the mega-conflicts are themselves rather paradoxical. The extent of destruction of capital and loss of output in the short run is rather clear, but the recovery of the European economy after the Second World War is a more complex question, on which an excellent general source is Dornbusch, Nölling and Layard [1993].

During the Second World War Germany is estimated to have lost 30% of its 1938 capital stock, mainly through bombing [Wolf, 1993]. For France it is estimated that the capital stock at the end of the war was 20 to 35% below its pre-war level, with 25% of the housing stock destroyed and 60-70% of the transport infrastructure [Saint-Paul, 1993]. Germany's industrial production in 1946 was reduced to 28% of its 1938 level, while the equivalent figures were 54% for Italy, 85% for France and 105% for the UK [Wolf, 1993].

The deeper question is what effect a traumatic war has on long-term economic performance. De Long and Eichengreen [1993] tell two powerful stories in reflecting on a chart (shown in the source) of economic growth in the century 1880 to 1980 in France, Germany and Argentina. During this century France and Germany suffered the two, devastating world wars, while Argentina, a moderately advanced economy in 1880, escaped both of them.

The first story is in the comparison between the country that suffered neither war, versus the two that were consumed by both of them. Argentina, at peace, sustained a smooth and dismal economic performance, with its trend growth rate slowing down after 1913. Both Germany and France, from 1960 onwards, had not only recovered the war losses to the trend level of output that would have been obtained by uninterrupted continuation of the pre-1913 rate of growth; the trend growth rate in fact accelerated substantially. A similar story is suggested by bringing Japan and the UK into the picture. Japan, deeply damaged by war, produced the biggest recovery miracle of all, initially under the firm guidance of General MacArthur. The UK, relatively little damaged, produced the most sluggish recovery.

The second story is that the recovery after the Second World War was far more successful than after the First World War in both France and Germany. The key differences between the two episodes concern, effectively, aid and trade: first, the crippling Versailles reparations imposed upon Germany after the First World War, versus the generous Marshall aid after the Second World War; and, second, the relapse into protectionism after the First World War versus the multilateral liberalisations of the OEEC, EEC, EFTA and GATT after the Second World War.

With these two external conditions - the Marshall aid and multilateral openness - set very favourably, economic policy in Germany and France seem to have offered show cases of, respectively, liberalism and state planning. By the late 'fifties these economic recovery achievements were consolidated and deepened with the launching of the EEC. Synergies were surely harvested as the population in Germany especially worked and worked, both for economic growth and construction of a new Europe, which, for society, was a clean and fresh departure after the horrors of the war period. "Support for European economic integration became a substitute for patriotism" [Giersch et al., 1993].

Relevant here are arguments of political economy and sociology combined, such as in M.Olsen's "Rise and Fall of Nations" [1982], according to which the very prosperous economy will in due course become slothful and develop sclerotic interest groups. The idea is one of alternating long cycles of dynamism and stagnation, a variant on the theme of Kondratief. In the early post-war period both Germany and Japan, the defeated, were motivated to make gigantic national reconstruction efforts. Meanwhile the victorious Britain had slow growth, for reasons ranging from the lack of need to replace the capital stock to more sociological factors like taking it easy after the war. Then in the 1980s and 1990s the pendulum seemed to swing again. Germany and Japan encountered obstacles to sustained fast growth, whereas the UK was driven by relative economic decline to take the liberalising therapy earlier.

In the USSR there was also a gigantic patriotic effort of scientific and technological development in the 1950s to 1970s, after unparalleled human and economic losses in the preceding decades.

The paradox seems to be that the greater the devastation caused by war, the greater the capacities of society to recover and reconstruct afterwards. This points to cautionary messages, especially for the economist. The economic destruction of war may not be so costly in the long run, because of society's springs of energy for reconstruction and recovery after the trauma of war. These sociological sources of economic growth seem only to be vaguely understood and even less captured by economic growth theory.

The economic role of refugees is another significant question. From 1945 to 1953 the west German population was boosted by 10 million refugees [Wolf, 1993], many from east Germany but many having come from elsewhere in central Europe, for example the 3.5 million Sudeten Germans expelled at the end of the war from Czechoslovakia. Wolf enumerated the several qualities of these immigrants that were favourable to growth: willingness to work hard and long hours, their high human capital value, their extreme mobility and their demand for durable goods starting with nothing. In Finland also there was a very large resettlement task with the arrival of 400 000 Finns from the part of Karelia seized by Stalin, representing a 10% addition to the labour force [Paunio,1993].

Europe was also the theatre of the most costly ever Cold War. In the NATO alliance the arms build-up saw defence budgets rise to a share of GDP about twice the level to which they have dropped after the end of the Cold War. The European countries of NATO, which spent 4.6% of GDP on defence in 1960, had cut this to 2.5% by 1994 [Sivart, 1996]. The comparable figures for the US were 8.8% of GDP in 1960 and 4.3% in 1994.

In terms of current prices the defence budgets of European NATO countries amounted in 1994 to $130 billion. If defence spending were now continuing at the share of GDP experienced at the height of the Cold War it would be costing about another $100 billion for European NATO countries. By the same calculation the United States would be spending over $200 billion more.

The costs of regional conflicts may be quite as devastating, proportionately. In Bosnia the recent war saw GNP cut to 10% of its pre-war levels. Here 70% of the industrial plant were destroyed. Unemployment rose to 80%, aside from the 3 million refugees and 200,000 lives lost [IISS, 1997]. In Serbia, just hit by sanctions, output in 1996 was reduced to half the 1989 level, 3 million pensioners were not receiving their pensions. In October 1995 the government of Bosnia-Herzgovena submitted its estimate of reconstruction costs for aid from the international community: $9 billion for reconstructing the transport system, $9 billion for re-equipping industry, $4 billion for reconstructing housing, and $4 billion for displaced persons and refugees, just for a country of 4 million population.

The case of Northern Ireland offers an example on the costs of relatively low-level conflict: apart from the human cost of 2,786 lives from 1969 to 1989, the subvention to the economy to compensate for the direct and indirect economic damage to the region rose by 1993 to a level 60% above the UK average, even excluding military expenditures [O'Leary and McGarry, 1995]. The extraordinary vulnerability of modern cities to terrorist bomb attacks is illustrated by single explosions in the commercial centre of Manchester and the financial centre of London in the mid-1990s, costing many hundreds of millions of pounds to repair. Apparently there is no space in the financial city of London now left unmonitored by security television circuits [Schulte, 1996].

But the economist is still left puzzled by the costs of conflict. The human losses in Europe have been so enormous that it seems superfluous, or even immoral to count economic losses as well. But when the economic losses are examined the calculations run into deep methodological and theoretical difficulties, since the costs of economic destruction so obvious at the time of the violence lead on to the mysterious but often very powerful, dynamic processes of recovery. The economist is left disarmed. Maybe he is better employed simply at his normal business of keeping economic policy on a reasonable track, averting economic disasters that provoke political violence.

3.4 Europe's 21st century

At the end of the 20th century Europe's security agenda changes totally, as the prospects of world war and ideological and hegemonic conflict recede over the horizon. The security system has to change accordingly to handle the new security agenda.

What type of conflicts and violence seems likely in the decades ahead? A valuable survey of the prospects for political violence in the European Union up to the year 2025 has recently been drawn up by P. Schulte [1996]. This points to the all-European security agenda for the period ahead, taking especially into account the kinds of tensions and conflicts that are visible or likely in central and eastern Europe.

With the disappearance of threats of world war, the new sources of conflict become much more varied. The emphasis shifts from outright inter-state conflict, even if the risks of this have not totally evaporated, and more to internal tensions of society which can have wider European implications. The frontiers between the concerns of the military, the police, the economist and politician become more and more overlapping. The enemy is not a foreign power but a range of societal ailments that can well undermine the working of civil society, threatening anything between its erosion to collapse.

A list of types of tension or conflicts, shown in Table 3.1, drawing on the schema of P. Schulte [1996].

Table 3.1: Categories of tension and actual or potential conflict

I. Nationalist-ethnic
1 Multi-ethnic	*Bosnia, Belgium*
2 Ethnophobic	*Le Pen-ism in France*
3 Separatist	*Basques, Chechnya, Northern Ireland*
4 Irredentist	*Russia in former USSR states*

II. Redistributive
5 National	*General strikes of workers*
6 Regional	*East Germany, N-S Belgium*
7 Sectoral	*Farmers and fishermen*

III. Radical opposition
8 Ideological	*Communist, fascist*
9 Ecological	*Anti-nuclear*

IV. Criminality
10 Mafia and corruption	*East Europe, Italy*
11 Disaffected groups	*Youth violence*

V. Anarchy
12. Breakdown of civil society	*Albania*

VI. External
13 Clash of civilisations	*Islamic terrorism, rogue states*

Source: derived from Schulte [1996].

The *nationalist-ethnic* set of problems is evidently the most real concern in practice as the 20th century draws to its close. It divides into several sub-species.

The *multi-ethnic* state is that in which the ethnic divisions are relatively equally matched in size. The issue may be about whether one group is to dominate, or whether power-sharing models can be made to work or not. Bosnia is a case that degenerated into all-out war,

Northern Ireland is that of a long stalemate in inter-communal violence, Belgium that of a tense but non-violent *modus vivendi*, Switzerland that of such ultra-democratic stability that violent conflict seems inconceivable.

The *ethnophobic* category is where a nationalist majority becomes aggressive towards an ethnic minority. While the epoch of Jewish persecution is now largely history, the Gipsy (or Roma) are a numerous underclass in much of central and eastern Europe, subject of grievances in several countries. In western Europe there are the massive new minorities from Africa and Asia. While these race relations are often remarkably positive, tensions are fomented by new-right political nationalists. The Le Pen party in France is an example, whose agenda includes expulsion and repatriation of the immigrants.

The *separatist* case is where the region with a well identified ethnic group wants to leave, without having a related group to join in another state. Separation was peacefully undertaken in Czechoslovakia in 1992; it was achieved *de facto* in Chechnya only after a terrible war and remains the objective of terrorist violence in the Basque territory and on a small scale Corsica.

Irredentism is the case where a separatist group seeks to join its ethnic brothers in another state, and is particularly dangerous when it involves poorly drawn frontiers, usually the outcome of an earlier war. Unfortunately the map of Europe has much irredentist potential, from the Hungarian communities in Slovakia and Romania, the Albanian communities in Serbia and Macedonia, and on to the Russian minorities in many of the states of the former Soviet Union.

The *redistributive* category of tensions, all about the struggle for income and wealth, may be thought of in terms of the national, the regional and the sectoral.

A dramatic example of *national* redistributive tensions arises in Russia and other former Communist countries, where pensioners have seen their savings wiped out by inflation and pensions and workers their wages often unpaid for months on end. Somewhat miraculously the reactions to these objectively very great social strains have on the whole been mild.

At the *regional* level political tensions can develop in depressed regions not only when they are neglected. In EU countries such regions are usually recipients of massive subsidies, becoming in some cases manifestly welfare-dependent, and ultimately to the point that the paying regions find their sense of solidarity stretched to the limit. Such is the case in Italy, with the north becoming less inclined to subsidise the south, East Germany where the transition has got stuck at a very high level of highly subsidised unemployment, and Belgium where Flanders becomes increasingly unhappy at subsidising Wallonia. Yet these tensions have not given way to violence.

At the *sectoral* level there is also a regular tendency in the EU for disputes over public subsidies or protected incomes to degenerate into low level violence, but still sharp in political effectiveness (farmers, fishermen, coal miners etc).

Radical opposition ideologies do not seem likely to achieve power. However old-fashioned Communists are by no means extinct as political activists in eastern Europe. Their possible alliance with undemocratic nationalists is a political scenario in Russia, even if a recurrence of the coup d'état attempts of 1991 and 1993 becomes more remote with the passing of time. However the Lukashenko regime in Belarus is capable of perpetrating or provoking political violence.

Within the EU *ecological* protest groups are causing low-level security headaches and economic disruption, such as in 1997 with the demonstrations surrounding the movement of nuclear waste in Germany and attempts to obstruct the movement of oil-drilling platforms in the North Sea.

The problems of endemic *mafia and corruption* in eastern Europe may now be rated as Europe's principal security risk alongside that of ethnic conflicts. The mafia problem has extremely wide-ranging implications. It can stifle economic growth and therefore threatens the economic transition. It can feed non-democratic political reactions. It seems to move across frontiers with ease, together with quantities of illegally traded narcotics, weapons and even nuclear materials.

Violence by *disaffected groups* amounts to be a residual category where the source of the problem is not so well identified. The main contemporary example is youth violence in towns and hooliganism. Control of football crowds, including across the borders of the frontier-free EU, has become a substantial task of the police. In France a more diffuse wave of juvenile urban violence has risen to worrying proportions, multiplying five times over the five years to 1997.

Anarchy is stronger and rarer stuff. It represents the complete failure of both government and civil society systems. Pure anarchy had seemed to be a largely theoretical concept for contemporary Europe, yet the example of Albania in 1997 came for a while close to this. In this case, following public discontent over the collapse of fraudulent pyramid savings schemes, the descent into anarchy happened with remarkable swiftness. Government ceased to function, arms were seized by gangs, shops pillaged and the country was at the mercy of local or regional groups, with a mix of regional civil war and local gangsterism. The episode shows what can happen when extreme economic hardship and injustices occur in a society with weak democracy and civil society.

External threats to Europe seem to focus now principally on aspects of Islam. There is occasional terrorist violence in France, allegedly representing the response of fundamentalist elements in North Africa to foreign policy positions taken over Islamic politics. "Rogue states" (Libya, Iraq, Iran) acquire missile and nuclear capabilities, maybe not yet with a range to reach much of Europe, but this is not inconceivable for the future.

While each item in the list may not seem all that threatening, bigger issues may arise through the combination and inter-action of tensions or more than one category. This is particularly so for the combination of ethnic minority situations with regional problems or irredentist relationships across frontiers, to which we now turn in more detail.

3.5 Checking out the ethnic flash-points

There are one hundred cases in central and eastern Europe where a minority nationality has a population in excess of 100 000 people, or 1% of the state's population. Most of these are listed in Annex table C, only omitting the very long tail of smaller Russian minorities. If a higher threshold of 5% of the state's population or 1 million people is

Table 3.2 : Main minorities in central and eastern Europe

Country	Minority	Number	% of nation's population	
EU applicants				
Czech Rep.	Moravian	1 356 000	13.2%	A
Slovakia	Hungarian	567 000	10.8%	B
Bulgaria	Turk	800 000	9.4%	A/B
Romania	Hungarian	1 620 000	7.1%	A/B
Estonia	Russian	475 000	30.3%	B
Latvia	Russian	906 000	34.0%	B
Lithuania	Russian	344 000	9.4%	A
=	Polish	258 000	7.0%	A
Other Balkan				
Croatia	Serb	582 000	12.2%	C
Macedonia	Albanian	479 000	23.1%	B/C
Serbia-Monten.	Albanian	1 687 000	17.2%	C
Bosnia Herzg.	Muslim	1 906 000	43.7%	C
=	Serb	1 369 000	31.4%	C
=	Croat	756 000	17.3%	C
CIS Europe				
Russia	Tatar	5 543 000	3.8%	B
=	Ukrainian	4 363 000	3.0%	A
=	Chuvash	1 774 000	1.2%	A
=	Bashkir	1 345 000	0.9%	A
=	Belarussian	1 206 000	0.8%	A
=	Mordvin	1 073 000	0.7%	A
=	Chechen	899 000	0.6%	C
Ukraine	Russian	11 356 000	22.1%	A/B
Belarus	Russian	1 342 000	13.1%	A
Moldova	Ukrainian	600 000	13.8%	A
=	Russian	562 000	12.9%	B
Georgia	Armenian	437 000	8.1%	A
=	Russian	341 000	6.3%	A
=	Azerbaijan	308 000	5.7%	A
Azerbaijan	Russian	392 000	5.6%	A
=	Armenian	391 000	5.6%	C

*Note: ratings by author: **A**=normal, **B**=serious tensions, **C**=conflict*

Source: Annex C

retained, there are the 31 instances listed in Table 3.2. The majority are problematic. If the cut-off were national minorities of 10% or more of the population there are ten cases. The numerous smaller cases are of course also important when any questions of principle and individual human rights are at stake. However they are much less likely to lead to collective conflicts, civil war and threats to inter-state peace.

Which of these situations are more vulnerable to becoming a source of conflict and danger for European security? A primary sorting would first distinguish between those cases in which the minority is regionally concentrated or dispersed, and secondly between those related to an irredentist power of another state or isolated. The most dangerous situation for its escalation potential is where the minority is concentrated on the frontier with an irredentist power. In practise such circumstances are virtually sure to be the result of an earlier war and may well represent deep historic enmities and unresolved grievances. Table 3.3 sorts out these cases.

Two further ingredients will raise seriously the probabilities of conflict: current economic difficulties resulting in social hardships, and a weak democratic order and set of civil society institutions and traditions. Then the classic political mechanisms of escalation can move into action. Emotions may be excited by the political leadership to the point that quiescent griefs and enmities are raised again to the level of hatred and even fanaticism. The leader becomes himself political hostage to the aspirations he planted with his people, such that he cannot afford to back down without certain political defeat personally.

These are a framework of ideas to be borne in mind as we now go on to review the map of Europe's ethnic fault lines, for assessing which are the serious risks for European security, and for understanding how other risky situations became stable and peaceful.

The objective is to form an overview of this vast ethnic mosaic, so as to judge where there are real risks to peace, and of widening tensions and conflicts. Is the map of Europe going most likely to see only a recurrence of unconnected bush-fires; or may linkages threaten escalation, leading to widespread war and destruction?

In the brief review that follows the main sources deserve special

Table 3.3: Typology of ethnic tensions or conflicts

	regionally diffuse	regionally compact
without neighbouring irredentist power	new Afro-Caribbean-Asian minorities in western Europe, Gipsy minorities in central Europe	Basques in Spain, Corsicans in France, Chechens, Tatar, Chuvash and Bashkir in Russia, Moravians in Czech Rep., Gagauz in Moldova, Muslims in Bosnia.
with neighbouring irredentist power	Russians in former Soviet Union states in general.	Russians in Narva(Estonia) and Sebastopol (Ukraine), Hungarians in Slovakia, and in Transsylvania (Romania), Armenians in Nagorno Karabakh (Azerbaijan), Albanians in Kosovo (Serbia) and Macedonia, Serbs and Croats in Bosnia, Azeris and Armenians in Georgia, Turks in Bulgaria.

mention. G. Brunner of the University of Cologne has compiled an exhaustive account of minorities in all countries of central and eastern Europe, including the former USSR [Brunner, 1996]. J. Bujajski has given a deeper account just for the central and eastern European countries, excluding the former USSR [Bugajski, 1995]. The international non-governmental organization, Minority Rights Group (MRG) of London, has published an invaluable collection of over 90 in depth reports on the situation of minorities world-wide.

- Western Europe

The EU stands for the historic reconciliation of former enemies. War between its member states has become inconceivable. None the less problems of low level violence are still serious in several regions, and some of the lessons of success stories of reconciliation are worth recalling as encouragement in relation to the many cases of unresolved tension on the map of Europe.

The success stories generally started as the typical European case where frontiers, brutally changed by wars, were left with poor ethnic fit [MRG, 1991]. Western Europe is hardly different in this respect from the rest of Europe.

Finland has a Swedish minority of 6% of the population, concentrated in South and Western regions, including the Aland Islands which are 95% Swedish. These islands have achieved a very high degree of regional and cultural autonomy, allowing earlier contention on questions of territorial sovereignty to be dissolved. The Swedish minority is supported by the equal status given to Swedish as one of the two national languages and its use in separate educational establishments.

The Finnish-Russian frontier is stabilised despite the Russian take-over at the end of the Second World War of the Finnish Baltic port of Vyborg and substantial slices of Karelia. Finland evacuated virtually its whole population in these areas, and the matter is closed politically.

The Danish-German frontier regions have long-standing mutual minorities, and the frontier was the subject of war in 1848-50, 1864, 1914-18 and 1939-45. The disproportionate size of the two nations has made symmetrical of treatment of the respective minorities difficult, and political tensions over the rights of the Danish minority on the German side of the frontier were still alive in the 1950s. The definition of the respective minority rights was made in two parallel, unilateral declarations made in 1955 in Bonn and Copenhagen, a form chosen to confirm the sovereignty of each nation. These acts of reconciliation (including for example special voting rules in Schleswig Holstein to ensure representation of the Danish minority in the Land parliament) were motivated in part by German's desire to smooth the path of its accession to NATO, an analogue of the implicit conditionality presently visible in NATO and EU enlargement processes.

Switzerland is a highly pertinent model for others in eastern Europe to reflect on, since its ethnic composition and divisions are the closest analogue to Bosnia and Dagestan, with comparability in terms of the number of main linguistic communities and also the patch-work of small minority communities and enclaves. Switzerland has four official languages, a confederal constitution and the most elaborate system of direct and decentralised democracy anywhere. All legislation can be altered either by referendum or individual initiative, with legislation that can be introduced by citizens. Several multi-lingual cantons have devolved cultural autonomy rights down to the village level (a formula that could have been a model for Bosnia, and might still be so in areas where there has not been irreversible "ethnic cleansing").

The case of South Tyrol in Italy has only recently become stable and peaceful, since up the 1960s there was inter-communal bitterness and separatist terrorism. South Tyrol, with its 85% German-speaking Austrian population, was passed to Italy at the end of the First World War, as one of the many poorly drawn frontier adjustments of that time. The Mussolini regime then embarked on a programme of cultural oppression and assimilation, banning German in any official use, destroying German schools, dismissing German-speaking government officials etc. When Italy was enabled none the less to retain South Tyrol after the Second World War, cultural autonomy for the German community was rapidly restored, and the region's political autonomy was greatly strengthened in 1972. The economic and social situation has drastically improved since, separatist violence has faded away and the leaders of South Tyrol promote the political concept of an integrated Europe of regions.

But western Europe still has three regions where efforts to quell secessionist violence have not yet succeeded: Northern Ireland, the Basque region of Spain and Corsica.

The nature of the conflict in Northern Ireland, hopefully now ended in 1998 after thirty years of bloodshed, had remained itself obscure to the most expert of analysts, as two quotations from McGarry and O'Leary [1995] suggest: "The conflict is variously held to be fundamentally theological, cultural, economic, or ethnic". Then, with a touch of Irish wit, a remark to underline the tragic absurdity of this violence: "Anyone who thinks they understand Northern Ireland is obviously confused". Repeated attempts to devise power-sharing formulae between Catholics and Protestants, and between London and Dublin, have eluded durable settlement until Easter day in April 1998. The settlement involved a new assembly in Belfast, new cross-frontier institutions and a completely new Council of the Iles. The latter includes representatives not only of Belfast, Dublin and Westminster but also of Cardiff and Edeinburgh, following the decision in 1997 to create these last two regional assemblies.

In Spain the Basque campaign for independence continues with minority support for the ETA movement which employs terrorist violence. With police action constraining ETA terrorism, the mode of violence shifts to more diffuse arson by disaffected youth gangs. Since the summer of 1997 public revulsion over Basque ETA assassinations seems to have been tipping the balance of regional public opinion in favour of non-violent politics.

In Corsica the National Front for the Liberation of Corsica announced in June 1997 a temporary cease-fire in its bombing actions, hoping that greater autonomy for the region might be agreed. Hopes for peace were again set back in February 1998 with assassination of the *préfet* of the department.

There is also a rich menu of regional issues in western Europe, where the political debate over regional devolution is active but non-violent. These include questions of stability of the Belgian federalism, of Italy's regionalism, the creation of parliamentary assemblies in Scotland and Wales, the autonomy of Catalonia in Spain and Spain's claims over Gibraltar.

Relations between the French and Flemish communities in Belgium have become tense again, notwithstanding the federalisation reforms of 1993. Unemployment rates are over twice as high in Wallonia, and the Flemish side wants to regionalise wage levels and social security, which Wallonia resists.

In Italy the separatist campaign by the Northern League is a protest over perceived misgovernment by Rome and exploitation of interregional fiscal transfers by the Mezzogiorno. However the Northern League in 1997 appeared to lack credibility as a secessionist force, winning only 15% in regional elections in April 1997, following 40% four years earlier. It has been speculated that a reverse for Rome's ambition to join the euro early could destabilise Italian politics, including over the regional divide. The civil society of Italy has long been vitiated by endemic corruption in state bodies and mafia violence in the south. Dramatic campaigns of purification have been under way in Italian national politics but the mafia problem seems still to defy solution.

Separatist pressures in Scotland have been entirely non-violent. In Wales nationalist pressures have already achieved recognition in the use of the Welsh language in education and public. Acts of violence in Wales have been limited to isolated burnings of English-owned secondary residences. Both Scotland and Wales are now to have parliamentary assemblies, following positive results from referenda in September 1997, with particularly extensive powers devolved to Scotland (with the normal constitutional powers of the state of a federation, together with attributes of nationhood). The central authorities of the UK here voluntarily led the process of devolution rather than resisting it, with only small separatist minorities wanting to go further to outright secession.

In Spain the long-standing autonomist demands of the linguistically distinct Catalonia and Galicia appear today reasonably satisfied or at least quiescent under the regionalised constitution.

Spain sustains a territorial claim over Gibraltar, imposing a variety of frontier restrictions and citing now the example of the return of Hong Kong to China. The UK rejects these claims, since under the Treaty of Utrecht of 1713 Spain only retains a first refusal should Gibraltar cease to be a British colony. It reminds Spain of this when Spain's full military integration into NATO is being concluded. Spain declared in December 1997 that it was in no hurry to complete its military's integration into NATO in the absence of British concessions.

In France, more important than the Corsican problem are the tensions between the immigrant North African community and the ethnophobic politics of the National Front party. The potential inter-action between Islamic fundamentalist terrorism brought on to French soil from Algeria and rising inter-ethnic tensions could escalate. The programme of the French National Front party for repatriation of foreigners would be divisive in relation to EU rules and policies of other member states. However the opposition to the nationalist programme is also strong, both in the government and in public opinion.

- EU candidate countries

The dominant trait among these countries is their strong motivation, expressed through their EU and NATO applications, to converge on normal European standards for the economy, politics and civil society. But this goes also with an inheritance of complex ethnic structures and historically fractious frontiers. In addition the former Communist countries have to withstand the strains of the economic transition with weak civil society traditions.

Poland, the largest country of the region, has had its frontiers relentlessly chopped up by history. But the post-communist period has seen confirmation, rather than questioning of the frontiers resulting from the Second World War. Within Poland the economy advances at the head of the transition countries. It has only one concentrated ethnic minority, 250 000 Belarussians in the eastern border area. Although Warsaw has rejected their demands for minority rights, the Belarus community appear rather content to be participating in Poland's relative economic success. There are also believed to be about 300 000 Ukrainians scattered in eastern Poland, without representing a minority problem.

There are significant Polish minorities in Lithuania (350 000), Belarus (4-500 000), and western Ukraine (250 000). There have been some unsatisfied demands for greater minority rights or local autonomy among these Polish groups, especially in Lithuania. In 1989 and 1990 the Polish minority in Lithuania pushed unsuccessfully for the creation of Polish national regions, while in March 1990 the six ethnic Polish members of the Lithuanian parliament abstained from supporting the Lithuanian Declaration of Independence [Wohlfeld ed., 1997]. This made for mistrust in Lithuania of Polish intentions. At the same time the Polish authorities in Warsaw signalled their concern for the treatment of the Polish minority in Lithuania. By 1997, however, there were signs that shared interests in NATO and EU enlargement were coming to the foreground, with the Polish foreign minister in March declaring that his country would do its best to get Lithuania included in the first wave. This was a positive, if only symbolic gesture, but none the less a good way to keep the focus on cooperation rather than tension. Among common concerns between these two countries is the Russian enclave of Kaliningrad, where the Russian military establishment amounts to the size of the entire Polish army. There are interesting projects for regional economic cooperation not yet secured, for example the Via Baltica highway which would go through these territories.

The reciprocal minorities on both sides of the Polish-Ukrainian frontier are considerable in terms of population, but politically these pose only minor issues compared to the strategic relationship between the two countries in the context of the EU and NATO enlargements and the role of Russia. The two Presidents declared in June 1996 evidence of *rapprochement* between the two countries: "The existence of an independent Ukraine helps consolidate Polish independence, while the existence of an independent Poland helps to consolidate Ukrainian independence." [Wohlfeld ed., 1997]. However the EU and NATO accessions of Poland will throw up several sensitive issues at the Polish-Ukrainian frontier, including trade and visa policies as well as questions of military alliance (see Chapters 4 and 5).

The *Czech-Slovak* divorce in 1993 set an example of peaceful separation. Subsequently within the *Czech Republic* the Moravians and Silesians have been demanding autonomy for their region, aiming at a federal constitution (in the 1991 census 1.4 million of 3 million of the inhabitants of the region declared their nationality to be either Moravian or Silesian). These pressures have not yet found a settled resolution, but the process seems likely to remain one of democratic politics. The issues are more about the degree of regional devolution of political powers than minority rights.

In January 1997 the Czech Republic signed a declaration of reconciliation with Germany, in which Germany apologized for the occupation of the Sudeten territory under Hitler and the Czech side regretted the offenses against the Sudeten Germans who were expelled at the end of the war. This agreement is intended to ensure against the risk of large-scale German requests for restitution of property, but is not yet operational.

The situation of the *Hungarian* minorities in Slovakia and Romania is a classic from the case book of European minorities. It concerns lands that were formerly part of the Hungarian empire, which was severely truncated after the First World War. Hungary reoccupied these areas during the Second World War, and had to cede them back again afterwards. The Hungarian authorities are concerned with the situation of their co-nationals. The Hungarians in Slovakia are mainly concentrated in communities on the Hungarian frontier, while in Romania their largest concentration is in the central region of Transylvania, which was controlled by the Austro-Hungarian empire after the withdrawal of the Ottoman empire from this area in the 18th century. In *Slovakia* the issue of minority rights of the Hungarian communities is tense, influenced by 800 years of history during which the Slovaks in this region were generally the underclass to the Magyars. But since 1993 the Hungarian community has had reason to complain over initiatives by the Meciar government that worsen their position on questions of language and local government; the EU Commission's opinion is also that reforms are called for [EU Commission, 1997].

In *Romania* the Communist regime of Ceaucescu severely oppressed the Hungarian minorities, trying to force their assimilation and resettling Romanians in their areas. In the first phase of the post-Communist period, from 1990 (when there were violent clashes between the Hungarian community and Romanians) to 1994 the Hungarian authorities of Budapest pushed for regional autonomy and improved minority rights for the Magyar communities, and there was episodic violence. But this situation greatly improved, following changes of government in 1994 in Hungary and in 1996 in Romania

[Wohlfeld ed., 1997]. By May 1997 tensions were substantially reduced, with signing of a Hungarian-Romanian friendship treaty confirming the inviolability of frontiers and following entry into the Romanian government of Magyar personalities of the "Democratic Alliance of Hungarians in Romania". None the less the government was still by the end of 1998 having difficulties in getting parliament and local authorities to accept this more favourable deal for the Hungarian minorities.

Overall the situation of these two Hungarian minorities should normalise as long as all three countries maintain their priorities to join the EU and NATO, and are therefore strongly induced to respect the norms of the Council of Europe and OSCE. But Slovakia lags. Hungary itself has adopted legislation protecting national minorities which is considered by experts in this field to be a model.

In *Bulgaria* about 800 000 people, or 9% of the population, are Muslim Turks, reflecting 500 years of Ottoman rule up until 1878. In the Communist period there was forced assimilation of the Turkish minority. This led by 1989 to violent protests and police repression, resulting in about 350 000 leaving the country for Turkey, of whom only about 135 000 returned after restoration of minority rights in 1990. The 1991 Bulgarian constitution has strengthened the political rights of minorities, and the EU Commission in its opinion of July 1997 agreed that the situation was much improved [EU Commission, 1997]. Mutual suspicions between Bulgaria and Turkey remain live and the relationship needs to be strongly influenced by the incentives and principles of modern Europe.

The Roma or Gipsy communities of central and eastern Europe are believed to total 6 million people, and constitute small but conspicuous minorities in many countries. These are culturally distinct, traditionally nomadic people, whose plight is characterised by poverty, low educational standards and social exclusion. During the communist period they were subject often to forced assimilation and human rights abuses. While their situation in Hungary has improved, there are serious problems still in Bulgaria, the Czech Republic, Romania and Slovakia, sufficient to have been highlighted in the EU Commission's opinions of July 1997, in addition to concern already expressed in the

Council of Europe and OSCE.

The *Baltic* states are the only EU candidate countries which have substantial Russian minorities. This makes a strong incentive to reach a settled situation for the Russian minorities there, but these countries have also understandable concern to bolster their new nationhood.

The *Lithuanian* case is generally considered to be settled, where the relatively small Russian minority has not been perceived as threatening enough to impede rather liberal citizenship laws. The Polish minorities there have been more vocal in complaints.

In *Estonia* the Law on Citizenship of 1992 set much higher hurdles for anyone who immigrated in the Soviet period, or for their descendants. There is also a language test in Estonian, with the result by 1995 that 30% of the population remained without Estonian citizenship. The EU Commission's opinion of July 1997 was that there should be measures to accelerate the extension of citizenship to the Russian minority.

Latvia took until 1994 to pass a comparable law on citizenship and 30% of the population was excluded from voting in the first parliamentary elections in 1994. The OSCE Minorities Commissioner has stated that in his opinion the law is too restrictive, suggesting that people born in Latvia should get citizenship automatically and that the language and history tests should be lightened. The EU Commission in its opinion of July 1997 added that there should be measures to eliminate discrimination in professional and political life.

The tensions over Russian minority rights in Estonia and Latvia are thus real, but waning with time. Russian nationalist political factions in the State Duma are still readily inclined to issue highly aggressive declarations, and trade barriers between Russia and the Baltic states are discriminatory, rather than preferential as for CIS states. On the other hand the position of the Russian minorities themselves is typically one of relative contentment with their material standard of living in the Baltic states, compared to if they were facing the prospect of returning to Russia. With Russia's present leadership these tensions seem unlikely to escalate, but the situation remains vulnerable if there were a serious political reversal in Russia.

Turkey harbours a multiple set of tensions or conflicts, concerning the functioning of democratic institutions, the inter-relation between politics and religion, issues of territory over the Aegean and Cyprus, and of minority rights issues of the Turks abroad and of the Kurds at home. While the business community integrates impressively with the European market, there is a political climate of national resentment over the apparently stalled EU application. There is thus an unresolved task still ahead, to fashion a stable place in Europe for this large and fast-growing people.

Turkey's EU application is undoubtedly affected by perceived uncertainty over the durability of Ataturk's legacy of the secular Muslim state, as reflected in the arrival of the Islamic party to power in 1996. This government was replaced in June 1997, but only after the army had pressured the Islamic party prime minister to desist in Islamic policy measures. In August 1997 a law was passed by a narrow majority to reduce the place of religion in schooling. In January 1998 the constitutional court took the ominous step of banning the Islamic party, despite its having the most populous support, on the grounds that it was undermining the country's secular constitution.

The Turkish army is itself instrumental in the repressive practices concerning the Kurdish minority, and the Council of Europe and European Parliament are highly critical of these human right abuses. Over a 14 year period Turkey has been depopulating Kurdish areas to the point of emptying over 3 000 villages [Sivart, 1996], with 18 000 killed, including the Turkish victims of Kurdish guerillas.

Turkish-Greek tensions also remain over the Greek Aegean islands and resources of the Aegean Sea, although these were alleviated in July 1997 by an agreement between Greek and Turkish leaders to deny the use of force or threat of force.

The current episode in Cyprus began in 1974 with the Turkish invasion of the northern third of the island, triggered by an attempted putsch by Greek nationalists seeking unification with Greece, itself then governed by a military regime. The Turkish minority in Cyprus had previously been badly treated. With the Turkish invasion 150 000 Greeks fled from their homes and land in the north, while 46 000 Turks fled from the south. The present dividing line, monitored by the UN, amounts to a Berlin wall, with complete separation of the populations.

The Greek part of the island has made enormous economic progress, with a GNP per capita of about Spain's level, much higher than Greece itself. The Turkish occupied area is economically depressed, its population of 150 000 including 35 000 Turkish military and 80 000 settlers brought in from continental Turkey.

Meanwhile political developments have made this situation increasingly anomalous. Greece became democratic and joined the EU in 1981. Turkey became an EU candidate in 1987. Cyprus became an EU candidate in 1990. Greece blocks Turkey's relations with the EU as long as northern Cyprus remains occupied militarily. Turkey makes various diplomatic threats if Cyprus were to advance faster into the EU than Turkey, possibly to block NATO expansion, possibly to annex northern Cyprus formally into Turkey.

The agenda for resolution of the Cyprus question is well established, with UN sponsored negotiations in 1992, which were suspended and then resumed temporarily in 1997: a federal constitution, protection of minority rights, demilitarisation, restoration of refugees' property rights, incentives for Turkish settlers to return. The gains from a settlement would be substantial, with modern economic development spreading to the whole of the island, accession of Cyprus to the EU and improved EU-Turkish relations.

In the contrary case there is the prospect of a grotesque return to antiquated international tensions as if of the 19th century, with Greek Cyprus planning to buy missiles and tanks from Russia, which is in turn only too willing to earn some money arming an enemy of its traditional rival Turkey. A recent study [Kramer, 1997] concludes: "in the long-run, such developments would almost certainly endanger Turkey's bonds with the West and could trigger a dramatic change in the strategic situation in the eastern Mediterranean and beyond."

In March 1998 Turkish frustration over its stalled EU application degenerated into angry and poorly judged polemic. As accession negotiations with five other applicants were formally opened, the Turkish prime minister chose to call Germany's preference for these other candidates a new *"Lebensraum"* policy, a remark that was only likely to escalate tensions.

- CIS Europe

Russia's legacy from its former empire and the Soviet Union is to find itself both "exporter and importer" of minorities on a grand and remarkably symmetrical scale, with 25 million Russians in the other former Soviet Union states and 27 million people of the minority nationalities within Russia.

By far the biggest and most complex issues arise with the *Ukraine*. There are two types of tension, one being the basic question of the Ukraine's destiny as between east and west, the other specific to Sebastopol, Crimea and the Black Sea fleet. The west of the country has been the centre of the Ukrainian nationalist idea for several centuries, whereas the east has a large Russian population. On the other hand one of the typical ingredients of European conflict is absent. The Russian-Ukrainian relationship at the historical and personal level is to a degree one of brotherhood more than enmity, with Kiev having been the first capital of the Rus in early medieval times. In mid-1997 visitors to the eastern Ukraine reported the absence of any powerful, pro-Russian separatist movement. The government in Kiev is dominated by personalities from eastern Ukraine. The language question has been handled tactfully and President Kuchma is reported as considering giving the Russian language greater status in the region.

The status of the city of Sebastopol has been disputed, Kiev regarding it as a Ukrainian city, Moscow recalling the special status given to it as a Soviet city when Khrushchev transferred Crimea to the Ukraine in 1954. But in May 1997 long negotiations over these issues and the future of the Black Sea fleet were concluded with signature of a set of agreements [Sherr, 1997]. Russia acknowledges Ukrainian sovereignty over Crimea, Sebastopol and the naval port there. Russia retains about four-fifths of the Black Sea fleet, buying part of the half earlier allocated to the Ukraine, and taking out a 20 year lease over the main bays and some hinterland. The Ukraine will receive a rent for the port facilities used by Russia and retains one bay outside the main port for its own fleet.

Economic tensions recur over gas supplies. In fact these have now eased, with the Black Sea Fleet settlement substantially financing debt service. However pipeline politics can work both ways, Russia holding the Ukraine under pressure for its vital energy needs, but the Ukraine having a hold on Russian export earnings with the gas pipeline to the West passing through its territory (although a new pipeline through Belarus will reduce this hold). The Ukraine for its part seeks to offer an alternative route into Europe for Caucasus and Central Asian oil and gas.

In a scenario with bad economic management in the Ukraine leading to dissent and division internally, combining with aggressive nationalist leadership in Russia, the ingredients for a major conflict between the two countries could exist. Fortunately this scenario has grown more remote.

Moldova upon independence in 1991 inherited a highly inflammable ethnic situation, with the majority of the population being Romanian of language and history, but with the Trans-Dniester land on the north bank of the Dniester river being heavily militarised and populated by Russians. Moldova has managed these dangers carefully. It has set aside the scenario of re-unification with Romania and adopted a liberally inclusive nationality law. Still, violence has not been avoided. The Russian military in Trans-Dniester sided with the putschists in Moscow of August 1991, having already in 1990 declared their region to be an autonomous republic which would remain part of the Soviet Union. By Spring 1992 these tensions escalated into a short civil war. Subsequent negotiations between Russia and Moldova led to plans for withdrawal of the Russian military. By May 1997 a political agreement between the Moldovan and Trans-Dniester authorities was signed and underwritten by Russia and the Ukraine; the region is to remain part of Moldova with a high degree of autonomy. But the reality is that Trans-Dniester becomes an archaic little museum, or zoo of the nearly extinct Soviet communism, producing mainly arms for delivery to undesriable destinations.

In the *Northern Caucasus* of the Russian Federation there are seven republics with a bewildering patchwork of clan divisions, who have been fighting Russian imperial expansion and each other for centuries. These Caucasian communities are heterogeneous, with Caucasian, Turkish and Iranian language groups.

Chechnya's declaration of independence in 1991 was followed by four years of *de facto* independence, but the region's provocative lawlessness and promotion of arms and drugs trade triggered the Russian invasion in late 1994. This campaign achieved notoriety for its brutality matched only by its ineffectiveness. The capital Grozny was largely destroyed with massive bombing and shelling. Fanatical fighters on the Chechen side inflicted heavy casualties on the poorly trained Russian conscripts. But the Chechen side incurred heavy casualties. In all 30 000 lives were lost before a peace was struck by General Lebed in September 1996 and Russian troops were withdrawn by January 1997. The OSCE mission in Chechnya played a commendable part in brokering early talks between Russia and the Chechens. The situation, however, has hardly stabilised. In April 1997 the Russian interior minister was reporting pressures in Southern Russia for pogroms, to expel remaining Chechen minorities in the light of recurring terrorist acts in the region. By mid-1997 the constitutional status of Chechnya was still being disputed, Chechnya claiming full independence and Russia offering a Tatarstan-type sovereignty.

The scale of the Chechen conflict prompts the question whether the other autonomous republics of the region might similarly see explosions of violence. There is no other example of an ethnic group so resolutely resisting Russia for centuries [MRG, 1994]. Three other republics (Dagestan, Karbardino-Balkaria and Karachai-Cherkessia) are each divided between two or more Caucasian ethnic groups, in addition to a large Russian presence or degree of russification. Dagestan is the most complex with ten ethnic groups, one of them overlapping the frontier with Azerbaijan. However its lack of a potentially dominating group, or an outside irredentist neighbour, seems to result in a rather peaceful caution in ethnic relations. In the other two cases Russia can mediate. In all cases there are very sensitive property questions relating to the rights of families deported in the Stalin period, and who returned to find their lands occupied by another ethnic group. Ingushetia, which seceded from Chechnya in 1991, not wishing to follow it into independence, has been in a different conflict with Northern Ossetia over a border dispute and armed clashes in 1992, which Russian force disarmed. There has been a massive displacement of refugees, causing enormous economic difficulties for these small republics. Overall, each of these North Caucasian republics continues to harbour serious ethnic tensions, but conflicts seem likely to be restrained by the Russian presence or political caution of local leaders.

The largest minority group in Russia, the *Tatars*, with 5.5 million population, have achieved a very high degree of independence within the Russian Federation, at least for the state of Tatarstan. Its capital Kazan was the centre of the Mongol power which dominated Russia in the middle ages, and the Tatars became Muslim from the tenth century. The adoption of the 1992 Constitution of Tatarstan and the Treaty between it and Russia in 1994 was surrounded with pressures and tension, but violence was avoided, thus offering the model of a peaceful alternative to the Chechen tragedy. Taken together the Constitution and Treaty are masterpieces in political ambiguity on the degree of sovereignty of Tatarstan in relation to the Russian Federation. However for the future it is not to be excluded that Islamic influence could increase further, and a next government might possibly push for full independence. Such developments are, on the other hand, much less likely with the next most important groups descended from the Mongols, the Bashkir and Chuvash, also in the Volga basin. Their regional centres have less autonomy, given that these groups lack majorities in their own regions. The Buryat Republic between Lake Baikal and Mongolia, also with a Mongol ethnic base, shows no sign of pushing for radically increased autonomy.

Overall the prospects for political stability between the Russian Federation and its main ethnic minorities appear to have improved, perhaps under the demonstration effect of the contrasting examples of Tatarstan versus Chechnya, and also following the defeat in 1993 of the attempted White House putsch, which largely dissipated secessionist sentiment in the Ural and Siberian regions. But such progress should be considered only provisional until the economic and social situation shows more solid improvement.

In *Azerbaijan* the Armenian populated enclave of Nagorno-Karabakh has been fighting a war of independence since 1988. Mediation attempts by the OSCE could not solve the problem, although there was an incomplete cease-fire since 1994, giving way to resumed fighting in 1997. In practice there is a land corridor joining the region to Armenia. Turkey sides with Azerbaijan by blockading Armenia. In November 1997 a settlement was apparently reached between Azerbaijan and Armenia with the aid of intervention by presidents Yeltsin and Chirac.

Georgia since independence has been torn by two secessionist movements. The region of Southern Ossetia waged a civil war in 1991-92 to secure its autonomy and to pursue unification with Northern Ossetia across the border in Russia. The Chechen war has at least dispelled for the time being moves in favour of border changes. In 1992 the region of Abkhazia proclaimed independence, and practically achieved this with some unofficial Russian military support, the Georgian population of the region fleeing and unable to return since. Since 1994 the peace has been kept by 1500 Russian troops, supporting 136 UN observers. But in political negotiations Abkhazia refuses to accept a place in a federal Georgia.

- Other Balkans

Only Slovenia avoided becoming embroiled in the new Balkan tragedy of the 1990s. This small, ethnically homogeneous state seceded from Yugoslavia after a minimal military confrontation in 1990. Slovenia makes impressively advanced grades by economic and democratic standards. It was rewarded by the EU Commission's proposal in July 1997 that accession negotiations be opened in 1998.

The recent war in Bosnia, from 1992 to 1995, finds its explanation in the combination of virtually every one of the criteria listed above as favouring ethnic conflict - historical enmities, poorly drawn frontiers, irredentist neighbours, weak democratic institutions etc. Bosnia was bequeathed by history to be the intersection point of three empires - Austro-Hungarian, Ottoman and Russian - and three cultures - the Catholic Croat, the Orthodox Serb and the Muslim Bosnian. Sarajevo was of course the site of the assassination of the Austrian emperor, triggering the First World War. The region also suffered the worst of ethnic atrocities in the Second World War.The 1991-95 war of the Yugoslav succession was provoked by the Serbian president S. Milosevic, who enticed the Serbs into war with Croatia and Bosnia with the prospect of enabling all Serbs to live together in an enlarged Serbian state. The war resulted in 4 million displaced persons, 220 000 deaths, 23 000 missing persons and 160 000 wounded. The Dayton peace agreement of November 1995 produced in a highly complicated and precarious constitutional arrangement, with a tri-partite leadership of Bosnia-Herzgovena, on top of a Bosnian-Croat Federation alongside the Srpska (Serb) Republic. By 1997 these structures were functioning at best weakly. The area does not even have a customs and monetary union, refugees have not been able to return and war criminals are still at large. It is widely speculated that the Dayton peace would not last long after withdrawal of NATO forces, which is why its presence is being prolonged beyond mid-1998.

The stabilisation of some regions of both *Croatia* (Eastern Slavonia) and *Serbia* (Vojvodina), and respect there for their ethnic minorities remains elusive. The region of Eastern Slavonia remains contested between Croatia and Serbia. While Serbia agreed in 1995 that it revert to Croatia, its population will remain majority Serb, even after return of Croat refugees. To tidy up the frontier with Serbia it also seems that Croatia wants to clear the minority of Serbs remaining out of the Kraijina area.

Serbia's province of Vojvodina has a substantial Hungarian minority, dating from its time in the Hungarian empire. It is a typical, small central European story. During the Second World War Hungary seized this territory back, but then had to return it again to Yugoslavia at the end of the war. Milosevic reduced the Hungarian minority rights in the 1980s. Relations with Hungary are tense, although violence has so far been avoided.

Serbia's province of Kosovo is 90% ethnic Albanian in population and lost its regional autonomy in 1989 after Milosevic claimed the Serbian minority there was being maltreated. In 1996 the Council of Europe's parliamentary assembly denounced human rights violations against Kosovo Albanians. An increasing number of the Albanian population were reported by early 1997 to believe that armed resistance to gain independence will be required. The Kosovo Liberation Army apparently has 40 000 trained supporters ready for guerilla war. 340 000 Kosovo Albanians have sought asylum in western Europe. Violence duly exploded in early 1998, with 60 fatalities in February and March as Serb police attacked Kosovan villages and indulged in random killings, allegedly in pursuit of Kosovan guerillas.

Albania itself in early 1997 collapsed into a state of pure anarchy, following the failure of fraudulent pyramid savings schemes. The ensuing violence represented a general collapse of civic society in the absence of ethnic complications, reflecting the strains of the economic transition in the poorest of European countries combined with very weak civic culture. The EU could not agree to intervene in April to restore order, and this was left to Italy to do so at the head of a group of Mediterranean countries on behalf of the OSCE and UN. Elections were held in June 1997 under their supervision, and by August the socialists who won the election were able to appoint a new president. The larger part of the foreign forces were able to withdraw, having facilitated the return of democracy and the retreat of anarchy.

The Albanian minority in *Macedonia*, experienced erosion of their minority rights in the late 1980s, and today demand upgrading of their status to a constituent people rather than minority. In mid-1997 the town-halls in the main Albanian population centres began flying the Albanian flag and numerous injuries resulted from police intervention. Fears of secession to create a greater Albania in turn excite Slav nationalists. The prospect of civil war is not to be excluded.

3.6 Dynamics again

If the dynamics of integration were seen in the previous chapter to be well identified in theory and in contemporary European realities, how can we assess the dynamics of conflict? Are the two in some way symmetrical? What are their mechanisms? If integration has its structural explanations and rationale, can conflict also be explained as rational behaviour, in spite of its manifest destructiveness?

Given Europe's persistent capacity to be host to both integration and conflict to the highest degree, and to be capable of switching between them with alarming speed, we do indeed need to understand as best we can this awful paradox.

In fact some symmetry in models of integration and conflict is apparent. Of the nine structural factors presented in Table 2.1 as explaining integration, most can be reversed in sign to make for antipathy, disadvantages or dangers. Cultures may be quite different, and history may have left a legacy of mistrust and resentment, maybe even hatred. In the economic sphere, trade will be almost always mutually beneficial, but monetary integration can cause tensions as can unfair income redistribution - with violent seizure of assets one of the incentives for war. But more clearly still, the conditions for political integration can, when reversed, make for hostility and war over fundamental values and the quest for power.

But the models of the *dynamics* of integration and conflict are particularly interesting to compare. Both have their widening and deepening aspects (see Table 3.4).

The term *domino dynamics* can apply in both cases for widening. In the case of conflict the bringing into play of alliances is one such mechanism.

For deepening the mechanisms also have some symmetry. For integration to deepen there has to be a steady build-up of mutual trust between the parties. Fears and historical resentments can gradually subside, and the benefits of integration progressively harvested. But for conflict the dynamics are more dramatic. *Bloodshed dynamics* may be the shorthand name. With bloodshed a different psyche is brought into play. Revenge or defence of sacred values become dominant. It is as if the weights of the nine factors presented in Table 2.1 are suddenly changed. The conflict may involve staggering economic losses. But this becomes a secondary matter when immaterial matters of religion, pride and vengeance dominate.

The term *disequilibrium dynamics* can also apply for the deepening of both integration and conflict. For integration it is a matter of one step creating a functional need for further steps still to avoid system failure. For conflict it is a matter of retaliation and escalation, maybe initially with measured steps, but then the situation runs out of control as leaders become desperate for victory to ensure their own political survival and cynically exploit bloodshed dynamics.

Table 3.4 Integration and conflict dynamics

	Integration	*Conflict*
Widening	**Domino effect**, *as the periphery finds exclusion costly.*	**Domino effect**, *as alliances are brought into play*
Deepening	**Trust builds up**, *permits step by step deeper integration.* **Disequilibrium dynamics**, *as one integration step calls for further steps for system to remain stable.*	**Bloodshed effect**, *change of psyche demands vengeance.* **Disequilibrium dynamics**, *as retaliation and counter-retaliation escalate out of control.*
(Speed of dynamics)	**Slow**, *because of reliance on build-up of trust.*	**Fast**, *because of first strike advantage.*

But one vital aspect is not symmetrical, namely the speed of the two dynamics. Integration is a slow process, because it requires trust, which is slow to build up. Conflict moves fast technically, since the advantage lies with the first to strike, in traditional battles as well as the ultimate of nuclear war. The question is when the rules of the game are to change, from law to war. When the first strike happens, then the dogs of war are let loose and bloodshed dynamics can soon take over.

Thinking back to our review above of tensions and conflict in contremporary Europe, the major question is whether the dynamics of integration can be counted on to dampen, or even extinguish the dynamics of conflict. This has virtually happened within the EU, but the jury is still out for the wider Europe.

At times in the last years it has not been so clear which trend would dominate. The pessimistic model is one indeed of contagion and escalation in and between different theatres of violence. In the Balkans this model of contagion and escalation has certainly been conceivable, going beyond the former Yugoslavia into Albania, Bulgaria and even linking to Turkish-Greek conflicts. Bosnia raised this spectre in the early 1990s and Kosovo was a reminder again in early 1998. So also in the case of the Russian minorities in the "near abroad" it was conceivable that the political forces of Russian nationalism could develope a band-wagon effect. A contrary, more optimistic model is that the worst tragedies of the recent period, notably Bosnia and Chechnya, had salutary demonstration effects, diminishing political support for those inclined towards conflict. In addition the incentives of EU and NATO membership for central and eastern Europe are strong and clear in terms of the rules of civil society that are expected. And so a band-wagon in favour of these rules acquires momentum and the areas of violent conflict become islands that are increasingly surrounded by the rise of civil society.

It does now seem that the more optimistic model may well dominate. The key indicators for this have been several: the preparedness of NATO to stamp on war criminals in the Balkans, the approximate settlement of relations between Russia and the Ukraine, the disinclination of the Russian minorities in the Baltic states to play nationalist politics, and the strong EU enlargement incentive effect on central and eastern Europe. This does not mean of course that all the problems are going to be extinguished soon, but that a strategy of building up the sinews of European civil society has a real purpose and chance of success.

4. Economics

The age of chivalry has gone. That of sophisters, economists and calculators has succeeded; and the glory of Europe is extinguished for ever.

Edmund Burke, *Reflections on the Revolution in France*, 1790.

The integrated Europe that overcomes conflict will be one in which there are commonly accepted ground rules of economics, politics and society, with an adequate legal basis and enforcement mechanisms. We divide these ground rules, in the next two chapters, between the domains of economics and security.

Within the economic domain we group the rules under four headings:

- *rules of open markets*
- *rules for macroeconomic stability*
- *rules of the social model*
- *rules of corporate governance*

The two dominating initiatives in rule-setting for the European economy, as it approaches the new millennium, are the EU's single market and the euro, its single currency. The single currency is the most challenging of the two, since the conditions for its success are more demanding. The European social model and adaptation of the labour market to the single currency are a key part of these conditions, but these are now reconsidered also in relation to the unemployment problem. The rules of corporate governance may be almost taken for granted in western Europe, but for these to be codified and become effective in the transition economies is a major task.

4.1 Rules of open markets

What is the agenda of action for integrating markets - for goods, services, labour and capital? An idea of the minimalist and maximalist agendas can be seen from the EU's Treaty of Maastricht, which listed the activities judged relevant for the single market completed in 1992. The list becomes increasingly extensive as one goes down it (Table 4.1). It is a convenient means for assessing the different degrees of market integration actually achieved in various European jurisdictions. The first heading (a) defines free trade, with elimination of tariffs and quantitative restrictions on trade. This was the level of the European Free Trade Area (EFTA), and is what is envisaged as a possibility between the EU and Russia. Heading (b), in providing for a common commercial policy, establishes a customs union, as is also shared between the EU and Turkey. Heading (c) defines a single market, removing all obstacles to the four freedoms - for the movement of goods, services, labour and capital. This is the level achieved now within the European Economic Area (EEA), which joins Norway and some others with the EU.

The very long tail of activities implementing or supporting the single market shows that the frontier between activities required or not for a single market is quite elastic. Some elements, such as competition and agricultural pricing policy, may be considered fundamental. Others, such as overseas development policy, are politically chosen activities with little functional link to the single market.

However this long list is the heart of the *"acquis"*, i.e. the stock of accumulated legislation of the EU, whose acceptance is a fundamental condition of accession to the EU. This mass of legislation is now the model for all the accession candidates of the EU. The technical assistance programmes of the EU to these countries amounts to a crash course applying this legislation. We spare ourselves here from descending to a finer level of detail. But its overall importance may be understood in summary by the findings of researches on the percentage of parliamentary legislation and governmental work at the national

Table 4.1: Rules and policies of the EU single market, and related competences

---

(a) the elimination, as between member states, of customs duties and quantitative restrictions on the import and export of goods, and of all other measures having equivalent effect;

(b) a common commercial policy;

(c) an internal market characterized by the abolition, as between member states, of obstacles to the free movement of goods, persons, services and capital;

(d) measures concerning the entry and movement of persons in the internal market...;

(e) a common policy in the sphere of agriculture and fisheries;

(f) a common policy in the sphere of transport;

(g) a system ensuring that competition in the internal market is not distorted;

(h) the approximation of laws of member states to the extent required for the functioning of the common market;

(i) a policy in the social sphere comprising a European Social Fund;

(j) the strengthening of economic and social cohesion;

(k) a policy in the sphere of the environment;

(l) the strengthening of the competitiveness of European industry;

(m) the promotion of research and technological development;

(n) encouragement for the establishment and development of Trans-European networks;

(o) a contribution to the attainment of a high level of health protection;

(p) a contribution to education and training of quality and to the flowering of the cultures of member states;

(q) a policy in the sphere of development cooperation;

(r) the association of the overseas countries and territories....;

(s) a contribution to the strengthening of consumer protection;

(t) measures in the spheres of energy, civil protection and tourism."

Source: Treaty on European Union (Maastricht), Article 3, 1992.

level occupied by applying these rules and policies. According to Leonard [1997] 60 % of national legislation is now driven by EU policies, and two-thirds of the time of policy officials in several ministries.

The rules of the market are thus onerous but clear for the EU itself and for the accession candidate countries. By contrast the future market regime between the enlarged EU and the rest of Europe is highly unclear, with problems looming up as a consequence of the next EU enlargement.

Every EU enlargement raises problems of how third parties are affected, as the new member states align their external policies on those of the EU. Such issues arose with the UK in relation to the Commonwealth, with Spain in relation to the US, and with Finland in relation to Russia. But these issues will be qualitatively much more important in central and eastern Europe because of the high sensitivity and of the frontier between the future enlarged EU and the European countries of the CIS (Russia, Ukraine, Belarus and Moldova - RUBM for short).

In the labour market the EU will have to face up to the same logical issues that NATO has had, in trying to enlarge to the east without offending the interests of the next ring of excluded countries. The freedom or not of movement of people, however, may become a more real question than the largely hypothetical one regarding NATO's defence guarantee. Practical issues will arise from the actual situation in which Poland and all the rest of central Europe have a visa-free relationship with both RUBM and the EU, while the EU and RUBM require visas of each other (Map 12).The result is a system that may be likened to a *canal lock*, in which Poland is the lock and has barriers that can open or shut with RUBM upstream and the EU downstream. The two barriers are never open together, since the flow of water would flood the system. However RUBM nationals make good use of the freedom to move in and out of Poland, for commerce and to enjoy the relatively high standard of living there. The visa-free regime tolerates a large amount of "grey migration", with a mix of commerce, tourism and informal employment. Polish nationals move in and out of EU countries visa-free in the same way. The amount of "grey migration" seems to be quite large, but it also seems to be mutually acceptable and beneficial.

The system has considerable merit as a positive factor for all-European integration, since the RUBM can profit from the openness of Poland in the same way that Poland can profit from the openness of the EU. If Poland were today to join the EU with a simple, mechanical application of the *acquis,* it would introduce visas for the RUBM and so re-install a West-East block barrier of the most personal kind.

The measures to avoid unintended damage could be of two types, either deferral for Poland of the application of the EU external visa regime for RUBM, or liberalisation of the EU's policy towards the RUBM, or a combination of both, such as deferral until the moment when liberalisation is possible. Until then the model of Poland as a central European *canal lock* has much to be said for it.

Similar issues are going to arise on a more complex scale in the markets for goods and services. The EU will first have to manage its differentiated approach to accession candidates in a non-divisive way. It would hardly be a good idea for Estonia's accession to the EU, maybe a few years ahead of Latvia and Lithuania, to introduce new trade discrimination between the Baltic states. Similarly it is highly undesirable that new discriminations be introduced between the participants in the Central European Free Trade Area, which in 1997 already included Poland, Hungary, the Czech Republic, Slovakia, Slovenia and Romania, with negotiations under way to include Bulgaria.

Bigger issues still will arise in relation to the RUBM. For example Poland claims that as of 1997 its import regime for the RUBM is more liberal than it would become by applying the common external tariff and policies of the EU. It may not be that Polish tariffs are lower than those of the EU, but its non-tariff barriers such as anti-dumping rules are probably less stringent. But the larger issue will be the entry of the accession countries into the whole single market system, which will then give Poland complete access to the EU market, whereas the RUBM would then be subject to new relative, if not absolute, disadvantages.

This problem could be substantially attenuated. First, as of today the next step in the trade policies of the RUBM is due to be accession to the World Trade Organisation (WTO). This would already be beneficial for trans-European trade, since it would automatically constrain the use of non-tariff barriers, such as anti-dumping duties. Second, the EU and RUBM could go ahead with the clause for considering free trade that is contained in the Partnership and Cooperation Agreements (PCA). The PCAs, identically for the RUBM, set 1998 as the date for consideration to be given over whether to open negotiations for a free trade agreement. (A thorough Russian appraisal of the PCA is provided by Y. Borko [1997]).

However a bigger proposal can be advanced to avoid that EU enlargement aggravates afresh the divisions between the EU and the rest of Europe. This would consist of proceeding with free trade agreements between the EU and RUBM, but going further in extending and multilateralising them to embrace the whole of Europe not in the EU. This would mean creating an All-European Free Trade Area (AEFTA). It would imply a drastic rationalisation of the several sub-regional preferential arrangements, such as the rump EFTA, the Central European Free Trade Area, the Baltic Free Trade Area and miscellaneous bilateral arrangements. A sweeping initiative like this would have important advantages over a jumble of sub-regional and bilateral preferential agreements: first, the policy would be clear enough to penetrate the awareness of business and politicians; second, the principle of a significant all-European economic initiative would resist the growth of the political mentalities of blocks and exclusions; third, at the technical level the multilateralisation of such agreements is desirable in the compact European space so as to avoid incompatible rules of origin between sub-blocks, and so facilitate deeper integration of production and trade structures.

Such an initiative could be coupled to the ambition for later on of widening the European Economic Area (i.e. the EU single market extended to non-member states). Phased objectives could be elimination of all tariffs in an All-European Free Trade Area by the year 2010, and an All-European Economic Area by the year 2020.

We pursue these ideas further in Chapter 6 in a specific institutional context, that of a proposed European Civil Society, embracing a comprehensive set of economic and political commitments.

There is also a Mediterranean dimension to be brought in. The EU agreed in 1995 to create a free trade zone with the southern Mediterranean countries. In principle this should be done by the year 2010. The motives are analogous to the reasons for similar measures with RUBM: to support the economic development of populous neighbouring countries and so reduce the dangers of their political instability and migratory pressures. The same logic of multilaterisation would apply for this even wider European economic space, becoming a Greater Euro-Mediterranean Free Trade Area, matching developments in Asian Pacific Economic Cooperation (APEC).

4.2 The euro policy quartet

In Chapter 2 we discussed Padoa-Schioppa's *inconsistent quartet* of economic policies in the European Monetary System. This concerned the conflict between pegged exchange rates, free capital movements and national monetary policies. The inconsistency was eliminated by unifying monetary policy entirely with the euro.

But in the euro area there will be a new policy quartet to focus on, governing the functioning of the euro area - monetary, budgetary, social and regional policies (as presented schematically in Table 4.2). The dangers of this new quartet proving inconsistent are considerable.

Within the functioning of the euro area there will be natural tensions between the four blocks of policy competences shown in the table. These tensions will be of two types: clarifying how the policy-mix actually works, and who leads or follows in the coordination process.

Crucially the monetary-budgetary policy mix, resulting from the policies of the European Central Bank and the Ecofin Council will jointly determine the euro's external exchange rate and therefore the international competitiveness of the trading sectors. The resulting exchange rate evolution, combined especially with social and labour market policies and wage bargaining outcomes, will determine the rate of unemployment. Regional policies will have a role in balancing the

Table 4.2: Economic policy competences in the euro area

Monetary policy	Budgetary policy
Exclusive competence of European Central Bank; \n\n except exchange rate regime and policy, decided by Ecofin Council. ECB retains a voice in exchange rate policy	Ecofin Council applies Stability and Growth Pact by qualified majority vote; \n\n elements of tax policy by unanimity; otherwise national competence
Labour/social policy	**Regional policy**
EU Social Protocol, employment chapter of Amsterdam Treaty; \n\n otherwise national competence, also for wage policies (if any)	EU Regional and Structural Funds; \n\n otherwise national competence

medium-term outcomes geographically. This will give rise to many issues of explicit or implicit coordination between the actors of the four blocks.

But beyond the formalities of coordination there will be issues of strength. Who will set the name of the game, who will lead and who will have to react and adjust? At the level of constitutional choice the name of the game is already clear. The European Central Bank (ECB) will be in a position of great strength by virtue of the clarity and single purpose of its mandate to maintain price stability, combined with its high degree of independence. The other policy competences are diffused between levels of government. Moreover for budgetary policy the rules of the Stability Pact will actually reinforce the leadership role of the ECB, by reducing the risks of policies challenging its priority of price stability [Artis and Winkler, 1997]. The character and performance of the euro area will therefore be revealed, first, as the

ECB uses its great powers and, secondly, as the other relevant actors adjust to the euro environment. These are the issues reviewed in the next sections.

4.3 Rules for macroeconomic stability

- Qualifications for the euro area

The composition of the euro area, as decided in May 1998, is a new seminal step in redrawing the map of Europe. It builds on the culture of the European Monetary System, which already saw intense monetary policy coordination and convergence over some twenty years, in spite of its crises and ups and downs. But the euro will be something in a different category, with a massive concentration of monetary policy power and massive symbolic clarity, as the realm of the euro banknote comes to reveal itself in everyday life.

The formal qualifications for membership of the euro area were established in the Treaty of Maastricht (Table 4.3). In the years since signature of the Treaty in 1992 these criteria have had a massive influence on the stabilisation policies of all EU countries, whether aspirants to be members from the start or not. The key criteria are the requirement for central bank independence, the rate of inflation, the budget deficit and public debt. The interest rate criterion is only secondary, since it depends on the first criteria, and is not adding anything. The value of the exchange rate criterion has been thrown into doubt after the exchange rate crisis of 1992, when the fluctuation margins became so wide to be of little meaning. All countries are now set to assure the independence of their central banks, including the UK after its May 1997 change of government.

By 1997 it was already clear that there had been an extraordinary effort of convergence on price stability and sound public finance. All countries had inflation rates under 3%, except for Greece, and even here the performance was rapidly closing in on euro norms after decades of notorious macroeconomic instability. The budget deficit

Table 4.3 Criteria for admission to the euro area

---

1. *Independence of the European Central Bank and each of the national central banks in the system from governments or EU institutions.*
2. *National budget deficits not to exceed 3% of GDP, except when authorised in exceptional circumstances.*
3. *National public debt not to exceed 60% of GDP, unless it is diminishing at a satisfactory trend rate.*
4. *Inflation rate no more than 1.5% higher than the average rate for the three lowest rates in member states.*
5. *Long-term interest rate no more than 2% points higher than the average for the three lowest rates of member states, for the year before the time of decision over eligibility for participation.*
6. *Observance of the normal fluctuation margins of the Exchange Rate Mechanism of the European Monetary System for two prior years, without devaluation.*

Source: Treaty of Maastricht, article 109j, and protocols

ceiling of 3% proved troublesome for many countries, but the main story was one of unprecedented convergence on low deficits. This included countries which had for much of the eighties been running deficits around 10% of GDP or more, such as Belgium, Ireland and Italy, and whose public debts rose to over 100% of GDP as a result. Even Greece was coming within sight of the norm, after a mega-deficit of 14% of GDP as recently as 1993.

One could also say that there had been a certain convergence in the level of political discourse over public finance, a convergence only on the average rather than the outstanding. The first period of preparation for the euro according to the Maastricht criteria was marked by many speeches from high priests of sound public finance, principally German finance minister Waigel, who warned about any creative accounting and loose interpretation of the scriptures. The sermons seemed principally to be addressed by the Germanic northerners to the unreliable Latin southerners. This traditional image of cultural divide was undermined when it became apparent that Spain, Portugal and even Italy were in reality converging on the Maastricht norms. France, on the other hand, included in its 1997 budget a notoriously large raid on the financial reserves of France-Telecom, which the Commission promptly endorsed as being in order. In July 1997 France's new Socialist government discovered that it had inherited a deficit significantly over 3%, and produced later a revised budget deficit profile that would only meet the Maastricht 3% in 1998. For his part Waigel was having difficulties also in respecting the 3% deficit limit and so he tried to raid the reserves of unrealised profits on the Bundesbank's holdings of gold. The President of the Bundesbank objected indignantly, and Waigel had to withdraw. The rest of the EU were left uncertain of the meaning of Waigel's former statements that 3% means 3.0%.

The public debt limit of 60% of GDP is manifestly not going to be a binding constraint on admission to the euro. The Maastricht rules already allow for higher levels, as long as there is a declining trend. More important is that the conventionally used figures are quite meaningless, since they exclude the contingent liabilities of state pension schemes. In practice such contingent liabilities amount, for example, to over 100% of GDP in Germany and France [Chand and Jaeger,1996]. In central and eastern Europe there are also formidable pension funding problems also [Ambrus-Lakatos and Schaffer, 1997].

In March 1998 the Commission and the EMI duly submitted their statutory reports on the conformity with the Maastricht criteria of the countries wishing to join the euro area on 1st January 1999. On the basis of its forecasts for 1998 the Commission was able to declare that all 11 countries wishing to join from the outset were going to meet the troublesome 3% of GDP budget deficit target (Table 4.4). There were grumbles, especially in the EMI report, about the high public debt levels in Belgium and Italy, but no dissent from the basic political decision for all these countries to proceed (France, Germany, Italy, Spain, the three Benelux countries, Austria, Ireland and Portugal). In May 1998 the European Council ratified these conclusions.

How far off qualification by these same standards are the accession candidates and other European countries? Table 4.4 shows that the

Table 4.4: Performance in relation to main stability criteria of the Maastricht Treaty

	Inflation %	Budget deficit % GDP	Public debt % GDP
EU (1998)	**1.9**	**-1.9**	**73.9**
Belgium	1.3	-1.7	118.1
Denmark	2.1	+1.1	59.5
Germany	1.7	-2.5	61.2
Greece	4.5	-2.2	107.7
Spain	2.2	-2.2	67.4
France	1.0	-2.9	58.1
Ireland	3.3	+1.1	59.5
Italy	2.1	-2.5	118.1
Luxembourg	1.6	+1.0	7.1
Netherlands	2.3	-1.6	70.0
Austria	1.5	-2.3	64.7
Portugal	2.2	-2.2	60.0
Finland	2.0	+0.3	53.6
Sweden	1.5	+0.5	74.1
UK	2.3	-0.6	52.3

Other Europe (1998, or latest month in 1997)

Bulgaria	30.0	-2.0	
Czech Rep.	9.5	-0.5	
Estonia	8.5	2.0	
Hungary	14.9	-4.8	
Latvia	6.6	-0.0	
Lithuania	6.8	-1.4	
Poland	13.4	-3.8	
Romania	60.0	-4.2	
Slovakia	7.0	-3.0	
Slovenia	8.8	-1.0	
Russia	14.7 July	-6.7 June	
Ukraine	0.6 June	-5.5 March	

Source: EU Commission, Spring 1998 forecasts.

deficit situation is in most cases already within the 3% limit. Estonia even manages a small budget surplus, and the Czech Republic a zero balance. Only Hungary has an "excessive deficit", to use the language of Maastricht. Inflation problems are more serious, especially in Bulgaria and Romania, but the Ukraine has shown how fast inflation can be stopped. Elsewhere the inflation rates are not so far off the standards set for euro members, such that an adequate convergence cannot be envisaged over a medium-term period.

However these figures do not adequately reflect the shakiness of financial stability of the transition economies, where the banking sector is weak and external debt burdens are often still grave. A succinct guide to these aspects is offered in the assessment of rating agencies, as shown in Table 4.5 for all European countries on a comparable basis.

The optique of the rating agency is specifically the chances of debt service problems. But this can be taken as a good proxy for the financial pressures that bear upon government and which make stabilisation policy more hazardous.

The story offered is that the most advanced of the EU accession candidates are marked A-, only one category behind six EU countries who are likely to qualify for initial euro membership. Four further accession candidates receive a BBB rating, in the same category as Greece. Russia achieves a BB+ rating, having made enormous progress in monetary stabilisation. On these indicators alone, one could imagine a quite rapid convergence on the standards being set for admission to the euro area.

However none of these measures approach the deeper question whether the countries in question fit the economist's criteria for membership of an *optimal currency area*, or at least an advantageous currency area (this was already discussed in a preliminary manner in chapter 2). Economists have been spurred into work on this methodologically difficult question by the prospect of the euro [Bayoumi and Eichengreen, 1996, Artis and Zhang, 1997, Gros, 1997, and Pisani-Ferry, 1997]. These studies all analyse multiple indicators of structural similarities or dissimilarities between Germany as the reference country, sometimes in comparison with the US.

Table 4.5: Sovereign Ratings, 1997

Austria	AAA	
France	AAA	
Germany	AAA	
Luxembourg	AAA	Lowest expectation
Netherlands	AAA	of investment risk
Norway	AAA	
Switzerland	AAA	
United Kingdom	AAA	
Belgium	AA+	
Ireland	AA+	
Spain	AA	Very low expectation
Italy	AA-	of investment risk
Portugal	AA-	
Sweden	AA-	
Malta	A	
Czech Republic	A-	Low expectation
Slovenia	A-	of investment risk
Poland	BBB	
Croatia	BBB-	Low expectation of
Greece	BBB-	investment risk, but
Hungary	BBB-	more susceptible to
Slovakia	BBB-	economic conditions
Lithuania	BB+	Possibility
Russia	BB+	of investment risk
Romania	BB-	developing
Turkey	B+	Investment risk exists
-	CCC	Possibility of default
-	CC	High risk of default
-	C	Currently in default

Source: IBCA, "Ratings", March 1997, London.

The most comprehensive study [Pisani-Ferry, 1997] looks at the stability of the nominal and real exchange rate, at the incidence of demand and supply shocks and at foreign trade structures and fluctuations. Many statistical tests were made by the several authors. In particular the notion of *clusters*, which is about structural reasons why countries group themselves together economically, is modelled precisely and quantified by Artis and Zhang [1997].

The conclusions of these studies may be summarised as giving the following indications:

- all agree that there is a natural core or cluster for the euro area consisting of six countries - Germany, France, Belgium, Luxembourg, the Netherlands and Austria;

- in second place, Denmark and Italy are next closest to the core;

- thereafter the story becomes more complicated with divergences depending upon methodologies. Some studies would rate Portugal, Spain and the United Kingdom rather close to the core, like the second group, but others would place them further away. Ireland, Finland, Sweden and Greece are shown often to be quite far from the core group.

Compared to the political positions of the governments concerned, there is conformity within the core group between economic criteria and political intentions. In the second group Italy's enthusiasm to join the euro is reasonably supported, but Denmark's political scepticism questioned for its economic rationality. For the other countries, the political enthusiasts in Portugal, Spain, Ireland and Finland are receiving some warning that their economies could face some difficulties of adjustment in the euro area. The political sceptics in Sweden and the United Kingdom receive some understanding from the economists. Greece's political wish to join the euro, but only in some years' time, is consistent.

However the political sceptics should bear in mind that these indicators change, just as economic structures are always changing, and the euro will itself have direct repercussions on these. For example, a real difference in financial structure between the United Kingdom and the core group is the much greater dependence in the UK on variable interest rate borrowing [Pennant-Rea et al., 1997]. This means that there would be a difference in the effects of a given euro monetary policy in this country compared to the core group. However it is quite possible that this structural difference could quite rapidly diminish, especially if the government clearly chose to plan to join the euro within a few years.

In addition, as already mentioned, the judgement that might be based just on optimal currency area criteria may be overridden by *domino dynamics*. It is one thing for a number of countries to have different first preferences over the decision to create a single currency or not. But when it is decided that a core group will go ahead in any case, the periphery have to decide upon their second preferences. Then new arguments enter the calculation, notably the specific costs of exclusion form the core. These may include loss of influence in Europe's main economic and monetary policy and loss of market share as a location for mobile international investors seeking a politically risk-free place in the EU market. In practice it looks a plausible scenario that the Denmark, Sweden and the UK, cautious if not sceptical in their first preferences, will choose to opt into the euro sooner rather than later, as soon as the euro proves itself. The UK, which basically would have been happy if no one had thought about monetary union, already changed its position in autumn 1997 in this sense. For these countries the year 2002 has a natural attraction, in that the euro banknotes will then be introduced, ending the complication of parallel use of the euro and national currencies, and the proving of the new system will have been done. Also Greece had by late 1997 become seriously interested in joining the euro, so as to secure monetary stability once and for all, and its budget is now aimed at reaching the Maastricht norms faster than most observers were expecting.

Similar issues will be posed over a longer time horizon for the transition economies which are EU accession candidates. At what stage should the EU candidate countries aim to peg their currencies on the euro, and when should they contemplate actually joining the euro? This question has in fact been examined carefully by Halpern and Wyplosz [1997]. Their answer in short is that the transition economies should wait until their transition is very advanced, before either fixing irrevocably their exchange rates or necessarily trying to match the euro's standard of virtual price stability. Relative to the west European economies, the transition economies still have tumultuous changes in economic structure to achieve. This is the first objective fact which means that, if data were collected of the type reported above in the studies of Pisani-Ferry [1997] and others in relation to the optimal currency area theory, the results would surely be a low ranking in aptitude to join the euro in the near future.

But Halpern and Wyplosz [1997] present a more developed argument. Their analysis of the central and east European economies leads to a stylised model of the path of the real exchange rate through the transition period. The initial liberalisation of the formerly state controlled economies leads to a dramatic drop in the real exchange rate, certainly overshooting the level to be reached when the reconstructed economy finds a new equilibrium condition. This overshooting is only gradually corrected over a medium to long period, as the dollar wage level heads up towards a normal level for a European economy. This real appreciation may be achieved either by admitting a significant internal nominal inflation together with an exchange rate that remains nominally fixed, or by allowing the exchange rate to float upwards while domestic inflation is brought to a low rate. Either way these are bad conditions for entry into the euro, which would mean both virtual price stability and absolute exchange rate fixity together. In fact the policy choice of the transition countries seems to be to retain a lowish but significant rate of inflation until tax systems have become fully developed, since inflation gives an automatic tax to the issuer of the currency. It is therefore not surprising to note in Table 4.4 that the typical transition economies, excluding those whose stabilisation policies have been manifestly out of control (viz. Bulgaria and Romania) have tended towards inflation rates of the order of 8 to 20%. Exchange rate policy in the transition has typically gravitated towards managed floating or adjustable peg systems, allowing for the use of the DM or dollar as a nominal anchor, but not with absolute rigidity. Such systems could well increasingly take the euro as their anchor in the future. The criterion for judging when best to adopt the euro as the national currency is best deferred approximately to the time the economy's real wage level approaches its long-term equilibrium in relation to the EU average, rather like has happened in the case of Spain over the last ten years.

- *The monetary policy of the European Central Bank*

The critical concern most often heard is that the new ECB may begin with an unduly restrictive monetary policy, for two reasons. First, the ECB will give priority to establishing its credibility as guardian of Europe's monetary stability. This will require action in addition to words, for example to be seen to hold to a restrictive policy through a period of cyclical weakness when there could be clamours for a more expansionary policy. Secondly, in the initial period the behaviour of the euro's monetary aggregates may be erratic and difficult to interpret for the purpose of monetary policy targeting, due to shifts in portfolio preferences of international investors of financial assets.

These are certainly issues that warrant serious discussion. Neither argument is without some plausibility. However the initial price stability condition of the euro area looks like being highly satisfactory. The European Monetary Institute, in its *Annual Report 1996* [EMI, 1997] could note that the average EU inflation rate was already down to 2.6%. There is no evident reason why this performance should deteriorate in the foreseeable future, with no cyclical overheating on the horizon (except perhaps the UK and Ireland), but on the contrary a prevailing climate of determination to consolidate low inflation in the countries not yet clearly within the Maastricht criteria.

As regards monetary policy strategy the EMI sets out in its *Annual Report 1996* its assessment of five possible strategies (exchange rate targeting, interest rate pegging, nominal income targeting, monetary targeting and inflation targeting). It narrowed down the choice to the last two listed, prepares to implement either of them, but defers the actual choice of strategy for later when the euro area begins to function. This degree of freedom is consistent with averting what apprehensive critics fear, namely a dogmatic monetary targeting when the monetary aggregates may be behaving erratically at an early stage. On balance therefore this apprehension does not seem to be particularly strongly founded.

Meanwhile the EMI prepares in technical detail the instruments and procedures of its future monetary policy operations, including the means for open market operations, minimum reserve requirements and related reporting requirements for banks [EMI, 1997a].

Another concern for the years 1999 to 2001 is that the system itself could be wrecked by speculative movements between the national banknotes still in circulation alongside the euro. Such ideas are apparently influenced by the EMS crisis of 1992, but this is misplaced. These arguments seem not to recognize that the system will by then have changed categorically to one in which the ECB will be controlling aggregate money supply in the euro area, and any switch in preferences from Lire to DM, for example, will be met without limit, subject only to the aggregate money supply objective.

- Budgetary policy under the Stability and Growth Pact

The rules of the Stability and Growth Pact, agreed by the EU leaders in December 1996 as a supplement to the Maastricht Treaty, were refined in a Resolution of the Amsterdam summit of June 1997. Artis and Winkler [1997] give a detailed appraisal of these provisions. Critics mainly fear that an excessively rigid and restrictive budgetary policy may result. The main Maastricht rule is that budget deficits should not exceed 3% of GDP either for entry into the euro area, or in subsequent years, unless there are "exceptional circumstances" warranting some over-shooting. The Pact defined these circumstances with reference to recessions where there are drops in output of between 0.75 to 2%. If the drop in output were more than 2% "exceptional circumstances" would be recognised automatically. If the drop were between 0.75 and 2% the Ecofin Council would be responsible for deciding by qualified majority whether the circumstances were exceptional or not. In the event that the circumstances were not determined to be exceptional, then the member state concerned would have to agree with the Council a programme of corrective measures, failing which sanctions would begin to be applied. Initially these would be in the form of an interest free loan to the EU, and later returned or converted into a definitive fine depending upon whether the member state had adopted corrective measures deemed adequate by the Council.

The amount of the sanctions would be minimally 0.2% of GDP, maximally 1% of GDP and in between graduated in proportion to the excess deficit.

These rules of the Stability and Growth Pact are subject to two main criticisms. First is the economic argument that with a monetary policy addressed unreservedly to the defence of price stability, there is a corresponding need for a significant degree of macroeconomic policy flexibility with the budget. But this is indeed seriously restricted by the Pact. Second is the political argument that the process of levying financial sanctions on a member state could turn out to be extremely conflictual. It is easy to imagine, for example, a national parliament in a country with economic difficulties finding itself unable to assemble a majority for voting a supplementary budget to pay the sanction to the EU. Eviction from the euro area in the case of non-respect of the rules is neither provided for, nor would it be easy to engineer, especially after the euro notes and coins are in circulation and national monies withdrawn. However, if a conflict over non-compliance persisted, it is surely possible to envisage extremely serious political scenarios in which nationalistic political parties might raise the question of secession from the EU.

It is not certain that the Pact will run into serious operating difficulties of these kinds. A more positive view would follow two arguments. First, the entry into force of the euro with its Pact could become a defining point in European economic history, when the member states secured themselves permanently in a condition of sound and sustainable public finance. As the Amsterdam Resolution points out, medium-term budget balances should in any case be aiming in the next decades at least at balance, or even some surplus in view of increasing pension obligations due in the period 2015 to 2030 and which are currently under-funded in many European countries. Such structural balances would leave a considerable margin for cyclical variations in the budget deficit before the 3% of GDP limit were reached. And beyond that, the circumstances might indeed turn out to be exceptional. Secondly, the highly developed procedures now established for reviewing excessive deficits in the Ecofin Council

Table 4.6 : Budget policy rules of the euro area

Growth and Stability Pact, adopted by the European Council, December 1996. Main features:

(Supplementing the 3% of GDP maximum budget deficit rule of the Maastricht Treaty)
1. "Exceptional circumstances" automatically are recognized when the level of GDP drops by 2% or more.
2. Where the drop is between 0.75% and 2% the Ecofin Council determines by qualified majority vote whether the "exceptional circumstances" exist.
3. Where, in the absence of "exceptional circumstances", an excessive deficit fails to be corrected, the member state will be called upon to make an interest-free deposit with the EU of 0.2% of GDP plus one tenth of the excess of the deficit over 3% of GDP, with a ceiling of 0.5% of GDP.
4. Where the deficit remains excessive after continued procedures lasting two years, the deposit becomes a definitive fine.

Resolution of the European Council on the Stability and Growth Pact, June 1997. Supplementary points:

-"The Member States... commit themselves to respect the medium-term budgetary objective of close to balance or in surplus set out in their stability or convergence programmes....".
-"Adherence to this objective will allow Member States to deal with normal cyclical fluctuations while keeping the government deficit within the 3 % of GDP reference value".

Source: European Economy, No 64. Commission of the EU, 1997

and for graduated pressures for their correction may prove very useful in reinforcing the sanctions applied in principle in financial markets to deter extravagant borrowers. It is well known that financial markets do not apply very significant interest rate premia on sovereign borrowers until and unless the policies become rather disastrous. In practice the rules may be tested early in the life of the euro, since several countries will start with their budget deficits right up against the 3% of GDP limit, without the EU economy being in recession. The Ecofin Council as a body will surely want to preserve its own credibility by applying peer pressure on countries which risk breaching the rules. On the other hand, as pointed out by Artis and Winkler [1997], the Council may be faced by the dilemma situation of the Pact proving counter-productive, either by inducing pro-cyclical behaviour, or being shown to be ineffective (if overshoots of the 3% are allowed) right from the start. Decisions to order sanctions have to be taken by qualified majority, meaning that a blocking minority is relatively easily made up if embarrassment with the 3% limit were shared by several countries.

- The monetary-budgetary policy mix and the exchange rate

The outlook for monetary and budgetary policy in the euro area, as so far considered separately, leaves unanswered some important questions as to how the whole system will work. Will the euro area system have adequate policy flexibility to stabilise economic cycles? How will international monetary policy coordination be affected? How will finance ministers shape up in their task of representing the interests of government in the economic policy of Europe, alongside the formidable power of the European Central Bank? How will the internal coordination of economic policy work out, as between the EU level and national competencies, especially for the labour market, social and regional policies? These are the questions to be resolved by the instruments of the *euro policy quartet* (i.e the monetary, budgetary, social and regional).

A part of these questions will be answered in practice through the shared management by the Ecofin Council and the ECB of the euro's external exchange rate policy. The exchange rate is always at the crux of macroeconomic policy coordination issues. There are here issues of rules and of discretionary policy to be taken together.

Rules for the conduct of exchange rate policy are outlined in the Maastricht Treaty (Article 109). Decisions on the exchange rate regime with third countries, apart from the EU countries outside the euro for which a modified Exchange Rate Mechanism has been prepared, are to be taken by the Ecofin Council. In particular this concerns whether to switch between floating and pegged exchange rate regimes, and in the latter case, to decide on re-alignments of the pegged rates. Intervention by the ECB in exchange markets will be subject to "general orientations" by the Ecofin Council, albeit "without prejudice to the primary objective of the ECB to maintain price stability". The texts are open to the prospect one day of the ECB refusing guidance from the Ecofin Council to intervene in the market, if they felt their policy strategy or reputation were at risk. The first EMI President, A. Lamfalussy, confirmed this interpretation as follows "the ECB cannot be forced to intervene in the foreign exchange markets in situations or for amounts which in its own view would...put at risk its stability-oriented monetary policy..., by creating excessive liquidity domestically" (Financial Times, 20 May 1997). The Ecofin Council clarified its doctrine a little in September 1997, agreeing that the ECB will be "ordinarily" in charge, while ministers will only become involved if there are overriding political reasons or during financial crises.

Rules for the exchange rate system between the "ins" and "outs" of EU countries were decided in a Resolution of the European Council meeting in Amsterdam in June 1997 [Commission of the EU, 1997c]. A new European Monetary System will begin on 1st January 1999 alongside the euro. Central rate will be fixed between the euro and the non-participating currencies, surrounded by the same very wide fluctuation margins of plus or minus 15% as in the prior exchange rate mechanism. However narrower fluctuation margins may be adopted on a case-by-case basis. Participation in the new system will be voluntary for the member states outside the euro.

A main concern is setting up this new system is to avoid disruption of the single market by excessive exchange rate fluctuations or misalignments. The exchange rate movements of the British pound and the Italian lire in the mid nineteen-nineties were sufficient to trigger clamours for political tensions at the time of their extreme depreciations, with calls for protective measures by France. However the new European Monetary System may not cover the problem entirely. As a result there is legitimate debate over the search for more adequate rules. The main candidate in this regard is that the member states not in the euro should adopt suitable inflation targets to guide their monetary policy, as is already the policy of the Bank of England, and as proposed as a general rule by a number of economists [e.g. Pisani-Ferry, 1997]. This should exclude that the countries concerned embark on deliberate strategies of competitive devaluation.

Between them these rules - the new EMS and/or the inflation target - will extend the euro's area of monetary stability and influence progressively across the map of Europe. New EU member states from central and eastern Europe could be attracted by the new EMS with the wide margins of fluctuation until their transition processes have matured, and then join the euro. Other European countries may be inclined to use the euro increasingly as the reference for their exchange rate policies, and the dollar less.

Beyond these rules is the question how the actual policy mix within the euro area will evolve, and how the arrangements for international monetary cooperation will work in practice. Economists have devoted great attention to these issues, whose real importance is only exceeded by their analytical difficulty, and so cannot be explored in detail here. For present purposes two key points should be made.

The first is that the actual choice by the ECB and the Ecofin Council of a certain mix of monetary and budgetary policy will in any case influence the exchange rate of the euro against the dollar and yen. This will be the case irrespective of whether the euro authorities seek to have an active exchange rate policy or not. For example, the combination of a strict monetary policy, maintaining virtual price stability, with a low budget deficit will result in low interest rates for the euro-denominated financial assets, and so lower the demand for the euro and consequently the exchange rate. By contrast high budget deficits, combined with a strict monetary policy, will push up the interest rate and appreciate the exchange rate. Such exchange rate movements will impact directly on the EU's international competitiveness.

If at the outset the main concern of euro policy makers were over the economy's insufficient competitiveness world-wide, then a low interest rate - resulting from low inflation and low public borrowing - could well be a consistent policy choice through its effect in weakening the euro's exchange rate. But of course that is just one set of possible circumstances, and others will surely arise when the EU's overall budget policy stance needs adjustment, taking into account its likely influence on the exchange rate change.

This will call for a more developed aptitude for policy coordination within the Ecofin Council. The proposal to create a special formation of the Ecofin Council, called informally Euro-X and restricted to euro countries, may be seen in this light, as another example of *disequilibrium dynamics* at work. A respectable case for Euro-X is made with by the French minister of finance, Mr. Strauss-Kahn [Financial Times, 27 November 1997]. It is not to detract from the independence of the ECB, but rather to be able better to inform the ECB what actually is the macroeconomic strategy of budget policy in the euro area. But in addition the Euro-X is a new twist to the diplomacy of *domino dynamics,* since it is precisely this kind of exclusion from an important economic policy forum of Europe that worries the countries not joining the euro at the start, especially those like the UK and Sweden who consider they have something to say on European economic policy.

Apprehensions about possible policy bias in the system, such as the ECB being "obsessed" by monetary targeting at the expense of an appropriate exchange rate, do not seem particularly founded. If the recent policy of the German Bundesbank is any guide, it is notable that since 1996 there was a willingness to accommodate a very substantial depreciation of the DM against the dollar.

Another issue is about whether the arrival of the euro on the international monetary stage will tend by itself to increase or decrease exchange rate instability in relation to the dollar and yen. The official opinion of the EU Commission is, unsurprisingly, that the euro should not increase monetary instability in the world [Commission of the EU, 1997c]. However academic economists are not so sure. International monetary affairs will be less of a game in which a dominant US leads and the fragmented rest of the world of smaller players follows. The game will become a more symmetrical two-player business, in which neither the US Fed or the ECB will have incentives to subordinate their primary interest of internal price stability to the wider interests of governments or of the international community [Eichengreen and Ghironi, 1997]. More precisely it is argued that the inflation effects of exchange rate changes will be less important within a consolidated euro area than it is for small countries individually; therefore the ECB may be less worried by exchange rate volatility than the former national central banks [Cohen, 1997]. This conclusion is strengthened with the argument that the advent of the euro will probably see a considerable increase in the demand for euro-denominated assets internationally, and this could contribute also to successive reactions and overreactions in exchange markets [Alogoskoufis, Portes and Rey, 1997].

These policy mix and exchange rate issues will in any case require reform in the ways the EU is represented in the international monetary institutions and meetings. It will soon be obsolete and absurd for one of the world's two leading currencies not to be properly represented on the Executive Board of the International Monetary Fund, while half of its distinguished members will have no monetary policy or currency of their own to represent. Resolution of real issues of policy tension and coordination, both internally and internationally, will vastly increase the inescapable responsibilities of the Ecofin Council.

4.4 The labour market-social-regional policy nexus

- *The social model and the unemployment problem*

Unlike the good starting position with price stability, the euro area starts with its labour market, social security and often also its regional imbalances in serious trouble.

The rate of unemployment in 1997 was 11% in Germany, 12% in Italy, 13% in France and 22% in Spain, and still rising in France and Germany. By contrast Ireland, the Netherlands and the UK have cut their unemployment to 6%. Thus all four of the largest countries which want to be in the euro area from the start have large, unresolved unemployment problems.

As regards social security finance the problems typically combine very high rates of social security taxation, discouraging unemployment, with enormous unfunded future pension liabilities.

The most serious divergences in regional economic performance are now found in Spain, Italy, Belgium and Germany, where the worst performing regions suffer unemployment rates of around double, or at least 10 % points above the national average.

This set of problems, as long as they are not evidently in the course of being overcome, will surely translate into rising political tensions within the EU. There will be pressure for the macroeconomic solutions, namely an easing of monetary policy, where the problems are more microeconomic and structural failings in the labour market. The very acute regional unemployment in the four countries mentioned also is a warning to those responsible for the euro area. They are examples of how acute regional unemployment inequalities can develop within monetary unions, especially where wage rates are fixed at practically the same level throughout the territory. However, within these nations the budget transfers massive resources to equalize living standards to a high degree, even in the presence of the unemployment differentials. In this way the social tensions are dampened. Within the euro area, however, the regional redistributive mechanisms are rather small by comparison. This means that if wage levels were to be as rigid at the level of the euro area as they are presently within these countries, then the social tensions across the euro area could become extremely serious.

This situation is often argued as calling into question the *European Social Model*, and now more particularly the so-called *Rhineland Model*, in fundamental ways. The European Social Model has seen two attempts at a codification at the European level. The first was the European Social Charter of the Council of Europe, adopted in 1961, and extended in 1988 and 1996 (Table 4.7). The second was the "Charter of Fundamental Social Rights of Workers" adopted by the European Council in 1989, following President Delors' pledge to the European Trade Union Confederation in 1988 that the social dimension to the single market would not be neglected. This second "Social Charter" was in content similar to that of the Council of Europe, but with the difference that in the case of the EU there were also political pledges to translate these principles into binding

Table 4.7: The European Social Charter of the Council of Europe

The European Social Charter of 1961
Article 1 - Right to work
Article 2 - Right to just conditions of work
Article 3 - Right to safe and healthy working conditions
Article 4 - Right to a fair remuneration
Article 5 - Right to organise
Article 6 - Right to bargain collectively
Article 7 - Right of children and young persons to protection
Article 8 - Right of employed women to protection
Article 9 - Right to vocational guidance
Article 10 - Right to protection of health
Article 11 - Right to social security
Article 14 - Right of physically or mentally handicapped persons
Article 16 - Right of family to social, legal and economic protection
Article 17 - Right of mothers and children to social and economic protection
Article 18 - Right to engage in gainful occupation in another member state
Article 18 - Right of migrant workers and families

Additional Protocol of 1988
Article 1 - Right to equal employment opportunities on ground of sex
Article 2 - Right to information and consultation
Article 3 - Right to take part in the determination .. of working conditions
Article 4 - Right of elderly persons to social protection

Additional articles in the Revised Social Charter of 1996
Article 24 - Right to protection in cases of termination of employment
Article 25 - Right of workers in the event of insolvency of their employer
Article 26 - Right of workers with families to equal opportunities and treatment
Article 28 - Right of workers' representatives to protection
Article 29 - Right to consultation in collective redundancy procedures
Article 30 - Right to protection against poverty and social exclusion
Article 31 - Right to housing

Source: Council of Europe (1992), Publishing and Documentation Service; Report on the activities of the Council of Europe (1996), Strasbourg

legislation. In particular the Treaty of Maastricht of 1992 included a "Protocol on Social Policy" in which all member states except the UK pledged to implement the 1989 Social Charter (the UK's opt-out was cancelled by the Labour government after its election in May 1997). The rising unemployment problem in Rhineland Europe, or Germany, France and southern Belgium to be more precise (since Belgian Flanders and the Netherlands have managed much better) has led to intensifying debate about whether at least the Rhineland version of the European Social Model ought to be reformed. The EU Commission showed signs of fresh thinking in 1997, publishing a new policy statement in 1997 on "Modernising and Improving Social Protection in the European Union" (Table 4.8). The accent in this document is on making the mechanisms of labour law and social security more *employment-friendly*.

The political debate is often over-simplified and emotionalised in regard to the so-called Anglo-Saxon model. The essence of the European Social Model, which is documented elsewhere [Emerson, 1987], is that there is comprehensive social security for public health and income maintenance and labour market law which governs the rules of labour relations and employment contract (including recruitment and dismissal). In the US there is only a thin and incomplete social security system, with notable gaps in public health care, and little labour market regulation (meaning in practice much greater flexibility in recruitment and dismissal).

The difference between the UK and US within the so-called Anglo-Saxon model has in reality been much greater than some political speeches have suggested (especially when larded with the memorable political styles of former President Reagan and former Prime Minister Thatcher). A careful review of UK labour market and social policies [Robinson, 1996] shows that the UK in the seventies and eighties saw a trimming of social benefits and some revisions of labour market laws, but hardly a deregulatory drive into another paradigm.

The distance between the UK and the continent in terms of political rhetoric was reduced in May 1997 when the new government announced their intention to sign the EU Social Protocol, without

Table 4.8: "Modernising and Improving Social Protection in the European Union"

(*below are the objectives highlighted in the EU Commission's most recent policy statement on social protection)*

1. *Increase awareness of* **social policy as a productive factor.**
2. *Make social protection* **more employment-friendly** *by developing* **unemployment compensation schemes** *into employability insurance, in line with the move towards life-long earning.*
3. *Make social protection* **more employment -friendly** *by narrowing the gap between total salary costs and net take-home pay* **for low-skill workers**
4. *Make social protection* **more employment-friendly** *by increasing employment incentives as well as employment opportunities* **for older workers.**
5. *Make social protection* **more   employment-friendly** *by activating integration policies associated with* **social minima policies**
6. *Foster the* **adaptation of public pension schemes** *to the ageing of European populations*
7. *Provide a secure environment for* **supplementary pension schemes.**
8. *Revisit social protection systems to meet the* **care needs of dependent older people.**
9. *Improve the* **efficiency, cost effectiveness and quality of health systems** *so that they can meet the growing demands arising from the ageing of the population and other factors.*
10. *Adapt social protection to the new* **gender balance** *in working life and to changes in family structure.*
11. *Adapt the coordination system (for cross-border workers) to new forms of social protection and new needs in the field; avoid unnecessary complexity and remove barriers to* **cross-border mobility.**

Source: Communication from the EU Commission, 12 March 1997 (COM/97/102)

greatly changing the policies they inherited from the Thatcher period.

More broadly it is instructive to look at the policies of those EU countries who have adjusted onto a *reformed European Social Model*. Even in the heart of the Rhineland there has been visible reform, notably in the Netherlands, whose policies have come now to be regarded indeed as a new model case. Also Sweden, which extrapolated the European Social Model to breaking point, has been able to make very large and fast adjustments in 1995-96, from the moment when political consensus was reached that a major change was required.

Ingredients for reform of the *European Social Model* are diverse, depending on the starting point of the country concerned. The general prescription starts with rectification of glaring extravagances and abuses of social security mechanisms and of excessive rigidities in wage levels. It continues with a broader trimming of benefit regimes and easing of regulatory restrictions on employment. However the reforming countries have relied on varying packages of measures, as pointed out in a recent study on the Rhineland Model [Davidson et al., 1997]:

- the Netherlands, which had high labour costs, including very high payroll taxes, focused on achieving wage moderation through centralised bargaining and tax reductions, lowering minimum wages, especially for young workers, and scaling down payroll taxes especially on low-wage earners. It also tightened up on its notoriously generous granting of dubiously justified invalidity and early retirement pensions;

- the UK, with its history of troubled labour relations, gave priority to product market reform, privatisation and reform of labour law, curtailing excessive trade union and cutting the duration of unemployment benefits;

- Ireland, with high unemployment, took action to reduce the generosity of unemployment benefits, cut marginal tax rates, and improve human capital formation;

- Sweden was also able to make a dramatic reduction of its unsustainable budget deficit in 1995-96, including curtailment of a much abused sickness benefits scheme, to the point that the actual incidence of sickness of workers suddenly dropped quite remarkably;

- in Spain in 1997 it was agreed to reduce the extremely high cost of dismissal of workers and discontinue the fixing of wages at the national level, given the extremely high differences in regional unemployment levels.

By contrast the core Rhineland countries have been slower to embark upon adequate reforms, although there is increasing public awareness of the needs to do so. The German wage-bargaining system, highly unionised and centralised by industrial branch, does not lend itself to the type of tightly concerted coordination of wages policy seen in the Netherlands. However at least a debate on these themes is engaged as a national priority. In France, repeatedly in 1996 and 1997 the French governments, in examples reminiscent of the UK labour relations twenty years earlier, showed lack of resolution in tolerating the blockading of international motorway connections by truck drivers. The new Socialist government since 1997 is set upon a policy to reduce unemployment in part by reducing the average working week to 35 hours by the year 2000, without a loss of earnings. This approach seems highly unsuitable for a Europe with a declining population of working age, mounting problems of pension funding and a consequential need for measures to redress the declining ratio of active to inactive parts of the population. In Belgium straightforward debate about the economics of the labour market is still vitiated by political tensions between the two language communities.

The prospect of a classic confrontation between a strict commitment to price stability and the rigidity of labour markets will remain as long as the unemployment problem is not substantially resolved. It is therefore not surprising that the *1996 Annual Report* of the European Monetary Institute [EMI, 1997] gives particular attention to the need to alleviate labour market rigidities. Diplomatically the EMI cites examples of reform measures from most EU countries in the areas of unemployment benefits, employment protection regulations and social security payroll taxes. The starker facts are that the core euro countries have yet to confront these issues with sufficient force. The opportunity presents itself, with increasingly strong evidence of employment policy successes coming in from the reformist countries, and the EU Commission's re-think of the rules of social policy. This could aim at redefining a reformed EU Social Model, and creating a widening consensus over the adequate reform agenda.

There is growing recognition of the problem, as suggested by the inclusion of a new employment chapter in the Treaty of Amsterdam and the first-ever "jobs summit" of the European Council in November 1997 devoted exclusively to these issues. At least the language of political declarations moves towards a new synthesis of the European Social Model. The clearest text so far are the "Guidelines for Member States Employment Policies" addressed by the Commission to the jobs summit [Commission of the EU, 1997d], which was broadly endorsed in the conclusions of the summit. A notable change of emphasis is the highlighting of a high employment rate, rather than a low unemployment rate as the main challenge. The EU's current employment rate in 1997 was 60.4%. This should be increased to 65% in five years, heading later towards 70%, implying creation of 12 million new jobs. No such unemployment target is presented (a small revolution in itself). Attainment of the objectives rest on four "pillars": entrepreneurship, employability, adaptability and equal opportunities. These slogans are still of course far from the front-line action, but at least they change the basis of the debate and may be a due part of the long, heavy process of changing course for the super-tanker called "European Social Model". Also the EU's remarkable success of the 1990s, in achieving convergence on low inflation and budget deficits in preparation for the euro, is perceived now as a model for serious concerted action in the labour market area.

- Regional economics

There are particular reasons why regional economic trends and policies in the euro area have to be regarded as a major topic. Europeans do not like to leave their regions for economic reasons. They are apparently 25 times less likely to do so in response to wage differentials than the average US citizen [Puga, 1997]. The reluctance of Europeans to move from their region reflects cultural and ethnic attachments, which can become highly sensitive politically in the event of persistent economic difficulties regionally. The adjustment of regional imbalances within member states has of course not been able to rely on exchange rate changes in the past. In the future it will be the whole euro area that has to find regional adjustment mechanisms other than the exchange rate.

Actual regional trends in the seventies and eighties in the EU reveal an important and at first sight puzzling paradox [Puga, 1997]: *between* the member states there has been on average a positive convergence of GDP per capita levels. Inequalities have reduced; but *within* member states there has been on average a divergence, i.e. a widening of regional disparities.

This paradox seems however to have explanations. The convergence between member states, notably the catch-up by Ireland, Spain and Portugal, shows that the opening of markets combined with large-scale investment in modern transport infrastructure and other elements of modernisation, can be important ingredients of convergence success stories. On the other hand the long persistence and now aggravation of very high unemployment rates in depressed regions within several countries warns that regional investment aids may not be effective when combined with an insufficiency of regional wage differentials.

In Spain the south and western regions see unemployment levels of 30% compared to the national average of 21%. In Italy Sicily sees unemployment of 23% compared to the national average of 11%. In Germany the new eastern *Länder* see unemployment of 20% compared to the national average of 10%. In Belgium Wallonia has 13% unemployment compared to 7% in Flanders.

In particular the four countries wanting to join the euro with very high unemployment in their depressed regions (Germany, Belgium, Italy, Spain) have exhibited, at least until recently, a virtual total lack of regional wage flexibility. In the Italian *Mezzogiorno* in 1977 wages were 25% less than in the north; by the early 1990s there was virtually no difference. In Sicily unemployment is 23% compared to the national average of 11%. In Belgium wages have remained nationally negotiated and enforced without regional variation, even when over two decades the southern region unemployment rate has soared to over twice that of the north. In Germany the decision upon re-unification for 1 to 1 parity between the west and east marks caused immediate and uneconomic wage equality, which only now begins to be unwound. In

Spain, like in Italy, strictly national wage levels were enforced in all regions [Bentolila and Jimeno, 1995], even when unemployment in the south was reaching 30%; but in 1997 it was agreed to discontinue the centralised wage-fixing.

Moreover recent analysis of the dynamics of regional economic geography (Puga, 1997) underlines how difficult it is to correct the problems of depressed regions. Growing agglomerations develop specialisations by industrial sector, with dense networks between suppliers, producers and customers. Once established these specialisations become acquired comparative advantages, which are very difficult for other regions to out-compete in the struggle to attract mobile investment. The EU single market will see an accentuation of such trends, if the US pattern of much greater regional specialisation by sector is an advance indicator of what to expect.

Regional wage flexibility. Depressed regions will therefore - in the face of the new economic geography of industrial concentration and specialisation - have great difficulty in attracting new investment is the absence of wage differentials to offset their lack of comparative advantage. These regions on the whole do not lack investment in transport infrastructure, and the economic locations of Belgium and east Germany are not at all peripheral. However their lack of wage competitiveness, sufficient to attract new investment is clear. Further increases in investment in transport infrastructure and subsidies for private investment risks would only increase economic distortions and waste, with excessive capital intensity and erosion of competition policy principles. Where the regional unemployment rate is 10% above the national rate, one could think in terms of a 10% wage cut to bring the region in line in the long-run (such are the generally observed wage-labour demand elasticities). But if it was desired to get a sharp kick-start to regional employment recovery it would be more realistic for these four cases to envisage a 20% cut.

In fact something of this order of magnitude seems to be beginning in east Germany. An estimated two-thirds of employment in the new *Länder* now have wage rates set at the local or plant level. While east German wages fixed in industry-wide bargaining amount to 90% of the national average, those negotiated locally amount only to 77% of that level [*Financial Times*, Germany supplement, 18 November 1997, quoting Bundesbank sources].

This example suggest that when legal or conventional impediments to regional wage differentiation are scrapped, changes in relative wages may work through quite strongly, when regional unemployment is so high. General reforms of labour regulations and social security mechanisms in the direction of enhancing market pressures would also help. If results are not forthcoming, a supplementary mechanism could be conditional wage subsidies. There is a substantial economic literature on this subject [Snower and De la Dehesa, 1997], but little experience of such subsidies outside limited fields, such as youth employment schemes and measures to help disadvantaged groups. The key point for a scheme focused on the depressed region, whose wages were hardly different to the national average, would be to offer the subsidy as a grant matching the degree to which the negotiated wage fell below a national reference level. This would be a critical difference compared to the existing Italian scheme, which allows lower social security taxes in the *Mezzogiorno*, but unconditionally with respect to the wage level. In practise this subsidy seems to be entirely shifted into the wage level, which is virtually the same as in the North.

Shock-absorber. The euro area will also be confronted by increased tensions over responsibility for painful industrial adjustments as the single market integrates more and more completely. The well publicised case in early 1997 of the sudden announcement by Renault of the complete closure of a car factory at Vilvoorde in the Brussel suburbs illustrates the kind of situation which is likely to be repeated across the euro area. The Renault closure was a shock to the local economy, but it should not be considered as a shock to the EU system, but rather a normal part of the rationalisation of industrial specialisations across the regional map of Europe, as already mentioned above. The case none the less has salutary features for stimulating the reflections of policy makers.

The present regional and structural funds of the EU are not adapted to respond quickly to intense and narrowly localised shocks of this type. The ethos of these funds has been to deal with problems of long-term backwardness, or peripherality or structural decline of old industrial regions.

However the opportunity exists to adapt the funds to handle the sharp localised shocks, both for procedural reasons since the structural funds are due for revision by 1999, and because there is a model instrument already at hand in the workings of the European Coal and Steel Community (ECSC), which could be given general application for any sector through reform of the structural funds. Even the criteria and language of the ECSC Treaty in its Article 56 could be copied, for example "if fundamental changes in the ... industry should compel some undertakings to discontinue, curtail or change their activities", or if restructuring "should lead to exceptionally large reduction in labour requirements in the ...industry, making it particularly difficult in one or more areas to re-employ redundant workers", then the executive would be empowered to use both grant and loan finance "for the creation of new and economically sound activities". To serve these needs the structural funds should be endowed with larger financial reserves, to be held available for such eventualities. These grant funds would be used together with loan capital of the European Investment Bank or of the Commission.

4.5 Avoiding a new inconsistent quartet

The foregoing review of the policy system with which the euro will start is showing some risks of systemic fault, analogous to that which brought the downfall of the EMS. This time the quartet of features are those shown in Table 4.2, namely (i) the single currency, (ii) the rules of budget policy, (iii) the social and labour market model and (iv) the system of inter-regional redistribution. The particular risk is that the system may not have enough flexibility to adjust to economic problems, especially of employment, in specific regions or entire member states.

Each of the four system components can, in principle, be modulated by degree of fixity or adjustment capacity. Existing economic and monetary unions reveal some alternatives in terms of stable systems. For example the Federal Republic of Germany combines the national currency and a large federal budget with high-powered inter-regional equalisation transfers and very limited inter-regional flexibility of wages or social benefits. The United States has less inter-regional redistribution and more inter-regional wage flexibility. Within all EU states there is a strongly equalising inter-regional redistribution function and, mostly, very limited wage flexibility (the UK is an exception).

But as pointed out earlier in this chapter, several states very keen on joining the euro are in fact not managing their own national policy quartets well. Germany, Belgium, Italy and Spain have enormous unemployment problems in their depressed regions, all resulting from a defective combination of inter-regional equalisation transfers and rigid regional wage equality. France experiences the same syndrome in its small overseas territories.

The euro will be introduced in fact with an unusual quartet: (i) the single currency, (ii) constrained national budgets, (iii) rigid real wage levels and (iv) a small redistribution function for absorbing adverse economic shocks. The system, at its worst, could be an idiosyncratic blend of features from the EU and national systems, trying to maintain social model rigidities that have already caused grave regional unemployment crises, but without the cushioning of generous redistribution mechanisms.

The risk more precisely is that acute regional or national unemployment problems would appear to be without solution, leaving only the euro to blame. Political tensions would mount. In the extreme case there could be "exits" from the euro area. To leave a monetary union is not that difficult, as Ireland observed in 1978, in breaking with the British pound.

This is a warning , not a prediction. Most ministry of finance and central bank officials are familiar with these arguments, but this was also true for the first *inconsistent quartet* (section 2.4), and this time the stakes are higher. Political debate on this issues exists. Strategic mistakes are possible, but not inevitable. The question is how to weight the adjustment and shock-absorbing capacities of the four policy blocks. The managers of the euro will have a degree of freedom in the flexible external exchange rate, although dogmatic monetarists might contest this. There is, or could be some room for political discretion in application of the Stability Pact rules. There seems to be consensus that the aggregate size of the EU budget should not increase, but there is some room there to re-allocate agricultural and regional funds to meet euro area's adjustment problems (as argued in section 4.4). There is considerable room for labour market and social policy reforms to get more responsiveness to unemployment problems. The Rhineland's favourite child of today, the Netherlands, has shown what concerted real wage adjustments can do, together with correction of manifestly abused social welfare programmes. And the EU's *enfant terrible*, the UK, has shown how grave regional unemployment problems in depressed regions can be overcome with the aid of some regional wage flexibility coupled to investment in renewal of the economic infrastructure.

The most plausible reshaping of the new and presently *inconsistent quartet*, politically, would be to seek partial contributions from each of the four blocks. A more detailed review of these alternatives is offered by Obstfeld and Peri [1998], who speculate that the resistance to greater inter-regional real wage flexibility will create strong pressures for inter-regional transfer mechanisms. But they also point out the hazards of a "European Transfer Union" (ETU). The social and labour market policy block should remain the major candidate for reforming action. The new emphasis on employment policy at the EU level, reported above, arrives therefore none too soon. But this will be a programme with a lengthy time horizon of 10 to 15 years before full results should be expected.

4.6 Rules of corporate governance

The improvement of basic standards of corporate governance in central and eastern Europe, including the reduction of bribery and corruption, now emerges as a strategic priority for the second stage of the transition process.

The first stage, taking typically about five years, consisted of the primary acts of liberalisation and privatisation. The priority concern at the time was whether the animal spirits of private enterprise could be brought back to life rapidly, if at all. It took a few years for the animal spirits to be seen not only to spring back to life, but also to reveal themselves to be very wild animals. The first stage of privatisation led, for reasons now easily understood, to a rough and often violent struggle for the appropriation of assets being divested by the state. Even when this consisted of a democratic distribution of vouchers, there still remained thereafter the process of shaking down these share holdings into structures of control, which often took place according to the rules of the Wild East. Corruption and bribery, already a deeply established culture in the state controlled economy, developed a new lease of life, together with a horrific growth in some countries (especially Russia and the Ukraine) of mafia violence and contract killings of managers and bankers.

Data are now assembled by *Transparency International* from opinion polls of businessmen on the extent of perceived corruption, and are published for many countries. The results for European and some other countries are given in Table 4.9. While the international comparability of the numbers must surely be considered only very rough, there are none the less several interesting messages in the data.

A first group of virtually corruption-free countries of Europe are all small countries of the north-west of the continent. Then in a second category come all the G-7 large industrialised countries except Italy. These large countries are regarded as largely honest. This discrepancy by size, among countries of otherwise the same level of economic development, coincides with that already reported in Table 2.4 on the level of trustworthiness of different nationalities.

A third category, at around the half-way point in the scores between maximum and minimum of honesty, brings together both the weakest scoring EU countries (Spain, Greece, Belgium and Italy), where business men perceive real problems, and several central European countries (Poland, Hungary, and the Czech Republic). Comparison may be made with these countries' investment ratings (Table 4.3). There is in the corruption rankings a similar overlap of existing EU member states and the accession candidates. There are also here groupings reminiscent of the main cultural divides in Europe. The

Table 4.9: Corruption perception index, 1996-1997

	1996	1997
1. Denmark	9.33	9.94
2. Finland	9.05	9.45
3. Sweden	9.08	9.35
4. New Zealand	9.43	9.33
6. Netherlands	8.71	9.03
7. Norway	8.87	8.92
9. Singapore	8.80	8.66
10. Luxembourg	-	8.61
11. Switzerland	8.76	8.61
12. Ireland	8.45	8.28
13. Germany	8.27	8.23
14. United Kingdom	8.44	8.22
16. United States	7.66	7.61
17. Austria	7.59	7.61
19. Portugal	6.53	6.97
20. France	6.96	6.66
21. Japan	7.05	6.57
24. Spain	4.31	5.90
25. Greece	5.01	5.35
26. Belgium	6.84	5.25
27. Czech Republic	5.37	5.20
28. Hungary	4.86	5.18
29. Poland	5.57	5.08
30. Italy	3.42	5.03
37. Romania	-	3.44
38. Turkey	3.54	3.21
41. China	2.43	2.88
45. India	2.63	2.75
47. Mexico	3.30	2.66
49. Russia	2.58	2.27
52. Nigeria	0.69	1.76

Source: Transparency International , Annual Report [1996, 97].
Note: 10 is the highest possible score for the least corrupt, and 0 the lowest possible score for the most corrupt. The data are based on surveys of opinions of businessmen. The incomplete numerical ranking of countries in the table is because only data for a selection of non-European countries are extracted from the source.

Latin south-west scores badly compared to the Germanic north-west. But also the western Slavs score well compared to the Balkans (Romania), Turkey or Russia. The western Slavs in this indicator appear to have an economic culture already acceptable for club admission by west European standards, even if all this third category will be seriously concerned to improve their ranking. In the worst ranked EU countries, Belgium and Italy, the fight against corruption is already one of the very highest political priorities.

While Romania and Turkey head the fourth category, Russia scores a little lower still. By this point the corruption factor is recognized as a major factor deterring new investment and therefore becomes a brake on the resumption of economic growth. While data for the Ukraine are not available from this source, surveys specific to Russia and the Ukraine show the incidence of bribery to be even wider in the Ukraine [Kaufman, 1996]. Another detailed survey showed the incidence of bribery in the small business sector, for the obtaining of regulatory permissions and public services, to be twice as high in Russia as in Poland [Frye and Schleifer, 1996].

However as corporate structures have become more settled in the second broad stage of the transition, so also the owners and managers have to switch their behaviour from the "grab mode" to the "grow mode", since otherwise their assets will fail. This process leads typically to needs for external capital and western business connections, which in turn translate immediately into pressures to move towards Western standards of corporate governance.

The agenda for good corporate governance has become clearer and a rising, urgent priority for policy makers. The EBRD is now taking up a leading role for promoting good corporate governance, issuing guidelines which its clients would be expected to follow (see Table 4.7 for a summary of its contents). This becomes a new kind of microeconomic conditionality for the supply of international finance to the new private sectors of the transition economies, whose time has arrived in central and eastern Europe. Endemic corruption and mafioso criminality are the social and economic maladies that good corporate governance has to displace. The switch now from "grab mode" to "grow mode" should work steadily in favour of this displacement.

Table 4.10: EBRD guidelines on "Sound Business Standards and Corporate Practices"

---

1. Relationship with customers
- *consistent quality at competitive prices*
- *overall reliability of service*
- *long-term perspective, rather than short-term gains*

2. Relationship with shareholders and corporate governance
- *transparent share holding structure*
- *protection of minority shareholder rights*
- *protection of shareholder register*
- *audited accounts*
- *rules of shareholder meetings*
- *division of authority between management, board and shareholders*
- *responsibilities of board of directors*
- *disclosure of personal interests of board members*

3. Relationship with employees
- *respect labour laws*
- *respect health and safety standards*
- *respect rights to union activity*
- *effective consultation procedures*
- *clear pay and employment conditions*
- *concern for long-term welfare of staff (eg pensions)*

4. Relationship with suppliers
- *transparent purchasing policies*
- *severe sanctions for employees paying bribes*
- *arm's length relationship with suppliers*
- *pay suppliers promptly*
- *respect environmental conventions*

5. Relationship with the community
- *sensitivity to concerns of local population*
- *communicate with local interest groups*
- *sensitivity to environment*

6. Relationship with government
- *pay fairly computed taxes*
- *respect mandatory regulations*
- *obtain all permits required*
- *no bribery in dealings with government*

Source: EBRD [1997], "Sound Business Standards and Corporate Practices - A set of guidelines and recommendations".

An example from Russia in February 1998 illustrates this process at work. In the course of consolidation of the Russian oil industry Russian financiers Berezovsky and Potanin planned share issues by the Sidanko company, which would have massively diluted the value of the minority interests of some foreign investors. The share issue was challenged by the foreign interests, and their position was upheld by the Securities Commission in Moscow. Potanin then commented: "it is not possible not to respect shareholder rights. The issue is that the rules of the game are changing in Russia so quickly. This transaction with the Sidanko bonds was organised almost one and a half years ago".

Meanwhile the democratic process throws up also increasing clamours for cleaning up corruption and for security from extortion or contract killings by the mafia. Political leaders were by 1997 increasingly putting these issues into higher priority on governmental agendas in eastern Europe, from Russia to Bulgaria and Romania (two of which are marked severely in Table 4.7 and anecdotal evidence suggests that Bulgaria would be scored similarly).

For their part the industrialised countries agreed in 1997 to an OECD convention, under which each member state will introduce legislation to make bribery a criminal offence.

The rules or corporate governance thus now justify their place as a critical element in the building of a European Civil Society.

5. Security

I could not stop NATO's expansion, nor could I bang my shoe on the table like Khrushchev.
President Yeltsin to Jiang Zemin on returning from his Helsinki summit
with President Clinton, April 1997.

If NATO is the answer, what was the question?
European Professor of International Strategic Studies, September 1997.

Security is in this chapter defined as covering democracy and the protection of human rights including those of minorities, as well as inter-state behaviour and the use of the military to keep the peace. In contemporary Europe this set of issues is a seamless web. Democracy may be seen as the best of all instruments of defence against violence and war. The quality of democracy and sharing of related political values is also vital to the process of integration. Tensions involving national minorities and related frontier questions is the single most extensive threat to peace in the post-communist Europe.

This security nexus thus involves four inter-related sets of rules of civil society, each of which is set out in more detail later in the chapter:
- *rules of democracy*
- *rules of human rights and fundamental freedoms*
- *rules for protection of national minorities*
- *rules of inter-state behaviour on matters of security*

The European institutions concerned with security in this wide sense are several: the Council of Europe, the OSCE, NATO, WEU and the EU. These organisations all have differing but substantially overlapping memberships, and also in some cases overlapping competences. We defer to Chapter 6 the questions of coherence of this set of institutions, and first review the substance of the rules and how the institutions adapt to the new European environment.

5.1 Democratic institutions

- Rules of democracy

It is curious that the official institutions in Europe are so reticent about adopting a working definition of democracy. It seems that democracy is the first and foremost qualification for integration into Europe, that official institutions are able to decide admissions on the basis of recognising whether democracy is up to a minimum standard, but that this can be done without an official code or working set of criteria defining democracy. Those concerned with the promotion of the democratic ideal world-wide have the really difficult task to find a possible common ground between countries with very different cultures, but this should not be so in Europe.

We must use, therefore, the definitions of political scientists. One suitable formulation used in a review of central and eastern European democracies for the Council of Europe and the EU Commission, by Kaldor and Vejvoda [1996] drawing largely on the formulations of Dahl [1989], is that presented in Table 5.1. The list contains the obvious institutional headings - elected power-holders, free and fair elections, separation of powers - , and understandably includes also the rule of law and civilian control of the military. But the list then runs on into the domains of individual human rights, including freedom of expression and inclusive citizenship. Such rules of human rights in this chapter are discussed separately below, although of course the domains of democracy and human rights are parts of the same seamless web.

However the field of democracy becomes even more of a grey area when it is taken to embrace "associational autonomy" and related concepts. A currently influential branch of political theory emphasises the importance of *civil society* in the European tradition [Hall, 1995;

Table 5.1: Rules of democracy

---

1. Elected power-holders
2. Free and fair elections
3. Inclusive citizenship, with no exclusions based on race or ethnicity
4. Rule of law, with protection of the individual and minorities
5. Separation of powers - legislature, executive, judiciary
6. Freedom of expression and information
7. Associational autonomy
8. Civilian control of the armed forces

Source: Kaldor and Vejvoda [1996], supplementing Dahl [1989]

Cohen and Arato, 1989]. Gellner [1994], influenced by thinking in central Europe before the demise of communism, offered the following definition: "civil society is that set of diverse non-governmental institutions, which is strong enough to counterbalance the state and, whilst not preventing the state from fulfilling its role of keeper of the peace and arbitrator between major interests, can nevertheless prevent the state from dominating and atomizing society." Civil society thus means both deepening the culture of democracy and protecting against the "tyranny of the majority", to use a formulation by de Tocqueville. Cohen and Arato [1995] are a little more precise in their definition of civil society as: "a sphere of social interaction between the economy and state, composed above all of the intimate sphere (especially the family), the sphere of associations (especially voluntary associations), social movements and forms of public communication. Modern civil society is created through self-constitution and self-mobilization. It is institutionalised and generalised through laws.... In the long run both independent action and institutionalisation are necessary for the reproduction of civil society."

Civil society is thus a concept of democracy that deliberately goes deep down below the mechanisms of government into the culture and traditions of society at a more private level. Apart from making any of assessment of the democracy of EU candidate states much more subjective, the concept is also relevant to the debate about the EU's own future constitution. It bears, for example, on the question how much centralisation of institutional power is appropriate over the next few decades. It leads on also into the concept of *cosmopolitan democracy*, which is an alternative to the federal paradigm for Europe's future, to which we return in Chapter 6.

-State of democracy

In spite of this lack of an official code of democracy, there is no shortage of practical evaluations, usually along the lines of the eight criteria in Table 5.1. The EU Commission's *"Agenda 2000"* document [1997] drew up its evaluations of the ten candidates for accession from central and eastern Europe, having access to the Kaldor/Vejvoda study. The Council of Europe monitors democracy in its member states. Its parliamentary assembly publishes occasional reports, but for a comprehensive annual source one has to rely on the US State Department's annual report on human rights [State Department, 1997]. This monumental document, 1500 pages long, is carefully researched and covers every country in the world, except the United States (despite this lapse the editors merit a Nobel peace prize). It reviews all basic criteria of democracy, and in greater detail the human rights record for individuals and minorities collectively.

These studies make it feasible to present summary assessments and overall rankings. As illustrated in Table 5.2, grade A marks a generally satisfactory functioning of democracy by commonly accepted European and western standards. Grade B signifies that there are problems of implementation, for example hindrances to respect of the constitution or weakness of the rule of law or of civil society institutions. Grade C signifies situations where the regime is basically undemocratic, either because of abusively authoritarian leadership, or of failings in the rule of law and of civil society, leading in extreme cases to anarchy or civil war.

The Kaldor-Vejvoda study presented grades for all eight criteria in Table 5.1. The formalities of democracy have been thoroughly introduced everywhere in the ten EU candidate countries. On the most basic criterion, election of power holders, all countries were graded satisfactory. The only criterion where there generally remain problems in all ten countries is over the rule of law and adequacy of the judiciary. A continued sense of individual insecurity remains in many countries.

On the inclusiveness of citizenship, Estonia and Latvia were faulted because of the severity of their laws for their large Russian minorities (minorities questions more generally are discussed later in this chapter).

On the separation of powers Slovakia was and remains clearly faulted because of the prime minister's abuse of the constitution. Criticisms made in the study relating to the situation in Poland and Romania in 1996 appear no longer justified in the light of the changes of presidencies in these two countries.

The freedom of expression was satisfactory in nine countries, only Romania being criticised for restrictions on information reaching non-urban areas. Similarly the freedom of association was graded satisfactory in nine countries, only Bulgaria being criticised for forbidding association on grounds of ethnicity.

Finally on civilian control of the armed forces eight countries were graded satisfactory, but Romania and Slovakia were criticised for the remaining role of secret police services.

Such was the assessment of independent political scientists. How does this compare with the official assessments made by the EU Commission in their *"Agenda 2000"* document [Commission of the EU, 1997]? The Commission agreed on the general extent of the need to fight corruption and improve the rule of law. Most countries were only otherwise faulted on individual problems, with a close correspondence to the Kaldor-Vejvoda findings. The need to curtail the secret police in Bulgaria and Romania is noted, so also the need to accelerate the naturalisation of Russian minorities in Estonia and Latvia.

The Commission judged Slovenia's democracy to be functioning remarkably well, and this must have influenced the political decision to propose this country for inclusion in the first wave of accession

Table 5.2 State of Democracy in Europe and OSCE

EU countries (all), (according to US State Department)		A
EU candidate countries		
Poland, Czech Rep., Hungary, Slovenia, Lithuania,		A
Estonia, Latvia,	citizenship issue	A/B
Bulgaria, Romania	recently much improved	A/B
Slovakia	constitutional irregularities	B/C
Cyprus	(divided island)	A
Turkey	role of army, religion in politics	B
Other Balkans		
Albania	anarchy in mid-1997, democracy being restored since	B/C
Bosnia H.	unsettled still	B/C
Croatia	auth. pres., media pressures	B/C
Macedn.	some electoral irregularities	A/B
Serbia	auth. pres., electoral abuse, media bias	C
CIS countries		
Belarus	auth. pres., denial of freedom of press and assembly	C
Moldova	no serious criticisms	A
Russia	some press bias in elections, weak rule of law	A/B
Ukraine	media bias and limitn. on freedom of association	A/B
Caucasus		
Armenia	electns seriously flawed, media bias	B
Azerbn.	electns. flawed, limited indep.of parlmt./press/assembly	C
Georgia	limited press freedom	A/B
Central Asia		
Kyrgyzstan	auth. pres., electoral and constitutnl. flaws	B/C
Kazakhstan	auth. pres., electoral and constitutnl. flaws	B/C
Turkmenistan	auth. pres., denial of press and political freedoms	C
Tajikistan	auth. pres., denial of freedoms, civil war	C
Uzbekistan	auth. pres., denial of press and political freedoms	C

Note: A= satisfactory; B=some problems; C=undemocratic; "auth. pres." signifies undemocratically authoritarian presidential regime. Grades A,B,C are the author's reading of the sources.

Sources: For EU-candidates, EU Commission [1997] and Kaldor and Vejvoda [1996]; non-EU candidates, State Department [1997].

negotiations. By contrast fundamental criticism is limited to Slovakia, where the government has not respected the competences and rights of the presidency and opposition, also refusing to respect judgements of the constitutional court.

The political assessment of the ten candidate countries of central and eastern Europe is thus clear. Apart from Slovakia, the Commission recognises in all other ten candidate countries credible commitment to the principles of democracy. Weaknesses in the practical functioning of the institutions that remain are expected to be overcome progressively with time and effort.

Of the two EU candidate countries not so far mentioned, Cyprus is divided by a "Berlin wall", of no constitutional legitimacy. In the southern Greek Republic of Cyprus, the democratic institutions work according to western norms. The EU's intention to open accession negotiations provoked protests from Turkey and threats of annexation of the northern part of the island. For Turkey itself the Commission in *"Agenda 2000"* recognises its parliamentary democracy, but rates it below the European norm regarding the treatment of human rights, the freedom of expression, the persistence of torture and non-judicial executions and ambiguities in the civil control of the military.

In other former Yugoslav states and Albania there is still an extremely unsettled and mostly unsatisfactory situation. Only Macedonia, in spite of its complex ethnic structure, sees something like a satisfactory functioning of basic electoral and parliamentary processes. Serbia (Yugoslav Federation) was suspended from the OSCE for its part in the Bosnian war. Most recently a C grade is justified for the constitutional manoeuvre of Milosevic, who in July 1997 evaded the problem of not being allowed to stand for president a third term in Serbia by getting elected for the Yugoslav Federation instead. In Croatia in June 1997 an OSCE team rated the referendum on presidential elections as "below minimum standards". In the Serb Sprska Republic of Bosnia-Herzegovena the President declared in July 1997 that "the functioning of legal order is in serious crisis in almost all areas". However in the Muslim-Croat Federation of Bosnia Herzegovena the 1996 elections were considered by international monitors to have been imperfect progress, with continuing acts of intimidation and ethnic conflict. In Albania the outbreak of anarchy in mid-1997 provides also grounds for a C grade, with complete breakdown of the rule of law and governmental processes. After the Italian-led forces had supported OSCE supervision of parliamentary elections in July 1997, the basic mechanisms of democratic government began to return to life.

However in Russia, the Ukraine and Moldova democracy is proving robust, imperfect certainly, but passing the basic tests of free and fair elections. In Russia democracy survived two challenges by the putschists of 1991 and 1993, and went on to observe vigorously contested parliamentary elections in 1993 and 1995, and the presidential election of 1996. Some bias of the media in these elections, and serious problems for the rule of law in society as a whole translate into a mixed A/B grade. Analogous problems exist also in the Ukraine, which nonetheless observed a freely contested change of the presidency in 1995. Moldova wins an A grade, since the usual problems of the young democracies appear there to have been moderated rather successfully.

The surprising outsider compared to this group is Belarus, a country which under the USSR experienced the highest levels of educational and technological performance. Its authoritarian president, Alexander Lukashenko, is responsible for unfavourable grades on most criteria of democracy, and an overall C grade. Belarus offers a contemporary reminder of what undemocratic eastern Europe can consist of. The president has amassed comprehensive powers since his election in 1994. He dissolved parliament with an irregular referendum in 1996, made himself cabinet minister for life, extended his mandate as president by two years and subordinated both judiciary and the legislature to his control. The presidential guard uses force against opposition politicians without judicial oversight. The security forces make arbitrary arrests and detentions, beat up prisoners and monitor politicians. The president even championed that he was confident of his prime minister's loyalty, because he knew, through bugging, what he said to his wife in private [State Department, 1997]. Such is a C grade political regime.

All three Trans-Caucasian states - Georgia, Armenia and

Azerbaijan - have applied to join the Council of Europe. It remains to be seen whether these countries make the grade. President Shevarnadze of Georgia carries a certain credit as a democratic politician, and his country gets an A/B grade, given still some problems such as press freedom. But in spite of the enormous difficulties of two regional wars of secession, the basic mechanics of democracy have functioned reasonably well. In Armenia, however, elections have been seriously flawed, warranting a B grade. More extensive problems for democracy are evident in Azerbaijan, with flawed elections and limited independence of parliament and freedoms of press and assembly warranting a C grade.

None of the Central Asian states have applied to the Council of Europe, although all are members of the OSCE. So far the leaderships in Central Asia have emphasised their attachment to other political models for maintaining stability, notably the loosely identified Asian model according to which the earlier stages of economic transition may better be pursued without too many political experiments. Of the five countries, Kazakhstan and Kyrgyzstan are graded B/C, their regimes being clearly authoritarian, but with limited breaches of human rights. However in Turkmenistan and Uzbekistan the regimes have gone further.

In Turkmenistan, probably the most authoritarian state in Central Asia, President Nyazov has established a one-party state and represses all political activity. The president controls the judiciary and parliament and indulges in a blatant personality cult. The government censors all newspapers, controls all media and prevents any real criticism of the government. Criticism of the government in academic circle is not tolerated. Public gatherings of political opposition is prevented. Security forces make arbitrary arrests and detentions, beating prisoners with impunity [State Department, 1997].

- *Outlook*

How does this overview of the present help us for the future map of Europe? For the EU and NATO accession candidates of central and eastern Europe, the achievements already of the nineteen-nineties look like credible commitments to the culture of democracy. The staged and conditional accession procedures make it highly likely that these countries will continue to converge progressively on western norms. The conspicuously deviant case at the present time, Slovakia, is sure to feel its isolation and encirclement by the culture of democracy, while this country has no obvious reasons of national culture to remain divergent.

A similar argument applies to Belarus, surrounded by the seriously democratic Russia and Ukraine on one side and the EU candidates on the other. It may only be a matter of time before this country too chooses to converge upon the norms of its neighbours, even if the replacement of the present authoritarian leadership may still be distant. For Russia and the Ukraine the democratic processes are sufficiently vigorous yet imperfect that there is every reason for the rest of Europe to work with them at the strengthening of the common framework of political and economic rules. In Russia there remain factions who like the idea of the perceived Asian model for deferring democratisation.

The Central Asian countries themselves are evidently converging together on some such Asian model, in which democracy as understood in the west is not the priority, compared to the longevity of incumbent leaderships. Azerbaijan, culturally close to Central Asia, shows signs of similar inclinations. Unlike the isolated cases of Belarus and Slovakia in the European heartland, there seems to be little reason to expect an early reversal of these trends in this Central Asian group. Georgia in the Caucasus, on the other hand, shows signs of moving towards the western political model, which is not inconsistent with its cultural history, this having being so distinct from that of its Islamic or Orthodox neighbours.

Finally in the former Yugoslavia and Albania, there is evidence of a slow and still patchy return towards political normality. Thus the outlook is not universally bad for democratic norms, and it might be expected that the zones of democratic culture in the region progressively expand.

- Monitoring democracy

These indications amply justify the work of the Council of Europe and the OSCE in the field of democracy, although there are questions of overlap and efficiency to consider in their parallel mandates. Both the Council of Europe and the OSCE participate in election monitoring, often alongside each other. Some rationalisation is here called for. The OSCE has its own specialised agency in Warsaw - the ODIHR (Office for Democratic Institutions and Human Rights). The Council of Europe has the clearest specialisation and widest mandate for the monitoring of democracy. There are separate monitoring activities of the Committee of Ministers (i.e. governments) and the Parliamentary Assembly. The Committee has the power to suspend a member state if it seriously violates its obligations for the rule of law and respect for human rights (Greece was forced to withdraw in 1969 during the regime of the Colonels; Serbia has not applied for admission since the demise of Yugoslavia). But its monitoring activity is closed to public view, which dampens the sharpness of its impact (although officials tend to argue, with questionable persuasiveness, that the more discrete pressures behind closed doors is the more effective).

The monitoring by the Parliamentary Assembly is public. It has begun now to prepare reports on the respect by new member states for their conditions of entry into the Council of Europe. For example, two of the first such reports were debated by the Assembly in September 1997, these concerning the Czech republic and Lithuania [Council of Europe, 1997a]. Since the democratic institutions of these two countries are considered to be functioning normally, the main contentious topics concerned citizenship and minority rights, and judicial, police and penal systems. The reports, and written replies of the governments concerned provide a good basis for political and public debate.

A timely question now is how best to give greater transparency and impact to the monitoring of democracy? At the level of analysis one idea would be to replicate for politics what the OECD does for economics; that is to produce an annual survey of each country on the functioning of democratic institutions and state of respect for human rights, at the same level of professional objectivity that the OECD has for years done for economic policy and performance. The first reports of the Parliamentary Assembly, just referred to, are promising, but so far lacking in comprehensive coverage. It is not evident yet sure whether this activity will acquire due consistency, with a reliance on ad hoc panels of parliamentarians. Consistent analyses, with solid methodology and comparability, would require a large input by the secretariat of the Council of Europe. It is a complete anachronism to have only the annual report of the US State Department, admirable as this document may be, as a regular and comprehensive source. The EU Commission's *Agenda 2000* document, in its detailed reviews of the ten candidate countries, makes a valuable, new contribution, especially if the promise is kept to do annual updates.

At the political level much greater leverage for the work of the Council of Europe can be obtained indirectly through the leverage of more powerful organisations, namely the EU and NATO. In fact this began to happen in 1997, for example with the conspicuous deferral of Slovakia from early accession negotiations by both organisations. The EU goes further, as should be expected of a civil political body. The Treaty of Amsterdam strengthened references to democracy and human rights as fundamental principles, and made it legally clearer that the EU Court of Justice could make binding judgements on compliance or otherwise of EC law with the Council of Europe Convention. In addition the Treaty of Amsterdam introduced a suspension clause, allowing the Council to vote by qualified majority to suspend the voting rights of a member state in the event of "serious and persistent breach" of democracy or human rights [European Policy Centre, 1997]. The EU has a policy for its general cooperation treaties with third countries of insisting on references to human rights and democratic principles, defined by reference to the basic texts of the OSCE, and allowing for measures such as suspension in the event of serious breach.

The EU and Council of Europe now hold meet regularly. At the 10th such meeting in September 1997 these parties (Council and Commission for the EU, Presidency and Secretary General for the Council of Europe) discussed notably developments in two non-EU member states - Albania and Belarus [*Press Release*, 15th September].

5.2 Human rights

Europe has an extraordinarily well developed mechanism for the protection of human rights. The European Convention for the Protection of Human Rights and Fundamental Freedoms was adopted in 1950 within the framework of the Council of Europe. The substance of the Convention is outlined in Table 5.3, which lists the rights and freedoms protected, as also extended by subsequent protocols. With Council of Europe membership extending progressively to virtually the whole of central and eastern Europe, the new member states are required to subscribe to the Convention and accept its jurisdiction.

The substance of the Convention and associated protocols is clear and indeed fundamental. It defines *rights* (to life, liberty, security, fair trial, appeal in criminal matters, respect for private and family life, marriage, education, free elections), *freedoms* (of thought, conscience, religion, expression, assembly, association, movement and *prohibitions* (of death penalty, torture, slavery, forced labour, punishment without law, discrimination, imprisonment for debt, expulsion of nationals, collective expulsion of aliens).

The European Court of Human Rights was set up later in 1959 to hear complaints of non-respect of the Conventions and to hand down binding judgements. (There is also a Commission of Human Rights, which has functioned as a court of first instance, but this is being now merged into the Court, in the hope of reducing procedural delays). The level of activity of the Court has built up strongly in recent years. Until the 1980s there were under 10 judgements per year. By the 1980s the number rose to 25-30 per year, and in the 1990s the number has risen so far to 30-87 per year. These judgements represent only the conclusion of the legal process. Much greater numbers of applications to the Court (or Commission) are made, starting with around 100 in the early years to several thousand per year in the 1990s. Applications can be made by a state, a person, a non-governmental organisation or a group of individuals over allegations of breach of the Convention. The judgements of the Court are final and binding; they cannot be overruled by the courts of member states.

Table 5.3: The European Convention for the Protection of Human Rights and Fundamental Freedoms.

The Convention
Article 1 - Obligation to respect human rights
Article 2 - Right to life
Article 3 - Prohibition of torture
Article 4 - Prohibition of slavery and forced labour
Article 5 - Right to liberty and security
Article 6 - Right to a fair trial
Article 7 - No punishment without law
Article 8 - Right to respect for private and family life
Article 9 - Freedom of thought, conscience and religion
Article 10- Freedom of expression
Article 11- Freedom of assembly and association
Article 12- Right to marry
Article 13- Right to an effective remedy
Article 14- Prohibition of discrimination
Article 15- Derogation in time of emergency
Article 16- Restrictions on political activity of aliens
Article 18- Limitation on use of restrictions on rights
Protocol No 1
Article 1 - Protection of property
Article 2 - Right to education
Article 3 - Right to free elections
Protocol No 4
Article 1 - Prohibition of imprisonment for debt
Article 2 - Freedom of movement
Article 3 - Prohibition of expulsion of nationals
Article 4 - Prohibition of collective expulsion of aliens
Protocol No 6
Article 1 - Abolition of death penalty
Article 2 - Death penalty in time of war
Protocol No 7
Article 1 - Procedural safeguards relating to expulsion of aliens
Article 2 - Right of appeal in criminal matters
Article 3 - Compensation for wrongful conviction
Article 4 - Right not to be tried or punished twice
Article 5 - Equality between spouses

Source: Council of Europe [1995]

Virtually all of the rights and freedoms listed in the Convention have been subject to cases referred to the Court [ECHR, 1995]. Those articles most actively used concern the right to fair trial, the respect for private and family life, the freedom of expression and the protection of property. However jurists point out [Jacobs and White, 1996] that there is hardly an article which has not spawned a case-law defining and clarifying the right protected. A comprehensive survey of cases judged in the years 1959-1994 showed that after 290 judgements in which violations of human rights were found, there were 107 instances where the governments concerned adopted general measures to comply with the judgement or adapt their case-law [Council of Europe, 1995].

The Court is making many judgements against the governments of EU member states. Two examples of June 1997 are illustrative. In *Halford v. The United Kingdom* the Court judged that the tapping of telephone calls of a former police official had violated Article 8 of the Convention on the right of respect for private and family life. In *Grigoriades v. Greece* it was judged that the military trial of the plaintiff on a charge of having insulted the army violated Article 10 of the Convention on the right to freedom of expression. These and many other cases may seem relatively trivial, but they are showing that while the EU member states have generally acceptable democracies at the level of high political processes, they are still recurrently fallible at the level of detailed application by the processes of law of individual human rights.

This is important politically for the non-discriminatory quality of the Council of Europe's work on the broad agenda of democracy and human rights. The new democracies of central and eastern Europe are understandably concerned that the all-European institutions should not be just policing mechanisms targeted at them alone.

Nonetheless the Court is likely to face a new tidal wave of cases of great gravity, as the Convention and its judicial procedures move into full effect in the new member states from eastern Europe. Some idea of this is offered in Table 5.4, which summarises the human rights situation in all OSCE countries. We use again a rough A, B, C grading for the situation in different countries. The Court is already extremely busy with the flow of cases from the A graded countries of western

Europe. As the two example of recent cases from the UK and Greece suggested, many of these cases are really about refining and perfecting the human rights regime, and correcting isolated cases of abuse. The EU accession candidate countries mostly come into the A/B, or B categories, meaning that there are far more widespread problems still, notably in the practices of security services, police, judicial and penal systems. The C category represents the situation where the Court could not conceivably handle the mass of potential cases of violations, since the systems in these countries are qualitatively out of line with European societal norms. But these are typically the cases of countries whose membership of the Council of Europe is not yet accepted (Belarus) or sought (Serbia), or not considered eligible (Central Asian countries). However even counties which are making enormous efforts of modernisation will need many years to transform their judicial and penal systems. For example the expert report on Russia's penal system, prepared before its accession to the Council of Europe, illustrated how prisons starved of adequate resources may not be able rapidly to throw off the *gulag* quality.

On the other hand the EU's Treaty of Amsterdam marked a reinforcement of the linkage between the jurisprudence of the EU and of the Council of Europe's Convention on Human Rights. In its first chapter on fundamental rights the Treaty states that "the Union shall respect fundamental rights, as guaranteed by the European Convention for the Protection of Human Rights and Fundamental Freedoms signed in Rome on 4 November 1950 and as they result from the constitutional traditions common to the Member States, as general principles of Community law" [European Policy Centre, 1997]. It goes on to confirm the Union's "attachment to fundamental social rights as defined in the European Social Charter signed in Turin on 18 October 1961 and in the 1989 Community Charter of the Fundamental Social Rights of Workers" (see Chapter 5 above on social policy). The Treaty also makes a declaration recalling that Protocol 6 of the Convention provides for abolition of the death penalty, noting that it has been abolished in most of the EU member states and is not applied in any of them.

The EU's own Court of Justice in Luxembourg is given competence

5.5 Human rights situation in Europe and OSCE

EU and other west Europe   A
but France, racial violence, increasing; Germany racial violence, declining;
   UK, police actions in Northern Ireland; Spain, security services re Basques;
   Greece, abuses in security and penal services.   EU
EU accession candidates
Hungary, Slovenia, Poland, Lithuania   A
Czech Republic,   but rough treatment of Roma   A
Estonia, Latvia,   citizenship of Russian minorities   A/B
Bulgaria, Romania govt. respects HR, but abuses by security, penal services A/B
Slovakia , abuses by govt./police/security services; minorities   B
Turkey, brutality with Kurds, more widely police/security services torture,
   killings, disappearances   B/C
Cyprus, except for frontier of Turkish occupied area   A
Other Balkans
Albania, numerous, serious abuses in political, judicial and penal system   C
Bosnia, ethnic cleansing and genocide condoned by authorities, loss of homes
     for refugees, abuses by security forces   C
Croatia, govt. record poor, abuse of Serb minorities   C
Serbia,   police brutality, killings, torture, ethnic repression   C
Macedonia, not bad, except for abuse of Albanian minority   A/B
CIS
Belarus, govt. record poor, abuses by security, penal services   C
Moldova, govt. respects HR, security/penal services harsh,   A/B
Russia, better after massive abuse of HR in Chechnya; judicial procedures
    weak, penal services extremely harsh   B
Ukraine, improving, but problems in police/penal/judiciary   B
Caucasus
Armenia, abuses by security services, arbitrary arrests, detentions   B
Azerbaijan, govt. record poor; abuses by security services   B/C
Georgia, improving, but abuses by security services, penal system   B
Central Asia
Kazakhstan., Kyrgyzstan, govt respects HR; abuses by security/penal service B
Tajikistan, police /security services torture; penal system life threatening   C
Turkmenistan, govt. serious abuses; also security / penal services   C
Uzbekistan, improving; limited freedoms; police/penal services   B/C

A =western norms, sometimes with exceptions; B = respected in principle but serious problems of implementation, more than isolated cases;C = human rights not respected, widely and gravely abused

---

Source: based on EU Commission, "Agenda 2000" [1997] and US State Department [1997]; grades by author.

to judge cases where actions of the EU institutions might themselves transgress the Convention of the Council of Europe. This is a weaker formula than some were advocating, namely that the EU should itself accede to the Convention. This formula was set aside because of likely problems of conflict of jurisdiction between the Courts of Luxembourg and Strasbourg. But still EU policy goes in the commendable direction of not to trying to monopolise European jurisprudence, nor re-invent the wheel; but, on the contrary, to exploit the value of a sister organisation and at the same time strengthen the tissue of the all-European civil society. In the beginning of post-war European integration, the year 1950 saw divergent European integration initiatives leading off in one direction with the European Coal and Steel Community and in another with the Council of Europe and its Convention; the end of the millennium sees the two finally moving back closer and reinforcing each other.

The overall assessment of jurists, to quote Jacobs and White [1996] is that "the European Convention has become the most sophisticated regional machinery for the protection of human rights..... The Contracting Parties have all accepted that individuals within their jurisdiction can raise a complaint before the Strasbourg organs if they believe that the State has not accorded them the protection guaranteed. Recent political developments in central and eastern Europe open the way to a truly pan-European system of human rights protection based on a compulsory and exclusively judicial system. These are huge achievements in the forty-five years since the Convention was signed".

The OSCE has its responsibilities under its "human dimension", but these are more political rather than legal in nature, and relate in practice more to collective disputes between states, or between nationality groups within states. The OSCE can therefore remain marginal to the work of the Council of Europe's Convention [Beddard, 1993].

A grim footnote is the reactivation in Europe of the War Crimes Tribunal mechanism used at Nuremberg, this time to try those responsible for genocide in Bosnia [Howen, 1993]. This new *ad hoc* Tribunal, instigated by the UN Security Council in 1993, was in early 1998 still trying to arrest their main targets (Karadzic and Mladic).

5.3 National minorities and conflict resolution

Of the 400 million people living in central and eastern Europe about one fifth are members of minority groups within their own country. Chapter 3 showed how many instances there are of tension or potential conflict, either because the frontiers are poorly drawn, or because of actual abuse of the human rights of minorities, or both.

Both the Council of Europe and OSCE have instruments to help resolve the tensions arising around the position of minorities, with a mix of complementarity of roles and competitive frictions (the member states have not yet helped resolve the inherent tensions).

The OSCE basic texts define the rights of national minorities in an adequate way, as indicated in Table 5.5. The "Copenhagen document" has been usefully complemented by the "Moscow Mechanism", the latter establishing the vital principle - for an integrating Europe - that serious breaches of human rights are not deemed to be just an internal affair. The OSCE also appointed in 1992 a High Commissioner for National Minorities (HCNM), in the person of former Dutch foreign minister, Mr. Max van der Stoel. The HCNM has developed *ad personam* an active and widely appreciated role. He visits tense areas, exercises an early warning function and through deployment of personal expertise and diplomacy tries to engineer solutions. His menu of situations visited and examined had by the end of 1996 included many of the critical areas reviewed in Chapter 3 [OSCE, 1996], including:

- Greek language education in southern Albania,
- citizenship and use of the Russian language in Kazakhstan and Kyrgyzstan,
- citizenship for Russians in Estonia and Latvia,
- the Albanian minority in Macedonia,
- the Hungarian and Slovak minorities in each country respectively,
- the Roma minorities in Romania and in central and eastern Europe as a whole,

Table 5.5: Rules of the OSCE regarding human rights and the rights of national minorities

---

OSCE, Copenhagen Document, on national minorities, 1990
- full human rights without discrimination and in full equality of law
- to belong to a national minority is a matter of individual choice
- rights of national minorities:
. free use of mother tongue in private as well as public
. own educational, cultural and religious institutions
. to profess and practice religion
. unimpeded contact within and between states
. to disseminate information in mother tongue
. own institutions and participation in international non-government.orgs.
- rights may be exercised individually or in community.

Moscow mechanism, Human Dimension meeting, 1991
*The participating states "emphasize that issues relating to human rights, fundamental freedoms, democracy and the rule of law are of international concern, as respect for these rights and freedoms constitutes one of the foundations of the international order. They categorically and irrevocably declare that the commitments undertaken in the field of the human dimension of the CSCE are matters of direct and legitimate concern to all participating States and **do not belong exclusively to the internal affairs of the State concerned."** (Emphasis added).*

Source: OSCE Handbook [OSCE, 1966].

- constitutional issues in Crimea, and problems of the Crimean Tatars,
- the Gagauz and Trans-Dniester regions of Moldova.

The legal force of the European Court of Human Rights and the European Convention on Human Rights, is not so useful for the redress of the collective problems of minorities. They are not protected as such by the Convention, only indirectly through the prohibition of discrimination. A new Charter on minority languages awaits ratification. More fundamental, however, is a new Framework Convention for the Protection of National Minorities (see Table 5.6). Ratification has progressed to the point that entry into force is imminent. A monitoring mechanism is provided. It remains to be seen how far the Council of Europe can add reinforcement to the work of the OSCE in this area (versus the peril of duplication and confusion of functions, which the political authorities seem to have done little to avert).

The range of possible remedies for insufficiently protected national minorities is well reviewed by Brunner [1996]. National constitutions and laws protecting and positively supporting the position of minorities are fundamental. Such legislation becomes more adequate in central and eastern Europe and the Hungarian constitution is considered a most advanced model. The Council of Europe's new Framework Convention provides points of reference for national legislation. Larger problems may have to be resolved through enhanced regional autonomy or in extreme cases exercise of the right to secede as an act of self-determination. Border revisions are another extreme measure. Population exchange against the will of the population concerned is inadmissible according to international law. Events in Bosnia and Croatia have provided tragic examples in practice, illustrating how inconceivable such "solutions" are for the chequered map of Europe.

Since 1991 the OSCE/CSCE has been actively engaged in missions to help prevent conflict and mediate crisis management in many states of the former Soviet Union and central and eastern Europe.

While the normal OSCE decision-making principle is consensus, there are mechanisms permitting the dispatch of missions in "cases of clear, gross and uncorrected violation of OSCE commitments", for example in 1992 when the objection of former Yugoslavia were overruled. The dispatching of a mission also does not require consensus, and the dispute conciliation procedure can go ahead on the basis of consensus-minus-two.

Table 5.6: Framework Convention for the Protection of National Minorities of the Council of Europe

---

(The Convention was signed in 1995 and will enter into force when ratified by 12 countries, which is expected before the end of 1997.)

Article 1 - Rights of national minorities an integral part of human rights
Article 2 - Shall be applied between states
Article 3 - Rights individual as well as in community with others
Article 4 - Discrimination prohibited; effective equality to be promoted
Article 5 - Culture to be promoted; refrain from unwilling assimilation
Article 6 - Promote mutual respect; protect against discrimination
Article 7 - Freedoms of assembly, association, expression, religion
Article 8 - Right to manifest religion
Article 9 - Media in minority language unhindered
Article 10 - Use of minority language in private, public, upon arrest
Article 11 - Use personal name in minority language; in displays
Article 12 - Education and research to foster knowledge of culture
Article 13 - Right to set up private educational establishments
Article 14 - Best endeavours for schooling in area with minorities
Article 15 - Participation in cultural, economic and public affairs
Article 16 - Respect proportions of populations in traditional areas
Article 17 - Right to contacts across frontiers; to join non-govt. orgs.
Article 18 - Favours agreements between states to protect minorities

---

Source: Council of Europe, European Treaty Series No 157 [1995].

There have been eleven field missions operating in recent years:
- former Yugoslavia (Kosovo, Sandjak and Vojvodina), concerning the human rights and democracy in areas with minorities;
- Macedonia, concerning border issues and inter-ethnic relations;
- Georgia, concerning the conflicts in Abkhazia and Southern Ossetia;

- Moldova, concerning the status of Trans-Dniester;
- Tajikistan, to facilitate dialogue between conflicting political forces;
- Estonia and Latvia, concerning language and citizenship issues;
- Ukraine, concerning nationality and constitutional aspects of Crimea;
- Bosnia, election and human rights monitoring post-Dayton;
- Chechnya, facilitating negotiations between Chechen and Russian parties;
- Azerbaijan-Armenia, concerning the war in the Nagorno-Karabakh enclave (visiting missions of the "Minsk Group").

From the list it is apparent that the OSCE is at least present in the most troublesome regions of tension or conflicts. Of course its means are those of conciliation, not military force of the type ultimately required in the Bosnia case. Its comparative advantage is the legitimacy of the OSCE in the all-European environment. For putting more leverage behind its work, the EU or NATO or major national powers have to support the OSCE operations politically. This is, however, not impossible. An example may be taken from the Chechen war of 1994-95. The mediation of OSCE in this war was strongly supported by the EU. At the time the EU was close to implementing a new trade agreement with Russia. In fact the EU, under pressure from the European Parliament, refused to implement the agreement until certain conditions relating to the Chechen war were met, including the establishment of an OSCE mediation mission there. After a while the OSCE mission started up in Grozny and made a notable contribution, and the EU-Russian trade agreement was then implemented. The "Moscow mechanism" (Table 5.5), under which abuses of human rights are not exclusively to be regarded as *internal* matters, was usefully activated here with some irony of circumstance.

5.4 Policing Europe

The completion of the EU single market triggered two mechanisms of *disequilibrium dynamics* for the integration process. The first to be taken seriously was from the liberalisation of capital movements, which led to the single currency (see section 2.5 above). The second is from the freedom of movement of people, without frontier checks. There is now a delayed impact from the freeing of movement of persons. The Treaty of Maastricht did make a gesture in 1992 in creating the so-called "third pillar" of the EU to improve cooperation in the fields of justice and home affairs, and so cope with the consequences of abolished frontiers. These provisions were widely criticised at the time for their institutional weakness, notably in staying outside the jurisdiction and decision-making procedures of the EU's "first pillar", which governs the single market. Moreover a sub-group of countries had signed in 1990 the Schengen Convention on the abolition of frontier checks, but also outside the jurisdiction of the EC.

In addition the turbulence of the post-Communist transition has created huge new demands for trans-European movements of people: of refugees, of persons simply wanting to compensate for their former impossibility to travel, of persons wanting to leave very difficult economic and social conditions, and finally of criminals looking for profit from illegal trade in narcotics and arms, and for havens for money laundering and for escape from prosecution or pursuit by other gangs.

It became quickly evident that the committee structure of the EU's "third pillar" was not making adequate progress in responding to the new agenda. As a result consensus emerged to make important changes in the system in the Treaty of Amsterdam. Contrary to the tendency in the preceding period to fragment the EU under its three pillars and other *ad hoc* arrangements, the Treaty inserted activity for the progressive establishment of an "area of freedom, security and justice" in the main institutional structures. The text, in the new Article B, states as its objective "to maintain and develop the Union as an area of freedom, security and justice, in which the free movement of persons is assured in conjunction with appropriate measures with respect to external borders, immigration, asylum and the prevention and combatting of crime." The Treaty goes on to list the actions to be taken in the next five years under EC jurisdiction concerning the free movement of persons, asylum and immigration [European Policy Centre, 1997].

There are also reinforced provisions within the "third pillar" for police and judicial cooperation in criminal matters. While this domain remains inter-governmental, there are also in the Amsterdam Treaty measures reinforcing the European Police Office (Europol), aiming at building up this agency's operationality within five years. Europol is hardly yet designed on the scale of the FBI of the US, but these developments have all the hallmarks of evolutionary potential for the decades to come. The realities of cross-frontier criminality will drive this.

In addition the Amsterdam Treaty incorporates the Schengen system into the EC jurisdiction under the new "flexibility" provision permitting limited opting-out from specific initiatives, in this case the UK and Ireland wishing to retain frontier checks and this being accepted because of their island geography.

Overall these provisions amount to a significant transfer of competences to the EU level, with a finely negotiated mix of standard EC jurisdiction under the "first pillar", the new flexible EC jurisdiction for Schengen and elements of intergovernmentalism for police and criminal matters under the "third pillar".

However the system between the EU and the rest of Europe remains poorly developed and uncertain. Already (in Chapter 4) we drew attention to the visa-free travel possibilities between on the one hand Russia, Ukraine, Belarus and Moldova (RUBM) and on the other hand central and eastern European countries which are candidates to join the EU. The automatic extension of EU immigration and visa rules to the acceding countries will mean aggravating the social exclusion of RUBM nationals from "Europe". As also in the field of trade and defence policies, EU enlargement is going to pose sensitive issues for the rest of Europe. The agenda for cooperation between the EU and RUBM on cross-border criminality begins to develop, given concern over drug and arms trafficking, money laundering and illegal immigration. But the responses are so far fragmented between bilateral cooperation, the EU and NATO, and thin in effect. At its October 1997 summit the Council of Europe [1997b] resolved to reinforce work on its all-European version of the EU's "third pillar", under the heading of "security of citizens" covering the fight against organised crime, corruption, money laundering, the prevention of drug abuse and protection of the child (viz. transnational paedophile rings).

5.5 Military security

- Three security maps

Europe's security system has its three clubs and maps - NATO, OSCE, WEU. The 1990s have seen increasingly intense activity to adapt these to the post-Communist situation. They represent three different concepts of Europe which may be either complements or rivals: NATO as the US-led and essentially west European power structure, which now expands east as the candidate nations demonstrate their qualifications to join the western club; the OSCE as the all-European structure committed to common rules and values and avoidance of a new block mentality; the WEU as the embryonic defence arm of the European Union.

NATO's reforms of the 1990s are about extending the organisation's role geographically and functionally, given on the one hand the political obsolescence of its original task to face down the Soviet threat, and on the other hand the emergence of new security concerns of lesser magnitude. NATO's roles might be described now (and substituting ordinary for official language) as being divided into three departments: i/ the *Major War Department*, ii/ the *Lesser Conflicts Department* and iii/ the *Cooperation Department*.

The Major War Department takes as its primary terms of reference the Article 5 collective defence guarantee. Its mechanisms are both nuclear and conventional weaponry. Its resources are national armed forces committed to the alliance and NATO's own facilities by way

Table 5.7: Lexicon of European security organisations

NATO:

- Comprises US, Canada and 14 European member states, with 11 candidates for accession from central and eastern Europe.

- Article 5: the guarantee that an attack on one member will be treated as an attack on all. Exclusive to full NATO members.

- Combined Joint Task Force (CJTF): capabilities made available for intervening in other, normally lesser conflicts or peace-enforcement operations. Capabilities will include headquarters command and control and ear-marked military combat units. Operations open and flexible in terms of participation. Operations may be undertaken for and/or led by WEU, in agreement with NATO.

- European Security and Defence Identity (ESDI): NATO name for discussion and actions confined to European members of NATO.

- Partnership for Peace: NATO's programme for broad cooperation with non-member states.

WEU:

- The West European Union comprises 10 EU member states, and is defined as "an integral part of the development of the EU".

- Article V: equivalent in principle to NATO article 5.

- Eurocorps: specific and generic name for multi-national military capabilities among WEU member states.

- Petersberg tasks: humanitarian, rescue, peace keeping, crisis management and peace-making.

CSCE/OSCE:

- Conference for Security and Cooperation in Europe, established with the Helsinki Final Act of 1975, converted into "Organisation ..." in 1994. Comprises 55 member states, effectively all European countries except Serbia (suspended), plus the US, Canada and Central Asian countries of the former Soviet Union.

- European Security Architecture: OSCE name for discussions and negotiations about the general development of the European security system.

---

of headquarters, control, command and communications systems, intelligence operations etc. While the Major War Department was initially intended to handle European "world war" threats, it recently supported the UN-sponsored action in the Gulf War against Iraq, which only marginally touched upon the territory of a member state (Turkey). Also for Bosnia some facilities of the Major War Department were mobilised, notably its air strike capabilities including linked intelligence and weapon guidance systems, and its command and control facilities for the post-Dayton army presence.

NATO's enlargement is only a politically sensitive matter with regard to this Major War Department, with Russia remaining an outsider. But if Russia were to be a member there would be two enormous implications. First, Russia's war machine would be placed under integrated command and control of NATO, a condition that Russia might not be willing at this stage to accept. No Russian politician has proposed this, and Russia has not applied for full NATO membership. Second NATO's Article 5 guarantee of collective defence would be extended to Russia's frontier with China, which NATO members might not be willing to take on, to say the least.

The Lesser Conflict Department is officially known in NATO-speak as the Combined Joint Task Force (CJTF). The CJTF is intended to handle the same tasks as those appearing on the so-called Petersberg list of the WEU, but may also go into militarily heavier peace enforcement missions, of which the Bosnian intervention of NATO is an example (even though not formally so since the CJTF mechanism was still in the course of being created). The CJTF can call upon most of NATO's common facilities and its national armed force committed to NATO. However the most original feature is that CJTF sees now the creation of its own, specialised headquarter facilities in three regional commands (central and southern Europe and the Atlantic fleet) as well as at SHAPE headquarters at Mons in Belgium. Part of the regional headquarter facilities will be mobile headquarter units that can be deployed at short notice to, or nearer to conflict locations.

The operations of the Lesser Conflict Department are, as a matter of policy, open on a case by case basis to participation by non-NATO countries, such as other European countries including the neutrals,

NATO candidate countries as well as Russia and Ukraine.

It is also open to operating in WEU-led mode. The CJTF headquarter centres will have multinational staff from all NATO countries, and will as a matter of policy be organised in such a way that would permit European (WEU) nationals to lead specifically designated operations. These individuals would be "double-hatted", i.e. they could switch between working under NATO or WEU political control. Moreover national missions to NATO may also be "double-hatted" (e.g. the whole of the UK mission to NATO is assigned also to WEU). Subject to the explicit agreement by consensus of the NATO Council, such WEU operations could use NATO assets and resources. The consensus rule means of course that the non-WEU countries (US for example) would retain a power of veto over the WEU's use of the NATO facilities.

The CSCE, originally negotiated with Brezhnev's Soviet Union, has proved a surprisingly adaptable framework agreement, spanning the Cold War through to the post-Communist period and continuously evolving its set of rules (Table 5.5 summarises the key principles). Its adaptation has been both real and symbolic (changing its name to the OSCE in 1994 as part of an attempt by Russia to give it a greater role). The OSCE has conceived security in a comprehensive sense, from military aspects including disarmament negotiations to conflict resolution and peace-keeping and human rights issues. Agreement on its three so-called "baskets" - the politico-military, human and economic dimensions - proved indispensable for the initial bargain of the Helsinki Final Act of 1975. In practise the politico-military and human dimensions have developed importantly, but the economic dimension has not found room for real substance alongside the several economic organisations open to all or many OSCE member states (IMF, IBRD, EBRD, WTO, OECD).

At the Budapest summit of OSCE in December 1994 Russia tried without great success to win support for a substantial strengthening of the organisation, notably through creation of a European Security Council. This restricted grouping of OSCE countries would have been analogous to the UN Security Council, to become the key forum for strategic dialogue and policy development in the European theatre.

*Table 5.8: OSCE basic principles for behaviour of states and governments
Helsinki Final Act, 1975*

1. *Sovereign equality, respect for the rights inherent in sovereignty*
2. *Refraining from the threat or use of force*
3. *Inviolability of frontiers*
4. *Territorial integrity of states*
5. *Peaceful settlement of disputes*
6. *Non-intervention in internal affairs*
7. *Respect for human rights and fundamental freedoms, including freedom
     of thought, conscience, religion and belief*
8. *Equal rights and self-determination of peoples*
9. *Cooperation among states*
10. *Fulfilment in good faith of obligations under international law*

Source: OSCE Handbook [1996].

The OSCE is working to give substance to its idea of a "European Security Model for the 21st Century". The President-in-Office of the OSCE, Danish foreign minister N. Petersen, declared to the summit meeting of the Council of Europe in October 1997 that this should lead to "a Platform for Cooperative Security", building on democracy and human rights, and broadening cooperation between NATO, the EU, the Council of Europe and the OSCE. The general idea seems to be going in a desirable direction, but concrete proposals seem not yet to exist, or to be in circulation. However the proposals presented below in section 6.4 may help.

The WEU has a long history as the Cinderella of European defence organisations. Europe was already zig-zagging its way towards an own defence identity early in the post-War period, alongside the setting up of NATO. The Brussels Treaty of March 1948 formed a collective self-defence alliance between France, the UK and the Benelux countries, three weeks after the Communist *coup d'etat* in Prague and three months before the beginning of the Berlin blockade. By December 1948 the Brussels Treaty partners joined the US and Canada to begin negotiations leading to signature in Washington of the NATO Treaty in April 1949. In 1950 NATO became operational, while in February 1951 France proposed creating a European army. This led to the signing of the European Defence Community Treaty in Paris in May 1952, but the French assembly refused to ratify this in August 1954. The WEU was then formed in October 1954, with the participation of Germany and Italy as well as the Brussels Treaty countries.

The WEU remained largely dormant until 10 December 1991, day of signature of the Maastricht Treaty, but also, at the same place and time, of a Declaration by WEU ministers stating that the "WEU will be developed as the defence component of the European Union and as a means to strengthen the European pillar of the European alliance". WEU ministers progressed in defining their operational responsibilities at Petersberg in Germany in June 1992. The Petersberg declaration innovated in specifying the limited tasks, apart from questions of mutual defence, for which military units of WEU member states could be deployed under WEU authority. These are for :

" - humanitarian and rescue tasks;

  - peacekeeping tasks;

  -tasks of combat forces in crisis management, including peacemaking".

Military units are assigned as "forces answerable to WEU" (FAWEU), and these include several multilateral formations, including the Eurocorps and several other specialised units. The Eurocorps, commanded by a French general, consists of army divisions from France, Germany and Belgium, a French-German brigade, a Spanish brigade and a smaller unit from Luxembourg. The annual exercise of the Eurocorps in 1996 mobilised 8 500 soldiers, 3 300 vehicles and 20 helicopters [WEU, 1997].

- NATO-WEU-EU trio

Definition of the WEU's political relationships with the EU and NATO is a special diplomatic art form, spanning the views of countries which wish to maximise or minimise the relative roles of the EU and NATO. The Maastricht Treaty considered the WEU to be "an integral part of the development of the EU", a crucially weaker formulation than would have been "an integral part of the EU". The same issues were much debated at the 1996-97 Intergovernmental Conference, where France and Germany proposed to merge WEU with EU. This was unacceptable to the neutral, non-WEU member states as well as the UK. As a result the Treaty of Amsterdam retains the Maastricht wording quoted, together with the weak supplement (in Article J.4): "The Union shall ... foster closer institutional relations with the WEU with a view to the possibility of the integration of the WEU into the Union, should the European Council so decide." The Treaty of Amsterdam none the less integrates the Petersberg tasks of the WEU into its definition of the capabilities available to the Union for its common foreign and defence policy. Moreover, as a final finesse, it allows member states of the EU which are not members of the WEU still the right to participate in Petersberg tasks, also contributing on an equal footing in planning and decision-taking in the WEU. (Examiners in schools of European studies will for years pose questions of the type "To what extent is the WEU part of the EU?", and students with prior training in metaphysics will have an advantage). The serious point in these semantic and juridical manoeuvres, far from the battlefield indeed, is that the former real divergences of defence policy such as France's distance from NATO command structures and the traditional neutrality of some small countries, are gradually melting away, with new common defence structures being prepared.

The EU-WEU-NATO relationships were given a political boost in January 1994 at a NATO summit. The two parts of Brussels began speaking together for the first time. The key concepts were [NATO, 1995]:

"We give our full support to the development of a European Security and Defence Identity which, as called for in the Maastricht Treaty, in the longer term perpective of a common defence policy, might in time lead to a common defence compatible with that of the Atlantic Alliance."

"We support strengthening the European pillar of the Alliance through the Western European Union, which is being developed as the defence component of the European Union."

"We therefore stand ready to make collective assets of the Alliance available, on the basis of consultations in the North Atlantic Council, for WEU operations undertaken by the European Allies in pursuit of their Common Foreign and Security Policy. We support the development of separable but not separate capabilities which could respond to European requirements and contribute to Alliance security."

"As part of this process we endorse the concept of Combined Joint Task Forces as a means to facilitate continuing operations, including operations with participating nations outside the Alliance."

The NATO summit in Madrid of July 1997 reviewed progress in making these ideas operational and concluded as follows [NATO,1997]:

"We are pleased with the progress made in implementing the CJTF concept, including the initial designation of parent headquarters, and look forward to coming trials. The concept will enhance our ability to command and control multinational and multi-service forces, generated and deployed at short notice, which are capable of conducting a wide range of military operations. Combined Joint task Forces will also facilitate the possible participation of non-NATO nations in operations and, by enabling the conduct of WEU-led CJTF operations, will contribute to the development of ESDI within the Alliance."

"We reaffirm, as stated in our 1994 Brussels Declaration, our full support for the development of the European Security and Defence Identity by making available NATO assets and capabilities for WEU operations. With this in mind, the Alliance is building ESDI, grounded on solid military principles and supported by appropriate military planning and permitting the creation of militarily coherent and effective forces capable of operating under the political control and strategic direction of the WEU."

The NATO summit in Madrid also clarified its enlargement policy, with invitations to begin accession negotiations extended to Poland, the Czech Republic and Hungary as the first wave from 12 applicants. The goal is for membership to become operational in April 1999 on the occasion of the next NATO summit, which is due to mark the 50th anniversary of NATO's founding treaty. The Madrid summit also, however, saw the Latin NATO countries pushing for the accession of Slovenia and Romania. While the US refused, it was agreed as follows: "We will review the process at our next meeting in 1999. With regard to the aspiring members, we recognise with great interest and take account of the positive developments towards democracy and rule of law in a number of south-eastern European countries, especially Romania and Slovenia" [NATO, 1997].

In response to Russian protests over NATO expansion, a bilateral "Founding Act on Mutual Relations, Cooperation and Security" between NATO and Russia was signed in Paris in May 1997. This provides for extensive cooperative activities and a political forum in the NATO-Russian Permanent Joint Council. An analogous "Charter on a Distinctive Partnership between NATO and the Ukraine" was signed in July 1997 at the Madrid summit [for both texts see: NATO, 1997]. These developments show a *hub and spoke* pattern of relations between the main European power centre and the periphery; a familiar pattern also seen in the economic field with the EU's Partnership and Cooperation Agreements with Russia and the other CIS countries. This contrast with the idea of all-European structures, as in the OSCE, or the more restricted proposal for a European Security Council advanced by Russia in 1994.

- Bosnia again

Sometime this diplomatic ballet of the NATO-WEU-EU trio should translate into some real example of concerted, military action, like NATO cooperating with WEU leadership for execution of a specific task. That sometime could have been with the mid-1998 deadline for the end of the SFOR operation in Bosnia. A simple end to the operation became too likely to lead to a renewal of civil war. The debate on what to do was well rehearsed in public, partly because some main actors of the Dayton regime are now in independent positions, for example Ivo Daalder, Carl Bildt and Pauline Neville-Jones who recently contributed to an analysis of "Bosnia after SFOR" in a journal [IISS, 1997a].

This debate reveals some essentials with great clarity. The American participant, Daalder, says: (i) the Dayton map must be changed. The Sprska Republic should be cut in two, half effectively left for the Serbs, and the other half integrated into a multi-ethnic Bosnian state. (ii) The US Congress will require that the US combat troops withdraw. The Europeans should take over the military operations, the US just offering supporting services. (iii) If the Europeans don't pull their weight, the US Congress will be very annoyed and become isolationist.

The Swedish participant, Bildt says: (i) There is no such thing as an instant peace. The renewed division of Bosnia would be disastrous, a recipe for new ethnic cleansing and new wars, for example in Kosovo and Macedonia. (ii)" In purely military terms, a European force would be enough. But the experience of the war years, with the perception that European efforts were constantly undercut by American political manoeuvres, makes such a solution impossible even to contemplate in any of the capitals".

The British participant, Neville-Jones, says: (i) Dayton is a US-designed agreement, which it forced on Europe, and is now a mess. Washington is not free to dump it on others to implement at a time of their choosing. (ii) The European message to Washington should be:"we're here if you're here".

This is a pathetic state of affairs for Europe. It is quite possible that there be cases where a European view on a matter of policy in Europe is sounder, benefiting from proximity of view and interests (although the recognition of Croatia at the outset of the Yugoslav crisis is widely believed to have been a blunder). But it is also quite possible for the US to leave Europe, which Europe cannot do. Bildt says that in purely military terms, this is a feasible task for the Europeans alone. In fact the operation seems to be perfectly suited for a WEU-led CJTF operation, along the lines of the communiques quoted in the last section above. But in addition Europe would indeed have to take responsibility for the political choices. What are its diplomats for? It is clear that the Bosnian case calls for the integrated deployment of civil, economic and military instruments. Neither economic sanctions and incentives nor NATO missiles and tanks can solve the problem on their own. Synergies between different branches of policy are called for, in the sense used in general terms in Chapters 2 and 6 when discussing the case for coincident jurisdictions, rather than overlapping but differentiated ones. "Synergy" is an important concept in these European affairs, but often one that is very hard to pin down concretely. But Bosnia supplies an example, moreover one of vital interest to all of Europe.

It would have been easier for the WEU to take up the initiative in Bosnia if it had gained some operational experience first, for example in suppressing the Albania anarchy in the summer of 1997. The UK and Germany refused to support Italy and the other EU Mediterraneans to undertake a policing action there. In fact Italy did the job. But this was another simpler case where "synergies" could have been very powerfully at work. Albania is the country where the thirst for normal civilisation is so strong that its opinion polls show more support for the EU than in any other country. An EU/WEU policing operation, associated with the prospects of economic assistance and later progressive integration with the EU, would have had a perfect logic.

But the WEU was still the Cinderella for the Albanian ball of 1997, and so also it seems likely to remain for the 1998 Bosnian ball, since a modified NATO force is being decided.

- Elementary effectiveness
Another example. The European members of NATO were in 1996 spending $187 billion on military defence, less than the $ 271 billion of the US, but still a massive resource. This buys much sophisticated equipment, especially in nuclear and air force domains, and employs 1.5 million active-duty manpower. However the effective capacity to deploy military power at any distance from home is extraordinarily small, given that investments have not been made in heavy lift aircraft and dedicated cargo ships. A recent analysis [O'Hanlon, 1997] concluded thus: "What power can Europe project today? Over a period of days or weeks, it can move several thousand troops, principally British and French, and dozens of fighters. But its real weakness would manifest itself in the period from two weeks to three months after a crisis began. During that time the US could deploy large amount of

equipment.... Europeans might deploy nothing in that time, unless aided by US strategic transport, and would probably get armoured forces to a distant theatre such as the Persian Gulf only after several months. Even then, beyond a couple of divisions, they would rely on the US for in-theatre logistics support."

This assessment was illustrated in practice in the Gulf War of 1990-91 and in Bosnia in 1994-95. European capabilities have not improved much since. Much debate has focused on the political weaknesses of the EU's Common Foreign and Security Policy, including such questions as majority voting or unanimity in the EU Council, and the links between WEU and EU. Yet the more elementary weaknesses in physical military capabilities seem to be too hidden behind these political debates, and the impressive high-tech military investments of the major European countries in virtually unusable resources. From Bosnia to Albania to Ruanda the needs have been for flexible and rapid deployment of substantial but rather traditional military forces.

The generally recognized objective is for Europe to become more self-reliant for diverse risks of low-intensity conflicts in the post-world-war, post-communist era. There are ways in which this could be done if greater rationality were introduced into Europe's procurement policies and organisation. In fact the political framework has already been well advanced, as already discussed, with the possibility of WEU-led CJTF operations consistent with WEU's political competence for the Petersberg tasks. What might this mean in practice, if one could escape for a moment from the inertia of existing structures?

Let us suppose that EU political leaders agree that they cannot and should not remain so dependent on US facilities for deployment of their expanded rapid-reaction units. They overcome the hesitations of the mid-nineties that caused them to defer building the Future Large Aircraft (military heavy lift project). They judge that about 100 heavy lift aircraft and a dozen large roll-on roll-off military ships need to be built and made available as a common capability. Their advisers are in fact agreeing with the estimates of O'Hanlon [1997]. The budget for these and associated investments is 50 billion euro, which they decide to spend over a five year period. The European Arms Procurement

Agency negotiates terms with Airbus as main contractor for the aircraft, and the EU competition Commissioner approves of this support for his policy to limit the global monopoly ambitions of the Boeing civil-military group. Common financing is required, since the aircraft will be allocated to the WEU Heavy Lift Command. EU political leaders agree that the time has come to make some economies in the agricultural and regional funds of the EU budget. A new budgetary chapter is created for military procurement, and 10 billion euro per year is transferred from these other chapters, without therefore increasing the budget total. For economy as well as political reasons it is apparent that valuable cooperation can be developed with Russia, whose Antonov 124 is an outstandingly capable heavy lift aircraft for 100 ton loads, and had already been chartered successfully for a number of EU food aid operations.

While some will dismiss such suggestions as fantasy, the point is to consider what initiatives over a medium to long-term future would be intrinsically cost-effective and politically valuable. It is also necessary to identify the practical ways of bridging the enormous, present gap between the EU's huge aspirations and economic capacity on the one hand and, on the other, its lamentable actual performance in the areas of foreign and security policy of interest to it. On time-horizons for important political mutations in Europe, it may be remembered that it will have taken a little over twenty years to go from the launching of monetary union as a political proposition by Messrs. Jenkins, Schmidt and Giscard d'Estaing to inception of the euro and European Central Bank. Of course the above suggestion is a much smaller and easier proposition than monetary union. It could be proposed any time now, with a year for political negotiation and five to ten years for deliveries.

- Geopolitics of a four player game

In due course, maybe in five or ten or fifteen years, fundamental factors could alter the strategic nature of the US presence in Europe and induce the WEU and EU to assume their natural responsibilities.

These fundamental factors would most likely come from changes in global geo-politics at the level of the four most relevant players -

US, EU, Russia and China. The present situation is basically quite a comfortable one from a European stand-point. The US is the ally. Russia has a remarkably friendly regime. China, though potentially erratic politically, is more of less cooperative, not yet very powerful and a long way away. This leaves the EU itself able to pursue its internal preoccupations with the euro and the enlargement process. How might this change? Table 5.9 offers a framework for some scenarios. The four players have, between them, six bilateral relationships which could proceed in several alternative modes: alliance, cooperation, engagement, integration, containment, friction and conflict.

From a European stand-point the most unpredictable player is also the furthest away - China. This could be re-assuring, were it not for potential knock-on effects via the other players. And Russia also is hardly yet in a safely stabilised condition. The main scenarios would then be marked by: I/ a benign world of cooperation between all four players, or II/ problems from China, or III/ problems from China and Russia at the same time.

How might the six relationships be affected ?

The EU-US relationship is solidly based on common values and economic ties. The US economy is as stable as could be imagined. On US priorities, while the presidency and governmental elite seems comfortable with the responsibility of the US as sole super-power and strategic actor in all continents, the same cannot be said of the Congress and grass-root political pressures. Vietnam is not forgotten and Somalia was a small, more recent reminder of the unattractiveness of getting sucked into intractable conflicts. Iraq and Bosnia have been two more recent and successful expeditions. Congressional constraints today seem likely only to sanction operations with good chances of short, sharp effectiveness.

There is the question whether the US and EU will actually sustain a sufficient level of consensus on policy priorities for European security, beyond the large agreement on fundamental political values. The recent debates over NATO expansion revealed in fact two important disagreements. The US pushed for NATO expansion when many EU governments doubted its advisability, on the grounds that there is no Russian threat justifying extension of the Article 5 guarantee to Poland and others. This could actually be counter-productive in generating support for old-fashioned Soviet types in the Russian Duma. Secondly, when the decision to enlarge was taken the US insisted on only three admissions, overriding the desire also to admit Slovenia and Romania on the part of the Latin NATO countries.

The argument here was that inclusion of these south-eastern countries could help consolidate the transition in a region where it is still precarious to say the least. In both cases the difference of opinion seems to reflect the difference in distance between the respective political constituencies -in the US and EU - from the front-line. The EU Commission's proposals for its enlargement, just two weeks after the NATO summit in July 1997, for its part extended into both the former Yugoslavia with Slovenia and the Baltic region with Estonia.

These considerations are of course serious, without however calling the alliance into question. But if China became a major threat, then the US could leave Europe much more to look after itself. Unless, however, there were problems with Russia at the same time, to which we shall return.

The EU-Russia relationship is currently cooperative but it is neither deep nor strongly anchored institutionally. Russia's political opposition, even a majority in the Duma, have different ideas to President Yeltsin. They espouse a more aggressive nationalism at home and in the former USSR states. There has also been a current of support for a less democratic Euro-Asian model, but its advocates may be thinking again in the light of the Asian crisis, which erupted in the second half of 1997. On the other hand there are those who would prefer deeper integration with Europe and resent that this has not proved possible so far. The EU-Russia relationship could therefore go either of three ways: warmer, the same or colder.

The EU-Chinese relationship is clearly the most remote of the three. It could be cooperative and business-like, or suffer if China's politics turned difficult.

Table 5.9: Strategic scenarios in a four player game

	I Globally cooperative	II China troubles	III China and Russia troubles
1. EU-US	Ally	Looser ally	Ally
2. EU-Russia	Cooperation	Ally/ integration	Friction
3. EU-China	Remote	Friction	Friction
4. US-Russia	Cooperation/ containment	Ally	Friction
5. US-China	Cooperation/ containment	Friction/ conflict	Friction/ conflict
6. Russia-China	Cooperation	Friction	Ally

The US-Russia relationship includes vigorous cooperation in economic and military matters, but it also has aspects of containment, as evidenced by NATO enlargement policy and strategic competition through activities in the Ukraine and the Caspian Sea region.

The US-Chinese relationship, like with Russia, is currently a mix of cooperation and containment, except that the weights may from the US standpoint be 1 to 2 for China and 2 to 1 for Russia. But China could impose a change in US priorities. Its emergence as an economic super-power seems only 10 to 20 years away, and with this will follow military capacity. The International Institute for Strategic Studies comments [IISS, 1997] "with the volatile mix of a strong economy and a struggling political system, the country veers from excessive confidence to paranoia about its ability to prosper free of external constraints." In 1996 the US deployed two aircraft carrier battle groups into the seas around Taiwan to deter Chinese threats to the island. While the handover of Hong Kong went smoothly in 1997, unresolved tensions exist in the China seas over islands (not only Taiwan) and off-shore concession areas contested by Vietnam, Philippines, Malaysia and Japan. If China became much more powerfully armed, which is virtually certain, and much more assertive or unpredictable, which is certainly conceivable, there are the makings of a fundamental re-orientation of global strategies of international relations.

The next question it would pose is for the China-Russia relationship, which has been reviewed recently by Anderson [1997]. The post-war period has already seen profound changes between episodes of intense cooperation and bitter tensions. In 1997 the accent is on trade for which there are large complementarities: Russia as a supplier of weapons and raw materials, China as supplier of consumer goods. But there are two other factors pointing in diverging directions.

The population over-spill from China into Siberia becomes quite substantial, is largely uncontrolled and could carry on growing. Russia's far eastern regions account for 36% of the country's territory with a population of only 7.6 million. Moreover this population had been declining with emigration, by 6% between 1992 and 1995 [Harada 1997]. Largely illegal Chinese immigration has resulted in the springing-up of new China-towns in many Siberian cities. At some point this could become threatening to Russia, maybe in terms of the social stability of affected areas, leading to tensions over the treatment of Chinese minorities (perhaps even becoming majorities in some areas). Also China has vital interests in Central Asia, with separatist minorities of Kazakh and Kyrgyz ethnicity in western Chinese provinces. China could become uncomfortably assertive as a competitor for strategic influence in the former Soviet Union states of Central Asia.

A factor going the other way is the natural solidarity between two nations of great power traditions, which resent being lectured and pressured by the west, especially the US, on political values such as democracy and human rights. Sentiments about the need to assure a multi-polar global power structure, about China's understanding for Russia's concerns over NATO expansion and about Russia's understanding for China's interests in Taiwan, have already been flowing with remarkable ease into the official communiques of bilateral Russian-Chinese summits of the mid-nineties [Harada 1997].

There are thus ingredients for either of two scenarios, in which a problematic China either allies or conflicts with Russia. Then the implications of Chinese affairs for the EU become important.

Suppose a post-Yeltsin Russia reverts to more nationalistic politics, with more assertiveness in relation to the near-abroad, coupled to an ideology of government which favours the Euro-Asian model, ie much less attachment to liberal democratic ideas. Both Russia and China will then be resenting western pressures, such as threats of economic sanctions, and concluding that by standing together these threats can be faced down. In this case the world will have set itself back a long way, with divisions and at least tensions and major risks for peace. The EU-US relationship will have to be hardened up again, although with front-line preoccupations over China, the US would surely expect the EU to do more to look after the European front.

In the alternative case Russia not only remains more western ideologically, but is also looking for allies because of its tensions with China, which is threatening Russia's Siberian territories and competing too effectively for influence in Central Asia. This is the scenario judged more likely by Anderson [1997].

Three conclusions seem to be suggested. First, the present, rather benign *status quo* in global geo-politics is not to be taken for granted. Second, the possibility of a large Chinese distraction for US strategic capabilities is to be taken seriously. Third, the conceivable instability of Russian strategic directions alongside a volatile China is reason enough to support a heavier political investment in all-European structures, to which the next chapter will turn.

6. Institutions

It may be that in Western Europe the era of the strong state -
1648 to 1989 - has now passed, and that we are moving towards
a system of overlapping roles and responsibilities with
governments, international institutions and the private sector all
involved but none entirely in control. Can it be made to work? We
must hope so, and we must try.
R.Cooper, The Post-Modern State and the World Order, 1966.

Who does what, and why, among the institutions of the new
Europe? How may they evolve, and what should be done to get them
to work well? We need a framework of concepts and theories to guide
us in this. First there is the question of categories and terminology, to
get beyond the *"unidentified political object"*, which a political
scientist recently felt compelled to call Europe and the EU in particular.
More fundamentally, we need to understand what is to be the
normative basis for discussing the role of the European institutions.
We try to do this with the aid of three paradigms:

- the *federal paradigm*, which takes a certain European territory as
given, and then goes about optimising the distribution of competence
for various policy rules between European, national and sub-national
levels;

- the *paradigm of cosmopolitan democracy*, which presupposes
that certain rules of civil society can be generally supported in
principle, and where the task is to find the means to secure their
application as extensively as possible in Europe, and indeed in the rest

of the world as well. Here the rules are given, while the map of their jurisdiction is the open question;

- the *management paradigm*, which takes both political institutions and rules as given, and where the issue is to get the institutions between them to manage to apply the rules as effectively as possible.

6.1 The unidentified political object

Contemporary Europe, and the EU in particular, is for political scientists such as P.Schmitter [1996] an *"unidentified political object"*. So far it flies. But it defies conventional categorisation. This is a warning. It invites two alternative interpretations. Either the EU is truly unique and will always be so. Or it is an immature political structure that will not stand the test of time until it has converted into some more solidly proven political shape.

A simple schema offering a little analytical order is presented in Table 6.1. It is a matrix 2 by 2, representing on the one hand the territorial extent and on the other hand the nature of policy competences. (I acknowledge Schmitter's terms and general idea, but offer a variant to his). The issue is how to describe an organisation where there are many territories which may group themselves either in a single union, or in diverse ways for different policy functions; and these functions themselves may be strongly or weakly organised. The four regimes are named *federatio, confederatio, condominio and consortio*. The Latin names suggest the broad ideas, but also allow for distance from specific, existing models.

At the territorial level both *federatio* and *confederatio* encompass the same countries. They have the same, fixed maps. The difference is that the functions of *federatio* are executed as standard policies, whereas *confederatio* allows for a degree of flexibility in their application by territorial unit, even allowing some opting-out, but not to the point of undermining the essential unity of the whole. This is consistent with the conventional distinction between federation and confederation, where the federal case recognizes a stronger legitimacy at the top level, compared to the confederal case where the states retain

Table 6.1: Models of multinational governance

	flexible territories	*fixed territories*
flexible functions	*CONSORTIO*	*CONFEDERATIO*
fixed functions	*CONDOMINIO*	*FEDERATIO*

political primacy. But in both cases there are sufficient inter-dependencies or synergies between the competences of the top level of government, such that the value of the unity of the whole more than offsets the loss of individual freedom of action of the states.

At the functional level *condominio* is where a given policy is operated with rather strong and permanent common mechanisms of law, or finance, or decision-making. This compares with *consortio* where the function is operated with a looser arrangement and may rely on cooperative behaviour for given periods rather than permanent commitment.

In the EU context, *federatio* would consist of unifying the three pillars of EU competence (economic and monetary union, common foreign and defence policy, justice and home affairs) and in particular integrating the WEU with the EU; and to have all policies apply equally to all member states. Integration dynamics may push towards *federatio*.

Confederatio is evident in the primacy of the member states in the Council as the most powerful institution. It is reinforced by the increased emphasis given to subsidiarity in the Amsterdam Treaty, as well as its introduction of the new flexibility clause with, in particular, opting-out arrangements for monetary, social, immigration and defence policies. These features are analysed in detail by Duff [1997, 1998], showing how far the model previously envisaged by Euro-federalists has been giving way in practise to something much more flexible.

Condominio is illustrated by NATO, a big and powerful organisation with its own assets and decision-making mechanisms. The euro area and European Central Bank would be another major example of *condominio* if its membership and decision-making bodies were to remain substantially different to those of the EU.

Consortio is illustrated by cooperative organisations such as the OECD or the Council of Europe, with overlapping but partly differing memberships and only weak powers over members. *Consortio* is also illustrated by specific enterprises like the European Space Agency, and other scientific and industrial clubs with optional membership and relatively easy possibilities to exit.

The question then is how to assess the relative advantages of these four types of structure for Europe, given that graduations in mixes between them are possible. In general this involves a trade-off between synergies that may be maximised with *federatio* and the individuality of preferences that can be maximised with *consortio*, with *confederatio* and *condominio* offering different compromises.

For Europe to be a meaningful political entity there has to be a substantial weight of either *confederatio* or *federatio*. To justify these concentrations of power, the synergies between competences exercised in the same institutions would have to be important. So what could such synergies actually consist of in the European context? There are two important types:

- synergies in achieving credibility and leverage for external policy. European foreign policy sees the interlocking of economic, monetary, political and security concerns. The relevant policy instruments may need to be deployed together in order to handle well strategic interests in relation to the world's major powers, or to bring to order smaller rogue states whose behaviour is objectionable or dangerous. For example the EU's policy in Bosnia was not powerful or credible enough; NATO's fire power had to be brought in to support diplomacy and economic sanctions.

- synergies internal to the politics, economics and societal development of the member states. An example is where "belonging to Europe" may mean accepting a whole set of political and economic norms that together transform society in a way that is democratically desired, but is not so easily achievable in new democracies without commitment to an externally fixed rule-book. The incentive of membership of Europe, with connotations of civilisation and economic prosperity, may now prove decisive in achieving momentum and credibility to such a transformation in central and eastern Europe. Earlier it was critical for consolidating peace and reconciliation in post-war Europe.

These synergies may be difficult at times to capture analytically, but there can be no doubt that there are major arguments here.

6.2 Three paradigms for Europe

-The federal paradigm

The important successes of federalism as a form of government, first in the United States and more recently in post-war Germany, has led to substantial literature in economics and political science on the benefits and techniques of multi-tier government [Oates, 1972]. This has identified a number of principles of relevance to all forms of multi-tier government, not just that with a federal-state-local shape. These principles are efficiency criteria for choosing the best level of government for a given task of public policy:

- *economies and diseconomies of scale.* Public goods or services become less expensive per unit when provided on an increasing scale, or vice versa depending upon technology and management variables. The defence sector is a main example where procurement of military equipment offers economies of scale up to the largest procurement unit (as in the US armed forces). The absolute size of military power is also decisive for victory in major conflicts. R & D investments in the aerospace sector, if viewed as a public sector concern, exhibits similar economies of scale. The organisation of markets also has key economy of scale characteristics, in the sense that only very large markets can allow both for economies of scale by private sector producers and competition. Diseconomies of scale arise when organisations become too large to be effective and too remote from the population they are intended to serve, leading especially to failure to respond to local tastes and priorities. Diseconomies of scale are suffered also where competition between jurisdictions is needlessly suppressed with loss of the benefits of experimentation and diffusion of best practices.

- *territorial spillovers*. This is where the benefits or costs of a public policy, or lack of a policy, fall substantially outside the territory of the jurisdiction in charge. Where the costs of a policy inaction, for example pollution, falls substantially on a neighbour's territory rather than on the home territory, then the jurisdiction in charge will not regulate the problem optimally. The assignment of taxes is heavily affected by spillovers. Import duties in a customs union cannot reasonably accrue just to the state with the ports. Nor can local taxes efficiently aim at highly mobile tax bases such as financial capital, and therefore have to concentrate on immobile property. The biggest example concerns the effects of macroeconomic policy, both monetary and budgetary, whose costs and benefits substantially spill over national frontiers in open and highly integrated economies. This is the basis of the case for monetary union and budget policy coordination in the EU.

- *subsidiarity* is a term now in use in the EU to represent the need to keep the level of government as low as is efficient, with a presumption against raising a task to the EU level unless there is a clearly demonstrated efficiency case for this.

- *synergies* between competencies. As already mentioned, this concerns where a combination of competences at a given jurisdictional level increases the pay-off from the whole set of policies. For example in international relations the possibility to combine political, economic and military leverage may increase bargaining power to the extent of creating critical mass in support of each policy instrument.

- *log-rolling*. Institutions that allow linked negotiations on multiple issues achieve a more efficient outcome by allowing the loser under one welfare improving scheme to be compensated by advantages obtained under another scheme. The idea here builds on the *Pareto-optimal* principle, according to which a measure is taken if it makes someone better off without making anyone else worse off. Log-rolling thus allows a high level Pareto-optimal solution to be found. However linked negotiations have their own hazards, notably that of complexity, such that there can be blockage in the system, or *grid-lock* as in a traffic jam (a condition not unknown in Brussels).

Federalism, as a specific form of multi-tier government, is based on some special assumptions. While the distribution of competencies is between three or four levels of government (federal, state, regional/ local), the federal level is usually presumed to represent the quality of nationhood or national identity. For Europe it would mean at least the stronger development of multiple identities (European, national, regional - as in section 2.4 above).

What would it mean for the EU to become virtually a federation or confederation? An exercise in scenario building along these lines was presented in the report of the MacDougall group [1977]. The approach here was to imagine an economic and monetary union, with also a defence function, but in which the inter-regional redistributive role of the modern state was replicated in the European Community with the smallest possible central budget. In the subsequent 20 years the EU model has moved substantially in this direction, but with some key differences. The essence of present trends suggests a model of an EU with four main functions, as sketched in Table 6.2, to which should be added adequate constitutional arrangements for democratic accountability. These four functions may be labelled *market, money, solidarity and security*. The model may be termed sub-federal, because of specific features departing from that of a standard federation.

The *market* function has already with the 1992 single market of the EC been raised to virtually the federal model of organisation of competences. The main rules of the single market - the four freedoms of movement of goods, services, labour and capital coupled to competition policy and regulatory policies - are solidly established at the EC level, and the decision-making mechanisms involve majority voting by the Council of Ministers and co-decision with the European Parliament.

The *money*, based on the euro single currency and European System of Central Banks, is certainly of classic federal lineage. More controversial are its supporting budget rules. The Stability Pact restraints on national budget deficits are not typical of federations, and the central EU budget is itself small by macroeconomic standards. These rules of budget policy are controversial, but innovation was inevitable by comparison with any previous federal model.

As for *solidarity*, the small size of the central budget raises the question whether the economic and monetary union will be able to function without a more typical federal redistribution mechanism between states. By way of scenario construction, the MacDougall group [1997] calculated the size of the EU budget if it undertook an equivalent degree of income equalisation, but with a budget that minimised the gross flows of revenues and expenditures passing through the EC level. Thus the redistribution function would be concentrated on direct transfers to the intended beneficiary states or regions. The degree of inter-regional income equalisation found in modern federations had been estimated in the range of 30 to 60%. To achieve this degree of equalisation with a minimal budget would require budget transfers of 2.5 to 4% of GDP. While the EU's actual regional and structural funds have increased significantly it is also clear that the present degree of political solidarity between member states does not permit the redistributive budget to be further increased substantially, if at all. The *"Agenda 2000"* white paper of the EU Commission [1997] projects an unchanged ceiling for the EU budget at 1.27% of GDP.

Whether this will prove a fatal mistake or not remains to be revealed. There are two arguments why the chosen system may work none the less. First, money is in the long-run neutral to the real level of economic activity. All European Union countries have now adjusted to

Table 6.2: Four functions of a sub-federal European Union

MARKET	MONEY
The single market exists with EU competencies comparable to classic federations. The system only calls for secondary refinement and modernisation of its regulatory functions continuously into the future.	*The European Central Bank and the euro are designed as classic federal institutions.* *The budget policy system departs from the standard federal model, with a much smaller EU budget but a higher degree of constraint on national budget deficits than in most federations.*
SOLIDARITY	SECURITY
The redistributive functions of the EU budget have developed considerably, but remain only on a small scale still compared to the inter-regional solidarity of the typical federation.	*For foreign policy EU competence develops in an evolutionary manner, as under the Amsterdam Treaty.* *For defence the integration of the WEU into EU and ultimately its emergence as the core of NATO, rather than its appendage, fits the federal model.*

the idea of permanent price stability. Second, economic structures now become so integrated that nation-specific economic shocks become less important. With regional employment differences within several member states unresolved by massive regional transfers, possibly worsened by them (Italy, Germany, Belgium), there should in any case develop greater wage flexibility between regions, sectors and enterprises (as was argued in Chapter 4).

The scenario for a European *defence* function becomes clearer. For the time being the US-led NATO remains the main mechanism. But the

WEU is developing as a European mechanism that can move harmoniously into NATO structures. The capacity and organisation to switch given operations between NATO-led mode and WEU-led mode are being created. It is conceivable, but not today on the horizon, that the balance could in the future switch predominantly to actions conducted in a WEU-led mode. A federal model for the EU would then see a joint funding or burden-sharing of WEU military capabilities.

One consequence of advancing to the sub-federal EU would be to increase the importance of the divide with the rest of Europe. It would also mean bigger resistance to admitting large countries of limited democratic experience. This would heighten the sense of exclusion for countries such as Russia, the Ukraine and Turkey, whose possible destabilisation represents the EU's largest security risks. For these reasons we also explore below how far one might go in developing the competences of an all-European organisation.

-The paradigm of cosmopolitan democracy

Cosmopolitan democracy is chosen here as an alternative paradigm to *federation*. It builds on the ideas of a *post-modern order* and *civil society* (the latter already introduced in Chapter 5). *Cosmopolitan democracy* is based on two essential ideas: first, the internationalisation of jurisdictions for the rules of the economy and political standards and, second, the banishing of *Realpolitik* and the distinction between, on the one hand the rule of law and morality within the democratic state, versus on the other hand the amorality of relations between states. Both *federation* and *cosmopolitan democracy* offer constructive responses to the pressures of globalisation and obsolescence of the old nation state. The difference is that *federation* opts for the coincidence of jurisdictions at the top level, whereas *cosmopolitan democracy* envisages a system of diverse and overlapping centres of political action controlled by groupings of democratic states [Held, 1995 and McGrew, 1997]. In this view for the new Europe the antithesis of *federation* is not old nationalism, but a more loosely structured cosmopolitan order.

The *post-modern* idea is important with its opposition to the *modern* state, although the terminology lends itself so easily to confusion that we prefer later to rely more on *cosmopolitan democracy* and *civil society*. The *modern state* is that whose essential features are traced to the Treaty of Westphalia of 1648. Of concern here are not the territorial and religious provisions of the Treaty, but rather that the defining characteristics of the nation state came then to be identified. This was to be a state whose ruling authority could legislate internally and would have a monopoly of the use of force either to keep the peace internally or go to war externally. The state would also represent nationhood. In the international order of modern states there was the distinction between internal and external affairs. The former was governed by the morality of law, whereas the latter was governed by *Realpolitik*.

This view of the world was early on challenged from within Germany itself by Immanuel Kant who advocated a cosmopolitan ideal: "...the greatest problem for the human species, whose solution nature compels it to seek, is to achieve a universal civil society administered in accordance with the right" [Kant, 1784, p.33]. But Kant had two more centuries to wait before something along these lines could begin to emerge.

The era of balance of power politics, and of major international wars is thus of the *modern* period, even if this may now be largely behind us [Coker, 1992]. Especially the prospect of nuclear war, developed to protect nations against other ideologies and dictatorial hegemonies, has practically disappeared from the European scene. The need to set the EU on the path of strategic development to become eventually a geo-political super-power is correspondingly weakened. As argued by Robert Cooper [1996], the US federation may prove to be the last outstanding example of the modern state, which combines the quality of nationhood together with a coincident jurisdiction for all of the four major tasks highlighted above (Table 6.2), and more. The US may continue to play the global policeman to deal with rogue states in the world. But its enormous investments in world war and even star war capacities, and the political structures to control them, may possibly wither away in operational utility, or at least not need to be reproduced in Europe.

As also remarked by Cooper, there is still the question whether the new Russia turns out also to become a modern state, or a post-modern one. Doubts on this score can be viewed as the only reason in principle to need to expand NATO to the east, to the exclusion of Russia.

The *post-modern* condition is also characterised by the evaporation of major ideological dispute. The *rules* of civilised and efficient societies are rather close to a matter of consensus. The questions are rather ones of the capacity of different societies to implement these rules and of strategies to facilitate convergence on them. The friction, actual or potential, between European civil society values on the one hand and those of fundamentalist Islam on the other, is a reminder that a global convergence of ideologies is some way off. But even here the instruments of European security need to be more in the area of encouraging secularism and cultural integration, rather than preparing for large scale wars. Also evaporating with the end of the main ideological confrontations in Europe is the need and possibility to mobilise national loyalties with supreme intensity, although this was necessary in the recent world wars when mass armies had to be sacrificed to defend the great causes.

In the *post-modern* world the focus therefore is on the *rules* of governance, which displace the international relations of *Realpolitik* and war. The system for developing these rules and organising their application is called *cosmopolitan democracy* by some political scientists [Held, 1995 and McGrew, 1997]. A more detailed description of this system has been offered by Held, and is reproduced in Table 6.3.

The mechanisms of *cosmopolitan democracy* lie in a multitude of overlapping networks, some of which are governmental but others belong to economic interest groups and to non-governmental organisations. The membership maps of these networks are diverse as opposed to their clear-cut concentration at the level of a federal territory (a whole mix of consortio, condominio, and elements of confederatio, to use the earlier language).

The interest of cosmopolitan democracy as a system is that it picks up some features of the actual European scene, and also offers in principle a progressive and enlightened alternative to the federal paradigm. In fact the contemporary European scene sees a compromise

Table 6.3: Characteristics of cosmopolitan democracy

---

1. Networks. The cosmopolitan order consists of multiple and overlapping networks of groups and associations involving the economy, regulatory and legal relations, civic associations, coercive relations, culture, welfare.

2. Clusters of rights and obligations. Groups and associations have a capacity for self-determination by a commitment to the principle of autonomy and specific clusters of rights and obligations. These clusters form the basis of an empowering legal order - a cosmopolitan democratic law.

3. Legal principles. These delimit individual and collective action within the associations of the economy, state and civil society.

4. Law enforcement. This is developed at a variety of locations and levels, along with courts to monitor and check political and social authority.

5. Democratic autonomy. The common structure for political action creates the agenda for long-term change and priorities.

6. Social justice. The modus operandi of production and distribution of resources must be conducive to, and compatible with the democratic process and common action.

7. Non-coercive principles, use of force. Non-coercive settlement of disputes is the main principle, but the use of force remains a last resort option, notable where tyrannical regimes deny democratic rights, or where circumstances spiral beyond control.

8. Citizenship. People can enjoy membership in the diverse clusters at different levels from local to global.

Source: D. Held, "Democracy and the Global Order - from the Modern State to Cosmopolitan Governance", Polity Press, 1995. The above is an edited extract from Table 12.1, p.271.

between the two paradigms. *Cosmopolitan democracy* is progressive in the sense of being in tune with the globalizing world tendencies, rather than reactionary like the nationalist. It is enlightened in being based on law and morality, rather than *on Realpolitik*.

The actual system in Europe may be interpreted accordingly in terms of the overlapping competences of the EU and several international organisations for the eight sets of rules that have been presented in preceding chapters, and summarised in Table 6.4. These rules are in substance generally in harmony with analogous rules formulated by the global institutions, but they are applied within Europe mostly with a higher degree of operationality. The EU is involved in almost all sets, but also striking is the diversity of institutions involved. We may call these the rules of a *European civil society*, since they are the foundations of Europe's contemporary civilisation.

Table 6.4: Eight sets of rules for a European civil society

POLITICAL, SECURITY

1. Democratic institutions	*Council of Europe, EU*
2. Individual human rights	*UN,Council of Europe, EU*
3. National minorities	*UN, OSCE, Council of Europe*
4. Inter-state behaviour	*UN, OSCE, NATO, WEU, EU*

ECONOMIC, SOCIAL

5. Market for goods, services ,capital	*WTO, EU*
6. Macroeconomics of money and budgets	*IMF, EU/euro*
7. Social model	*Council of Europe, EU*
8. Corporate governance	*EBRD, EU, OECD*

The setting is a Europe in which the nation state finds itself under tension from above and below, with demands to adapt to globalisation, Europeanisation and regionalisation all at the same time. The upward pressures derive from the technologies driving openness and internationalisation of trade and finance. The growth of the weightless economy, be it in traditional services or cyber-technology blurring the notion of goods and services, is making physical frontiers and distance less and less a restraint on international integration [Quah, 1997]. Meanwhile the downward pressures for regionalisation are supposed by sociologists to be linked to the same causes, since the globalizing and Europeanising trends are making governance more remote from the citizen, who wishes to retain a sense of belonging and of control over affairs and look to the regional and local organisations for this. A more specific argument of political economy is that the international integration fragments the loyalties of interest groups away from the national level, and regional interest groups become more relevant in the search for effective alliances [Casella, 1996]. Europe thus sees a fragmentation and layering of loyalties. While the modern state is deconstructed, its replacement is not necessarily the federal Euro-state, since Europe's nationality and regional structures mean that loyalties will always remain more complex. The location of state power has become more opaque.

- The management paradigm

The number and size of European and international organisations operating in Europe is such that management efficiency principles developed in the private sector, become also a useful paradigm. The ideas here may be more mundane alongside political theory. But they are none the less of first-rate importance, because the costs of malfunctioning institutions may be sufficient to offset the theoretical gains identified in the political and economic theory of government. Besides, in some policy domains there are choices between using alternative institutions and this can also be a competitive spur to efficiency. Finally, in the last decade principles of management efficiency have made unexpected strides into the workings of public sector agencies within national administrations, and there is every reason to draw on such experience at the European level.

A leading management textbook, *"Foundations of Corporate Success"* by John Kay [1993], offers some concepts for thinking about the efficiency of the set of European organisations. Kay analyses the source of *distinctive capabilities* of successful enterprises.

"Architecture is the first of the three primary distinctive capabilities. It is a network of relational contracts within, or around, the firm.....The value of architecture rests in the capacity of organisations to create organisational knowledge and routines, to respond flexibly to changing circumstances, and to achieve easy and

open exchanges of information. Each of these is capable of creating an asset for the firm - *organisational knowledge* which is more valuable than the sum of individual knowledge, - *flexibility and responsiveness* which extend to the institution as well as to its members."

"The second primary distinctive capability is *reputation.* Reputation is the most important commercial mechanism for conveying information to consumers. Reputations are difficult and costly to create but once established can yield substantial added value....*Brands* are a means by which the producer can establish the reputation of a product. They provide continuity. They may reflect a distinctive recipe."

"*Innovation* is the third primary distinctive capability."

"Few chief executives' statements have not included some reference to focusing on the *core business.* The core business is the set of markets in which the firm's distinctive capability gives it competitive advantage."

"Some competitive advantages are based not on the distinctive capabilities of firms, but on their *dominance or market position.* These are *strategic assets* for the firm concerned (*natural monopoly,..... incumbent firms,..... market restrictions*)".

"Specialisation allows many *niche* players to survive."

What happens when these evocative management concepts are applied to the set of European and international institutions? Does this help clarify thinking on directions for indeed the architecture of the system in Europe?

One can certainly say that the EU has a powerful architecture, with a distinctive ethos, corporate culture and organisational knowledge. It also has a dominant market position, and is even a natural monopoly. This, of course, is a warning about the normal hazards of monopoly, in terms of bureaucratisation and remoteness from consumers. The EU is positioned to derive great advantages from its virtually unassailable market power and potential for synergies between product lines. However the EU institutions may need big changes in management strategy to avoid problems of overload (we return to this later in the present chapter).

NATO also has a strong architecture, and a formidable reputation: this amounts to a crucial asset when it comes to military deterrence, but politically the brand is not so saleable in all market segments in Europe.

The IMF has a clearly branded product through its conditional macroeconomic assistance, with a strong reputation. Also this is the IMF's clear core product, with little dispersal of resources over miscellaneous services.

There are several organisations or specific functions which produce valuable niche services, whose distinctive products have good reputations. Such is the case for the European Court of Human Rights of the Council of Europe, the High Commissioner for National Minorities of the OSCE, and the Annual Economic Surveys of the OECD. The UN Economic Commission for Europe had a niche in the days of the Cold War to facilitate at least some minimal information exchange and personal contacts across the Iron Curtain. But this niche is now obsolete and the agency might best be closed down.

On the other hand the Council of Europe, the OSCE and OECD have very extensive, even sprawlingly diverse and sometimes overlapping interests. Serious questions can be asked whether there is a sufficiently disciplined concentration on core and niche products, with a weeding out of resources devoted to areas where there are less distinctive capabilities. The Council of Europe and OSCE are competing in the areas of monitoring democracy and minority rights. The member states do not seem to try hard to rationalise these activities, maybe because the diplomacy of so doing is enormously complicated in relation to the pay-off. A "wise persons" group, chaired by Mario Soares, has been set up in 1998 to sift through the issue and make recommendations. Also the OECD has difficulty in combatting the obsolescence of its working methods, as its membership becomes wider and more diverse, while the economic functions of the EU become deeper and wider. (A suggestion is made for the OECD at the end of the present chapter.)

The representatives of the member states on the boards, or councils, or committees of the European and international organisations may be thought of as shareholding members of the boards of multinational corporations. The main shareholders, maybe like large financial institutions with diverse holdings, can think strategically about several of their investments together. They can reflect on various restructuring ideas to get a better rationalisation or core activities, and different out-sourcing possibilities for the companies that have too many products. They may spot companies with a distinctive and well-branded product but weak market power, and look for strategic alliances to add value. These very basic management concepts may be more relevant to the European organisations than appreciated. For example the EU seems now to make an implicit strategic alliance with the Council of Europe, in putting its market power (in relation to accession candidates) behind the work of the "weak" Council of Europe in monitoring democracy and human rights, and of the "weak" OSCE in its work on national minorities in central and eastern Europe. (We return to these questions later).

The new technologies that render physical frontiers obsolete also offer opportunities to the managers of Europe's rules and policies. The board members of the different institutions could become adept at far more transparent, rapid and interactive communications, with the use of multi-media, multilateral video-conferencing facilities integrated with e-mail communication of documents. (To this also we return, at the end of this chapter).

These few paragraphs on management concepts suggest that they could well amount to a matter of great importance to the governance of Europe, with sizeable weight for these relatively mundane matters alongside the traditionally more noble issues of political and economic theory.

6.3 Three general purpose organisations

-The European Union

In the historical context of the post-war period, the EU now seems set in a mode of accelerating institutional evolution, with a sequence of Intergovernmental Conferences amending the Treaties and ground-rules.

A bird's eye view of the accelerating development of the institutions is evident from the barest summary of the successive

Treaties. After the three initial Treaties of Paris of 1951 (ECSC) and of Rome of 1957 (EEC and Euratom), the fusion treaty of 1965 put these three communities together to form a clearly general purpose organisation, not just a sectoral one, a shift from *condominio* towards *federatio*. The Single European Act of 1985 enhanced majority voting in the Council in order to help complete the single market and brought the European Parliament more into the legislative circuit. The Treaty of Maastricht of 1992 designed the institutions for the monetary union, including a classic federal central bank, and introduced the three pillar system of functions - Pillar I for market and money, Pillar II for foreign and security policy, Pillar III for justice and home affairs; it also allowed opt-outs in monetary and social policy domains. Overall Maastricht then accentuated elements of both *federatio* and *confederatio* at the same time. The Treaty of Amsterdam of 1997 developed all three pillars in evolutionary steps, strengthened the powers of the European Parliament in the legislative circuit and introduced a general flexibility ("enhanced cooperation") clause, thus making again for more of both *federatio* and *confederatio*. However Amsterdam failed to agree on crucial reforms to the Council's voting weights and the number of Commissioners and deferred these for the next treaty revisions, which are now programmed effectively from the turn of the millennium.

Scenarios for the maturing of the EU institutions may be sketched out with some clarity. The future is of course uncertain, but at least there is pattern of development and of institutional dynamics to be recognised, which is revealed by both the history of the last twenty years and the outcome of recent negotiations.

In the period until the year 2020 one can expect a maturing of the institutions along the sub-federal lines already traced. For the period 2020 to 2050 one can discuss something more federal.

For the period until 2020 we may attempt to describe the outlook for each of the four main institutions.

European Parliament. This institution now emerges somewhat surprisingly as that best set on new tracks, with plenty of room for maturing its effective functions within the newly revised constitutional rules. Its number of members is now given a ceiling of 700, whatever

Table 6.5: Results of the Treaty of Amsterdam, 1997

Institutional

1. Go-ahead for enlargement into central and eastern Europe
2. Comprehensive review of treaties and institutions before membership exceeds 20
3. Council: revision of voting weights with next enlargement
4. Commission: one member per state with next enlargement
5. Parliament: number limited to 700 maximum
6. Subsidiarity principle strengthened
7. Flexibility clause permitting "closer cooperation" by a majority but not all member states
7. Extension of assent and co-decision legislative procedures (increased role of Parliament)
8. Simplification of co-decision procedures
9. Council: extension of qualified majority voting
10. Commission: increased authority of its president
11. Reinforced role of Committee of Regions

Fundamental principles

12. EU bound by European Convention for Human Rights and Fundamental Freedoms
13. Member state's voting rights can be suspended with breach of human rights or democracy

Pillar I - Economic and Monetary Union

14. Employment chapter
15. Reinforced competencies for environment, public health and consumer protection

Pillar II - Common Foreign and Security Policy

16. Secretary-General of Council to be "Mr/Ms. CFSP"; new troika system
17. Policy planning and early warning unit
18. "Petersberg tasks" for WEU (humanitarian, rescue, peacekeeping, peacemaking, crisis management)

Pillar III - Area of Freedom, Security and Justice

19. Competences for the free movement of persons transferred to Pillar I
20. Incorporation of Schengen Agreement into EU jurisdiction under flexibility clause (no 7)
21. Possible introduction of qualified majority voting after five years

---

number of member states. The assessment of one of the Parliament's negotiators for the Amsterdam Treaty, Elmar Brok, may be quoted: "..if there is one winner in the Amsterdam Treaty, then it is the European Parliament, with 23 additional cases of co-decision added to the present 15 cases under the Maastricht Treaty, a simplified co-decision procedure putting the Parliament and Council on equal footing in the larger part of normal secondary legislation, agreement on granting budget rights to Parliament also in CFSP (foreign and security policy), the right of assent in naming the Commission president and in imposing sanctions on member states violating human rights being added to the present list of cases of assent comprising the acceptance of new member states, association treaties and others. In short, important decisions within the Union can in the future not be taken without the Parliament. The European Parliament has finally gained the status of a full parliament" (Brok, 1997). Even making allowance for a degree of triumphalism by the author quoted, it is evident that the Parliament now has an adequate legal basis for many years for filling out its role in the EU's political processes in practice, and for building up its own precedents, traditions and culture. The "democracy deficit" complaint is for the time being largely deflated at the level of the legal place of the Parliament in the system.

Council of Ministers. This institution has only begun to address its two main constitutional questions, the weighting of qualified majority voting and the role of the presidency. The revision of weights was attempted but failed during the Amsterdam summit of June 1997. The presumption is that the disproportionately high weights of the smaller member states will be reduced, or that a second majority criterion - of population numbers - will be introduced. The large member states can complain that with enlargement they risk becoming even more seriously under-represented, but the smaller member states will fight to prevent domination by the big countries. The failure of Amsterdam to produce a new column of weights means rather undramatically that the negotiation needed more time and greater proximity of serious consequences from continued impasse. A rendez-vous is set to fix the new weights before the next enlargement.

The Amsterdam Treaty did modestly extend the field for majority voting directly, and, more importantly perhaps, indirectly also by allowing for "enhanced cooperation", ie flexibility for a majority of countries to go ahead with a political initiative without participation of dissenting member states, but still using the EU institutions. The ground-rules for "enhanced cooperation" were specified to curtail risks of harming the interests of the dissenting member states.

The Treaty has been criticised because it did not deliver a greater extension of majority voting, with Chancellor Kohl backing away at the last minute, apparently under pressure from the Länder. However these critics do not always remember what political scientists have to say about majority voting. It is shown by Dahl [1989] that not so many democratic nations are fully majoritarian in their decision-making, many effectively being consensual because of their party structures, or retaining other constraints like the use of referenda (Switzerland) or upper chamber veto powers in federal states. Dahl argues that majority voting is sound practice under three conditions: i/ that the polity has homogenous political attitudes, ii/ that today's majority has a good chance of becoming tomorrow's minority and vice versa, and iii/ that matters such as language, religion and economic security are not at risk. Otherwise the chances of de Toqueville's *tyranny of the majority* may be very real. In the actual conditions of the EU the trend of reform of the voting rules is still significant and reasonably prudent.

The member states failed to address at all radically the weaknesses of the six-monthly rotating Council presidency system, namely lack of continuity and the limited resources of smaller countries. Of course the system has a positive quality, namely the importance of the presidential experience for each national government in turn - for about half its cabinet ministers and hundreds of its senior officials - in terms of diffusing expertise and a sense of responsibility for the EU system. Also it is regularly observed the small countries often produce outstandingly positive presidencies. As a result momentum for reform is for the time muted, or being met by more selective remedies.

One tendency is for the presidency system to allocate some specialised tasks to positions that do not rotate. The innovation of this type from the Amsterdam Treaty is for a Mr/Ms. CFSP, in the shape of the permanent Secretary-General of the Council. This will go with a reform of the cumbersome former *troika* system, in which the EU was represented externally on foreign policy questions by a committee of three Council presidencies (past, present and future) plus the external relations Commissioner. The new *troika* will be the present presidency, Mr/Ms. CFSP and the external relations Commissioner. This *ad hoc* innovation adds, however, to two others. Recently there has been increasing use of High Representatives for specific foreign policy tasks, for example in Bosnia successively with David Owen, Carl Bildt and Carlos Westendorp. There is also the long-established importance of the President of the Monetary Committee, held by a top treasury official or deputy treasury minister, elected for a period of about two years. This body has done much of the work of the Ecofin Council, especially in management of the European Monetary System and preparation for the euro.

An alternative idea promoted by Ludlow and Ersboll [1996] is for the small countries to constitute team presidencies, the lead presidency co-opting representatives of other small countries. While this idea did not receive endorsement in the Treaty of Amsterdam there was an informal development along these lines with the Luxembourg presidency of the second half of 1997 co-opting some officials from Belgium and the Netherlands into the presidency of some Council working parties. Overall these developments show signs of evolutionary response to an presidency question.

A more radical proposal for the Council presidency has recently been advocated by Jacques Delors [1997]. He proposed that a President of the Union be elected for three years by the European Council. He would be supported by two Vice-Presidents, one appointed by the present rotation system, the other being the President of the Commission. While the President of the Union would chair the European Council, the two Vice-Presidents would chair the sectoral Councils of Ministers. While Delors does not make this explicit, it might be imagined that the Commission President would chair the Councils with first pillar competences (especially economic affairs), whereas the Vice-President from a member state would chair the second and third pillar competences (foreign and home affairs), given their more intergovernmental character. This idea is rather interesting.

It would clarify the division of competences between the more supranational and intergovernmental domains but make an important change in institutional balance, partly in favour of the Commission.

Another issue for the Council is the proliferation of sectoral councils alongside the weakness of the General Affairs Council, manned by foreign ministers, to provide overall political direction and coordination, which in national capitals is assured of course by the head of government. A constructive proposal by Ludlow [1997] is that the General Affairs Council should become manned by personal representatives of heads of government or "Europe ministers", leaving the foreign ministers to get on with their normal business of genuinely external relations.

Commission. The number of Members of the Commission will be reduced to one per member state upon the next enlargement. The Commission has also undertaken to make an internal restructuring before the year 2000, with a regrouping of competences and consolidation for external relations in particular. How to conciliate the increasing number of member states and consolidated competences is not yet specified. However models exist in various national governments. Drawing for example on a combination of British and Russian examples, one can envisage the vice-presidents of the Commission as super-ministers, or like vice prime ministers in Russia covering large domains, with junior ministers working under them but none the less represented in the Commission (as in the cabinet or council of ministers). There could also be an accentuation of policy formation in restricted groups of most concerned Commissioners (as cabinet committees), with the plenary Commission sessions becoming more formal, and with a more limited agenda for substantive debate.

The Commission also announces its intention to prepare management reforms by the year 2000 (under the headings SEM 2000 for sound and efficient management, and MAP 2000 for modernisation of administration and personnel). Structural management issues under consideration include, according to the Commission's *"Agenda 2000"* document, the possibly wider use of external executive agencies.

The agenda for management reform in the EU institutions may be grouped under four headings: (i) languages, (ii) staff policy, (iii) procedures *between* the institutions and (iv) decentralisation *within* the institutions. These sound rather banal questions, common to any large international business. But they do amount to a critical mass of constraints on performance, which have to be addressed if the institutions are to fulfill adequately the constitutional role assigned to them. Put more bluntly, either these issues are fixed or the institutions will degenerate, the system eventually will fail and some other system will take its place.

The working language regime is enormously expensive in direct costs of translation and interpretation and indirectly in terms of delays and distraction of staff away from the real policy content of documents. Reforms are not that difficult to envisage. While all legislative texts will continue to be translated into all official languages, and parliamentarians must be able to speak in their national languages, this is not necessary for officialdom. All Members of the Commission, to be approved in future by the President, should be competent in at least two major European languages. Officials of national governments nominated to committees should also have language qualifications (the OECD and Council of Europe function in just two languages). EU member states are inconsistent when they allow very important bodies to function with minimal translation (European Monetary Institute and the Monetary Committee), while insisting on congesting the work of lesser, technical working groups with onerous language requirements as a matter of principle! All professional people in 21st century Europe must speak foreign languages, like reading and writing their mother tongue. Educated people from small countries already do this.

On staff policy the President of the Commission has already undertaken to finish with the ear-marking of senior Commission staff positions as traditional "captures" of certain nationalities (but has this reform happened?). The strict quota system of top jobs by nationality must also go. It does not exist in the IMF, which is politically a very important institution. The nationality ear-marking and quotas also has an insidious effect on individual loyalties, contradicting the creed of allegiance only to the EU institution rather than national interests.

Much of the heaviness of EU procedures, for example in contracting expenditures, comes from the efforts of member states to control the Commission's management tasks in their detailed execution, and to push for procurement quotas to the detriment of competition and quality in contract performance. This is seen in the abusive proliferation of the number and reach of so-called "advisory committees". In the maturing of institutional structures the European Parliament and Court of Auditors should be the detailed watch-dogs, leaving the Council to focus on the setting of policy and the Commission to get on with its tasks of execution.

The Commission is apparently considering both internal and external decentralisation measures. This is warranted. Recent years have seen very large management tasks grow up within policy departments, for example with technical assistance programmes to central and eastern Europe, where the departments concerned are drowned with contracting work to the exclusion of a balanced attention to the wider range of policy priorities. Agency mechanisms are the normal response to this problem, and a new specialised service is being established for contracting work for all development and technical assistance programmes.

Enlargement. The main purpose of the *"Agenda 2000"* document [Commission, 1997] was to assess the preparedness for membership of the 10 candidates from central and eastern Europe. This was done in great detail, to the point that the file of official opinions by the Commission amounts to a monumental 1300 pages. While dismissed for excessive bureaucracy by some commentators, these evaluations graded all the candidates systematically according to most of the *Rules of European civil society* (as in Table 6.4 above). The official criteria had been decided by the European Council in 1993, and covered democracy, human rights, minorities, the market economy and its external competitiveness, and capacity to adopt EU market legislation and macroeconomic performance. Although the evaluations may be questioned here and there on conceptual or factual grounds, this was one of the most comprehensive and strongest exercises in political and economic policy conditionality ever undertaken. If redrawing the map of Europe is effectively about extending the territorial coverage of the rules of law and norms of civic society, this is equivalent to the projection through much of central and eastern Europe of the *code*

Napoleon, mercifully this time without the blood-shed and with legitimacy.

The Commission judged in July 1997 that six countries were for negotiations to start in 1998: the three expected Visegrad countries - Poland, Czech republic and Hungary, as for NATO; Estonia was deemed to be a category ahead of other Baltic states in terms of economic reform and Slovenia also clearly more advanced economically and politically than other Balkan candidates. Cyprus had already been judged by the European Council to be ready for negotiations.

The Commission's proposals were endorsed by the European Council in December 1997, in spite of vigorous campaigning by the countries disappointed not to be in the first train. EU countries had diverse preferences on the matter, but no majority could be found to deviate from the Commission's proposal. However the pressures exerted by the countries not in the first train resulted in a decision to convene a standing conference of all candidate countries, although Turkey opted out of this after being faced with political conditions that it felt insulting or impossible to respect. (A thorough, independent analysis of the implications of enlargement has been published by Alan Mayhew [1998]).

Actual accession may begin in 2002 and continue in waves for the central and eastern countries and Cyprus until maybe 2010, making a 26 member EU. New candidatures may be expected between 2010 and 2020. For example, with accession of Slovenia and Romania their neighbouring states, Croatia and Moldova, may feel the force of the domino dynamics, with arguments of historical and cultural affinities in support.

Turkey's accession seems likely to remain beyond the horizon, unless the political regime normalises convincingly in terms of secularism, democratic control of the military and the treatment of minority groups. Albania, already with an association agreement, and Bosnia, Serbia and Macedonia would have to show a real conversion to the rules of civil society to get beyond the stage of association agreements. Malta will probably become firmly persuaded of the charms of being a small offshore tax haven and prefer to stay outside.

Table 6.6: Evaluation of EU accession candidates according to the Copenhagen criteria

---

Criteria from the Copenhagen European Council meeting of June 1993
- "stability of institutions guaranteeing **democracy***, the rule of law, human rights and respect for and protection of minorities";*
- "existence of a functioning **market economy** *as well as the capacity to cope with competitive pressures and market forces within the union";*
- " ability to take on the **obligations of membership***, including adherence to the aims of political, economic and monetary union".*
Evaluation of the EU Commission:

	Democracy, Human rights	**Mrkt. economy Competitiven.**	**Obligations of Membership**
Countries proposed for opening accession negotiations			
Poland	*OK*	*OK*	*will be OK if..*
Czech Rep.	*OK*	*OK*	*will be OK if..*
Hungary	*OK*	*OK*	*will be OK if..*
Estonia	*OK, but*	*OK*	*should be OK if..*
Slovenia	*OK*	*OK*	*should be OK if..*
Countries proposed for deferral of access negotiations			
Slovakia	*Unsatisfactory*	*could be OK*	*should be OK if..*
Latvia	*OK, but*	*difficulties*	*should be OK if..*
Lithuania	*OK*	*difficulties*	*should be OK if..*
Bulgaria	*OK recently*	*difficulties*	*limited progress*
Romania	*OK recently*	*difficulties*	*limited progress*

Cyprus   *Problems in north OK*   *OK*
(For Cyprus the Commission opinion of July 1993 was positive;
European Council of June 1996 decided to open negotiations within
6 months of the end of the last Intergovernmental Conference)
Turkey   *Unsatisfactory   OK but*   *OK*
(For Turkey the Commission opinion of 1989 was qualified.
Agenda 2000 updates the assessment)

Source: the abbreviated evaluations are the author's reading of the conclusions of "Agenda 2000".

The EU seems thus to be heading towards a stabilisation of its membership numbers at something approaching 30 by the year 2020. The unanswered question then is the EU's relationship with Ukraine and Russia. The EU is already highly sensitive to the problems of treating the accession candidates differently, as shown by its decision to initiate a standing conference with all candidate countries, except for Turkey's refusal. But the analogous issue in relation to Russia and the Ukraine seems not to register on the EU's priorities in more than a token way.

The *"Agenda 2000"* document also outlines how the EU's main spending policies should be adapted for the period until 2006, assuming enlargement early in the new millennium. The maximum size of the budget would remain fixed at 1.27% of GNP. Agricultural policy would see a continuing rebalancing of the policy mix, lessening price support and an increase in direct income aids. However agricultural spending would remain extremely high, rising to about 50 billion écu per year, leaving open the agenda for more radical reform to reduce these subsidies which become increasingly anachronistic in a context of severe budgetary restrictions under the Maastricht criteria. The structural funds would see a concentration on regions covering a lesser share of the total population, down from the present 51% to between 35 and 40%. This would permit a phasing-in of the funds for the new member states to the extent of 45 billion Ecu for the period 2000-2006 (including pre-accession aid), with a ceiling of 4% of GNP in each recipient country.

The long run. Assuming that the foregoing agenda for the next twenty years is soundly managed, one can speculate that in the period 2020 to 2050 the major issue will be, again but more intensely, the democratic accountability of the Council, Commission and European Central Bank. Proposals have been in circulation for the direct election of the presidents of the European Council and/or of the Commission. Either of these steps would represent an important move from the sub-federal towards the federal. The pressure for such initiatives would be intensified if the defence function were integrated into the EU, for example through the EU clearly taking over the WEU, and the WEU developing a core role within NATO, and the US largely withdrawing from the European theatre. The US leading role in NATO today is widely appreciated on both sides of the Atlantic, but not without warning signs of its potential unsustainability. The China factor has already been discussed (section 5.6). Given US Congressional pressures to limit physical and financial commitments in Europe, there is an increasingly obvious development of the "we lead, you pay" mode of military diplomacy presented by the US to its European allies. This is unsatisfactory and ultimately unsustainable.

-The Commonwealth of Independent States

This is about an organisation which exists on paper, which hardly functions in reality, and which is not a very good idea.

Since December 1991 the Commonwealth of Independent States (CIS) is intended to develop mechanisms for reintegration of the former Soviet Union states, minus the Baltic states. Upon the collapse of the Soviet Union the idea became to follow the model of the EC, and successive drafts of treaties were prepared drawing on the Treaty of Rome, which sounded a nice idea. In September 1993 a CIS summit meeting resolved to set up an Economic Union. In October 1994 another summit resolved to work towards a payments union, a free trade area, a customs union, a common market and a currency union. In addition a secretariat was set up and for the decision-making of ministers a system of qualified majority voting was announced, this following the model of the EU Council. But the jumble of overlapping objectives for economic and monetary integration was a warning that the leaders were not on firm ground. A realistic analysis of these developments by Dyker [1997] concludes severely: "It seems, then, that while the CIS leaders and their advisers were seeking to mimic the trappings of the EU system, they had little understanding of its inner workings, or of the implications and ramifications of those inner workings".

Efforts were made in 1992-94 by the CIS countries to establish a payments system along the lines of the post-war European Payments Union. However by the time that mechanisms had become advanced in their state of preparation the need was substantially reduced by the general convertibility of the rouble, although barter trade has remained important between CIS countries. Russia was careful to avoid monetary commitments that might lead again to its subsidisation of partner countries, which early in the post-Soviet period had serious inflationary consequences for rouble.

The CIS initiatives at the summit meetings of 1993 and 1994 were further confused by the parallel initiative in January 1994 of Kazakhstan, Uzbekistan and Kyrgyzstan to create a Central Asian free trade area. Then in January 1995 Russia, Belarus and Kazakhstan agreed to aim at a customs union, and were joined by Kyrgyzstan in March 1996, while this project was baptised the Community of Integrated States. However Kazakhstan's priorities remained ambiguous, as it refused in 1996 and 1997 to apply Russia's external tariff and thus denying the operating rules of a customs union. Moreover the Russia-Belarus relationship was given special ambitions for integration under the name of the Union of Sovereign States, primarily at the initiative of President Lukashenko of Belarus, whose lack of democratic behaviour, however, embarrassed most of Russia's leadership. The bilateral customs union between the two countries functioned only through the deployment of Russian customs officials to the Belarus external frontiers with Poland and Baltic states, while Belarus demands for a monetary union were refused by Russia out of concern not to get involved in subsidising its weak neighbour.

In general the CIS is hardly a suitable institution for helping modernise the ex-Soviet economies, compared to the rules of policy and influences brought by the IMF with its conditional loan packages for monetary stabilisation, or, in the field of trade policy, through accession to the WTO. The CIS has not really found its *niche* in the economic system, and seems unlikely to do so beyond limited technical measures in such fields as transport, energy and communications networks. The CIS has also provided a framework for military cooperation, notably for intervention in warring Tajikistan and also for restoring Russia's military bases in Georgia. Russia sees this military cooperation as its first line of defence, particularly in Central Asia and the Caucasus. But Georgia, for example, wants to replace Russian troops in Abkhazia by UN peace keepers. Russia resists this, showing that Russia's troops are not entirely guests.

In terms of stylised images of the emerging map of Europe it is quite misleading to suggest, as has been done in many official speeches, that the CIS is an analogue to the EU. In reality the CIS is a disfunctioning instrument, favoured by some conservative Russian politicians for gradual reassembly of the Soviet sphere of influence, if not domination. By the same token reformist politicians in Russia have little interest in the CIS, beyond a limited technical cooperation agenda.

A recent conference of Russian political economists [Galkin ed., 1996] analysed why, in the words of Y. Borko "no scheme or even more or less coherent concept of integration is possible". First, Russia needs quite different types of relationship with three zones of the CIS area: some specialised cooperation with Ukraine, Belarus and Moldova alongside their simultaneous movement towards closer relations with Western Europe; alliance relationships in Central Asia, with a mix of economic and military interests; and in the Caucasus special security concerns in relation to threats from Islam and aggressive competition from Turkey. The lopsided balance of strength, described by D. Furman as between "an elephant and ten pug-dogs" would inevitably generate conflict. In addition political integration was inappropriate with such a wide range of political regimes. According to V. Smirnov "the ruling elites base their legitimacy on the idea of government by the ethnic group after which the republic is named and its superiority over others, rather than the ideas of democracy and human rights cherished by Moscow liberals.... Since the idea of democracy cannot be the value basis for CIS integration, the problem is not just who would participate in integration but also what would be its ideology".

-The European Civil Society

This is about a European political entity which does not exist, but which could be a good idea.

The question is whether there is room for a multi-purpose European political entity beyond the European Union, which would be inclusive rather than exclusive and still have sufficient operational weight to be of strategic, geopolitical value. Put in other terms, it is the question whether there is a possibility to have a Europe that territorially includes Russia, the Ukraine and Turkey, the European Union and all that lies between, and where there is commitment to a sufficient number of the rules of European civil society for the members to feel that they are members of something important for the nation's political, economic and societal destiny.

Such seems to have been the idea of the late President Mitterrand, who called on a number of occasions for a "European Confederation". This was to be inclusive for the whole of the post-Communist Europe and devoted to fundamental political values. But the project was never spelt out in any detailed or operational terms. One concrete initiative was Mitterrand's sponsorship of what became the EBRD, but this is only a *niche* institution, although a valuable one. Moreover the attempt by Jacques Attali to use this bank as a base for wide-ranging European geo-politics lacked legitimacy on a monumental scale.

The idea of a European Confederation may still have a future, but it needs in any case a serious specification. The term *confederation* may be useful because it denotes a given territory which combines a wide set of functions of public policy, and is therefore more than a club or *niche* player. But the language is confusing in relation to a European Union which is itself still uncertain how far it becomes federal or confederal.

An alternative name, as vehicle for developing the idea, may be preferable: the *European Civil Society* (the origin of the term in political literature was indicated in section 5.1 above, drawing on Gellner [1994] and others). The name carries its own message, suggesting an attachment to the rules of civilised, democratic society, as opposed to a Europe of hegemons and *Realpolitik*. There is also an attractive resonance to the idea of a Europe that had both a *European Union* for a set of countries which for particular historical and economic reasons are already particularly closely integrated and a *European Civil Society* which embraced all European countries aiming at the same fundamental objectives. For the long-run it might be quite open how far the European Union extended its frontier towards encompassing the *European Civil Society*, or how many policies might be shared; i.e. how far the two might converge.

The obvious starting point, in terms of ideals and membership, is the Council of Europe. This is the only European body whose membership, actual and potential, fits well the contours of the wider Europe. Its present membership includes all the European Union, other west European countries, all candidates for European Union membership, Russia, Ukraine and Moldova. It envisages membership of all the former Yugoslav states as and when their political situations normalise, Belarus when its democratic credentials become acceptable, and the three Trans-Caucasian states in due course - Armenia, Georgia and Azerbaijan.

The Council of Europe already has its major specialisation in the functioning of democratic institutions and respect for human rights, as described in Chapter 5. It is based in Strasbourg and uses the same building for its parliamentary assembly as the European Parliament. Its flag is the original Euro flag, blue with twelve gold stars, subsequently adopted also by the European Union. The Council of Europe presents itself therefore with interesting qualities as a basis for the wider European identity: its actual or potential membership is suitable, its objectives and joint symbolism with the European Union admirable.

The problem with the present Council of Europe is that its competencies and operational activity is thin and, with the singular exception of the European Court of Human Rights, weak in powers of enforcement. But its competencies are also spread very wide, and there is serious overlap with the EU and OSCE. These problems are officially recognised, as shown by the appointment in January 1998 of a Committee of Wise Persons, presided by former Portuguese President Mario Soares. Anticipating their conclusions, here is a thought experiment to build upon the assets of the Council of Europe to create a much stronger *European Civil Society.*

A joint political initiative of the European Union and Russia proposes a summit meeting of the heads of state or government of the member states of the Council of Europe to create the *European Civil Society.* Institutionally the initiative draws on the early model of summit meetings of the European Community: the European Council met at the highest political level to give impetus to strategic initiatives, but without legal personality and therefore without passing legal acts. This allowed the leaders to invite or instruct the EC institutions to get on with the more technical legislative or policy operations. The model of these summits for the *European Civil Society* would be particularly appropriate since it avoids the need for negotiation over the statutes of institutions and allows for flexibility to take initiatives beyond the range of competence of the Council of Europe.

Meeting in plenary session the *European Civil Society* would have about forty countries around the table. Taking inspiration from both the UN Security Council and the G8 summitry (the old G7, now with Russia since Denver in 1997), the *European Civil Society* would also meet in restricted formation. This would be a G9, comprising all European countries with populations of 40 million or more (Germany, France, Italy, Spain and the UK from the EU, Poland soon to be in the EU, plus Russia, Ukraine and Turkey), together will full participation of the EU through its Council presidency and the Commission. Smaller EU countries would be represented by the EU institutions. This "Euro-G9" (or over-40 club) would have the task of inducing Russia, Ukraine and Turkey to join together with the EU in a civil approach to all-European issues. This is no small assignment, given the inheritance of rivalries between each of these three countries.

For the *European Civil Society* to gain critical substance and credibility it would need to add an economic agenda to the political and educational agenda of the Council of Europe. This could consist of (i) trade and single market policy, (ii) trans-European transport networks and (iv) macroeconomic policy cooperation. As a result there would be created a cluster of networks, more in the spirit of cosmopolitan democracy than federalism.

Trade and single market policy would concern first how to rationalise and multilateralise the present cacophony of sub-regional trade policy arrangements in Europe. A first benchmark concept would be, minimally, a tariff-free trade multilaterally for the whole area. This would mean a renewed and much expanded European Free Trade Area (EFTA), joined to the Euro-Mediterranean free trade area, agreed in principle for 2010. A second benchmark concept would be the European Economic Area (EEA), which offers full membership to the single market of the European Union, and goes deeply into the harmonisation of standards for goods and regulatory regimes for services.

The *European Civil Society*, meeting at summit level, could initially decide upon a conference to negotiate a comprehensive All-European Free Trade Area (AEFTA), which would embrace the European Union and all other member states of the Council of Europe. The *European Civil Society* would also give its blessing to the longer-term objective of an All-European Economic Area (AEEA), which would see progressive expansion of the existing EEA: i.e. membership of the EU's single market.

The Trans-European Networks are already being built, with financing from the European Investment Bank (EIB) and the EBRD, but with only modest extension beyond the EU candidate countries into Russia and other CIS countries. These networks concern roads, railways, ports, multi-modal transport connections, pipelines for oil and gas and electricity power transmission. There is work enough for two decades at least to develop these networks to their full potential. The *European Civil Society* would review progress of the existing Pan-European Conference of Transport Ministers and give fresh political impetus. The EU would instruct the EIB to open operations in all *European Civil Society* countries, lifting its present restrictions on investment in European CIS states.

The *European Civil Society* would also review implementation of the European Energy Charter, proposed in 1992 by the Dutch prime minister Lubbers as a project of all-European integration for trade and investment in the energy sector, and signed as a Treaty in 1995. Countries signing were virtually the same as for the EBRD, with the important exception of the US which withdrew at the end after long and difficult negotiations. One reason was because of doubts whether the US states could accept the jurisdiction of the Treaty.

Macroeconomic policy cooperation would focus on the monetary policy of the European Central Bank and the model of budget and social policies that are associated with it in the European Union. A successful launching of the euro will create a domino effect of widening participation by EU member states, and then of questions of exchange rate relations with other countries of the Council of Europe. The *European Civil Society* would invite the OECD to give adequate focus to the analysis of these policy issues. The OECD could service meetings between the EU economic and monetary institutions and the non-EU member states of the *European Civil Society*.

The *European Civil Society* would also take up issues of free movement or people, visas policies, asylum regimes and cross-border criminality, with an increasing need to integrate Schengen and Europol activities of the European Union with the central and east European countries. As the European Union itself begins to get seriously engaged on these questions, there is the real risk that the result will be to increase the height of the frontiers for the movement of people between the EU and the rest of Europe (as explained in section 4.1 above).

The *European Civil Society* would also deepen and make more concrete the educational initiatives of the Council of Europe. For example it would sponsor the creation of a network of European Schools in the major population centres of central and eastern Europe. These would be modelled of the European Schools of the European Union, which in Brussels and other EU centres have innovated in multi-lingual, multi-cultural education to a high level of academic achievement. Further extensions of the College of Europe of Bruges, for multi-lingual, post-graduate instruction in European studies, would be a further initiative, drawing on the experience of opening in Warsaw of a branch of the College of Europe. In addition there would be launched a European Scholarship Foundation, endowed to fund the graduate studies of brilliant young Europeans across the old west-east barrier. This would move central and eastern Europeans west, as well as west Europeans east. (Examples exist of international scholarship programmes that have over the course of a generation had profound impact on subsequent leadership groups, including US scholarships to young Germans after the Second World War, and the Rhodes Foundation which brings each year a few dozen students to Oxford University from the New World). Funding for these initiatives, of great importance for creating a network of enlightened future European elites across the whole of Europe, could be easily financed by a reorientation of the EU's Tacis and Phare funds away from the grant funding of commercial consultancy contracts which can now be left more suitably for purely private sector initiative. (This would mean a timely reform for the Tacis and Phare programmes, whose budgets could support extremely important initiatives in the educational field).

With the political linkage of these various functions assured through the *European Civil Society,* there would develop more powerful leverage for the political rules and ideology of the Council of Europe in the fields of democracy and human rights. As reported above, the EU in the Treaty of Amsterdam introduced an important new clause allowing for suspension of the rights of member states in the event of manifest abuse of the rules of democracy and human rights. An analogous procedure already exists within the Council of Europe, for suspension of a delinquent member. The innovation for the *European Civil Society* would be the capacity to suspend economic privileges, such as tariff-free trade, reimpose tariffs as applied between WTO partners and suspend new Trans-European Network projects etc.

The *European Civil Society* would be supportive of the activities of the OSCE in the field of conflict prevention and national minorities. The strictly military activities of the OSCE in the field of military capabilities or disarmament would be left to the high councils of OSCE, NATO and WEU. The WEU would adopt a policy of inviting other member states of the *European Civil Society* to join in missions in the Petersberg task category. However where the activities of the OSCE overlap with those of the Council of Europe, the *European Civil Society* would rationalise priorities. The search of the OSCE for a "European Security Model for the 21st Century" might well become subsumed in the *European Civil Society.*

How proceed concretely with the *European Civil Society* project as a whole? Two opportunities already present themselves conveniently on the official agenda for 1998 and 1999.

First, the EU has already agreements with Russia, Ukraine, Moldova and Belarus to consider in 1998 whether to proceed with negotiations for free trade (see section 4.1 above). This rendez-vous should become the occasion to raise the level of ambition and propose the All-European Free Trade Area.

Second, the Council of Europe's summit meeting in October 1997 agreed that measures to restructure the organisation should be prepared for a next summit in 1999 on its fiftieth birthday. That should be the occasion to launch the *European Civil Society* politically, setting as date for entry into effect the 1st January 2000.

6.4 The Euro-village

Many European and international organisations now have a say in the rules and policies that govern Europe at a multi-national level (most of them are represented in Map 17). How may the work of this complex system be affected by new information and communication technologies?

By the year 2010 multi-national coordination and governance has jumped ahead into the weightless world of electronic communication, with multi-media, multilateral video-conferencing of many categories of meetings and, of course, associated exchanges of electronic correspondence and documents. Each national capital has for large-scale multilateral meetings its official video-conferencing centre with a wall of TV screens, rather like a space control centre, with individual screens for different national capitals. These centres were initially called the Network of European Real Time Electronic Conference Centres, but the acronym was so awkward that the system was re-baptised the *Euro-village*, which captures its sense of proximity and intimacy. In addition all officials involved in the myriad committees and technical working groups of the EU and other European organisations have their own personal video-conferencing facilities available on their desks, with their PC work stations connected by Internet. The screen of the PC shows the live image of a few conference partners, alongside the texts up for negotiation. These technologies already exist and are spreading into use in the private sector [Bryce, 1996]. There is still a need for an extension of the ISDN cabling networks of telecommunication facilities, and improvement in resolution quality of images in order to achieve virtual meeting qualities. A further cheapening of the relative price of telecommunication facilities is anticipated and required for cost-effectiveness. The convening of meetings and distribution of texts is conveniently executed by E-mail, accessible to all relevant committee members and their staffs on-line in their offices. Textual negotiation is facilitated, as amendments are immediately available to all. Electronic voting is also executed automatically and instantaneously.

The switching of business between organisations is done almost with the facility of switching between layers in an ordinary windows programme of a personal computer (hence the imagery in Map 17). The distinction between formal and informal meetings is increased, with much formal business conducted through the *Euro-village* facilities. The informal meetings take place at weekends in agreeable places, and the cohesion of the different councils and committees is improved.

The *Euro-village* facilities have an influence on the conduct of business, beyond the reduction in travel costs. There is a considerable improvement in the efficiency, speed and transparency of policy coordination. Attendance at meetings can be organised with greater flexibility, with relevant staff more easily present. There is an extended system of observer status for many organisations. The system of rules and participation in oganisations becomes more integrated and generalised. The consequences of positions taken in one negotiation are more rapidly and transparently communicated into other linked negotiations. The sense of participation in European affairs in national capitals is enhanced, compared to the prior feelings of distance from what is being done "in Brussels". The mechanics of *cosmopolitan democracy* are greatly improved.

The business of the EU is considerably facilitated. The European coordination bureau of each prime minister's staff is able to enter into frequent real-time *Euro-village* negotiation, and their Brussels permanent representations are able also to observe these meetings on-line in their Brussels offices and then to take up outstanding business with the Brussels institutions directly afterwards. The technology facilitates a realisation of a long-standing idea that EU affairs be coordinated by "Europe ministers" directly representing prime ministers. Foreign ministers are able to resume their main really "foreign" policy responsibilities.

For non-EU countries of eastern Europe the *Euro-village* is used extensively in the work of the *European Civil Society*. For non-EU

Map 17: Europe of overlapping organisations

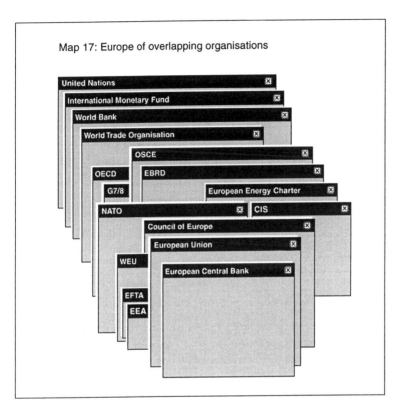

countries in central and eastern Europe the *Euro-village* offers particular advantages: a sense of inclusion in an important part of the all-European system, and access to governmental expertise in a far more flexible and economical way than through some present types of technical assistance contracts.

For example one can imagine the work of the OECD for the transition economies transformed. Replacing many unwieldy meetings in Paris of 25 to 30 countries, OECD would develop a speciality in arranging tailor-made video-conferenced seminars. For example, the Russian government wants access to expertise on highly specialised aspects of banking regulation policies. OECD arranges for four leading European experts in Brussels, London, Frankfurt and Paris to come on-line through the *Euro-village* facilities, with documents also distributed in real-time by E-mail during the seminar. Interpretation is also available on-line. Where appropriate such seminars could be open for observation at other *Euro-village* centres. This example suggests useful innovations. First, the techniques of policy dialogue and technical assistance could be made much more flexible and rapid in delivery, especially for relatively distant countries, compared to very expensive missions full of hassle for visas, air travel, hotels, and the laborious tendering of contracts to consulting companies etc. Indeed, many of the most qualified experts are often available for a consultation of a few hours without travelling from their home town, whereas they are not available at all for a four day mission. Second, the OECD, presently encumbered by a very unwieldy main mode of operation through vast committee meetings in Paris, could acquire a new lease of highly cost-effective life. The EU for its part could out-source such functions of the Tacis and Phare programmes to the OECD, which would become more of a technical assistance agency.

7. Conclusions - of Rules and Maps

Roll up that map of Europe: it will not be wanted these ten years.
William Pitt, on hearing news of the battle of Austerlitz, 1805.

To recapitulate and conclude, how may we order our thoughts for the future of the complicated Europe? A framework is offered under the headings *integration, conflict, rules, paradigms and maps.*

The dynamics of European integration are persistent and strong. We need to understand the nature of these driving forces, partly historical, partly economic, partly political. We need to set this alongside its opponent: conflict. For integration to proceed, and for conflict to be suppressed Europe needs some common rules, not too many but enough to secure a civilised Europe. We identify what these are in substance. The rules have then to be organised, which requires institutions. Europe has such institutions in abundance. To consider the development of these institutions we need to fit them with some political paradigms. But these institutions have different membership maps. Which map or maps of Europe are to dominate, if any? How is the map of Europe to be redrawn? This is the culminating question.

The millennium moves to a close with a largely episode of redrawing the maps of national frontiers peacefully. With the reunification of Germany in 1989, the break-up of the Soviet Union into twelve sovereign states in 1991, and the break-up of Czechoslovakia into two states in 1993, this new redrawing of the map of Europe has for the most part been remarkably successful, but for the disastrous break-up of Yugoslavia. However all these cases were still old-style politics of the nation state, and are no guide to the quite different process that lie ahead for the next decades in a continuous reshaping of the still immature organisation of Europe. While the nation state remains the primary focus of loyalties of the individual, many functions of the state devolve away from it both upstairs and downstairs, with supranational and regional devolution seeming both to be profound tendencies at the same time.

The summit meetings of the summer of 1997 amply illustrated the dynamics of widening three key membership maps. Amsterdam for the EU and Madrid for NATO put these two enlargement processes into higher gear. Denver set the seal on the conversion of the G7 into G8 to include Russia.

But within the EU and NATO there is also the deepening of their functions alongside greater flexibility in participation. In the monetary domain the selection process for the euro area looks like concluding with 11 participants by 1st January 1999. In the defence domain NATO's new department for lesser conflicts (officially the Combined Joint Task Force - CJTF) is able to operate in NATO formation, or under WEU leadership, or in other *ad hoc* formations. The EU, in having recourse in the future to the WEU for lesser conflict operations, gives the right to its non-WEU members to participate. In the domain of interior ministry affairs the Schengen club is incorporated into the EU jurisdiction, but still allowing some EU members to opt out and some non-EU countries to opt in. The organisations with the most extensive membership - the OSCE and Council of Europe - are at work on fundamental questions of security and civil society, but with some confusions of competence and modest powers. Yet interacting with more powerful governments and institutions they can be highly valuable organisations.

The new Europe also witnesses the need for integration of economic and security strategies, rather than their segregation as was the case in the old Brussels, where the EU and NATO never met. This is because of the nature of the current security agenda of the post-communist Europe. First there is the need for democracy and the rule of law to dominate the latent propensities for inter-ethnic conflict. Second there is the need for civic behaviour and sound corporate governance to overcome progressively the endemic corruption and criminality of the Wild East. The first means avoiding devastating costs of violence. The second means perhaps as much as the difference between continued economic stagnation and a growth rate sufficient to catch up with normal European standards of living within maybe 20 years.

These various developments still leave unanswered many questions about where the European system is heading more precisely, beyond noting an impressive profusion of institutional initiatives aimed at a civilised Europe. But what are to be its norms? How can we grasp more clearly the kind of system towards which Europe is heading, or which Europe really needs?

7.1 Sources of integration

How do countries actually form their desires to join the various clubs (the demand for integration), and how do existing club members assess their interests in admitting new members (the supply of integration)? The important arguments are in fact rather numerous. They may be grouped under the following headings:

Historical
- geography
- culture
- perceptions
Economic
- markets
- money
- redistribution
Political
- values
- power
- security

The *historical factors* are all about the affinity of peoples and how far they are willing to trust a sharing of responsibility for setting the rules with others. Proximity is the first factor. The prehistory of watersheds, rivers and seas had a big influence on subsequent cultural groupings - by language groups, religions and alphabets. Together geography and culture explain much of European politics. The alternating expansions of the EU between North and South is driven by such factors. We note how the objective criteria used by the EU for evaluating its accession candidates in fact resulted in priority for certain Baltic, Catholic Slav and former Austro-Hungarian states, but not yet for any Orthodox Slav or Muslim countries. We note how France led the Latin countries of NATO to push for inclusion of their kin in Romania, with the Anglo-Saxon countries of the North Atlantic unpersuaded.

Economic calculations over integration begin with the advantages of market openness, for which proximity is again a major factor. More demanding are the conditions for beneficial monetary integration, for which similarities of economic structure and behaviour and openness to migration flows are desirable. The controllers of access to the monetary stability club will also want to be sure that the money will not be debased by the influence of lax members. Marginal preferences for economic and monetary integration may be decided by the offer of financial advantages or redistribution mechanisms, providing insurance or compensation for possible economic losses.

Political assessments may be based first on the degree of commonality of political values. But the political elites will also be sensitive to the gains or losses of political power through integration, with subtle combinations of interests possible, for example some large states able to ally to achieve leadership, subject to the constraints of the voting power of small states which in the EU is disproportionately high. The calculation of security gains or losses is a final argument, but a complex one in a Europe which no longer has an obvious enemy, beyond a widespread concern for political instability and criminality in countries with weak rules of law and democracy.

If one thinks of the 40 or so sovereign states of Europe contemplating all of these arguments for integration from both demand and supply sides, it is evident why the integration process is hardly a simple matter. But the process is somewhat simplified by the formation of *core groups* with sufficient cultural affinities and commonality of interests and values. In practise Europe has two cores, first the

Rhineland group of EU countries and, second, Russia. The process is then further simplified by *domino dynamics*, according to which peripheral countries may find that exclusion from the core has greater risks of unfavourable outcomes than joining a core whose policies may not be their first best choice. Also there has been evidently at work in the EU a process of *disequilibrium dynamics*, according to which given functional steps of integration call for further steps if system failure is to be avoided (the single market leading to the single money, which will in turn intensify demands for greater democratic accountability of the institutions etc.).

7.2 Sources of conflict

The logic of integration, impressive as it is, was not strong enough to override Europe's capacity for violent conflict in the 20th century. In the last millennium the map of Europe has been redrawn drastically virtually every century, often with extreme violence. But in the 20th century this has been more than ever so. As recounted above in detail, in the 20th century Europe accounted for 75 million of the world's 110 million battlefield or war-related deaths, in addition to which there were a further 50 million civilian victims in the Soviet Union of the Stalin regime.

Both world wars and local conflicts caused devastating economic losses for the areas concerned. Although it may seem trite to quote monetary figures alongside the losses of life, the economic costs of conflict speak with massive force, compared to the marginal and often questionable results labouriously produced from many a cost-benefit analysis of options for adjustments of market and monetary systems in a setting of normal civil society. Losses of 50% or more of the entire capital stock were observed in local conflicts such as Bosnia and Chechnya, where GNP fell by 80% at the height of conflict. Public expenditure in Northern Ireland has to be 60% above the national average to try to maintain peace, counter unemployment and repair damages.

The causes of Europe's mega-conflicts of the 20th century may remain mysteries for historians and philosophers. The part of the individual responsibility - of the tyrants Hitler and Stalin -, versus the part that society in Germany and Russia was ready and willing to accommodate, will be debated for ever. The debates have in fact exploded in Germany and Russia since the nineteen-eighties. In both cases there was anti-Semitism, in both cases political factors opening the way for the tyrants (Germany's humiliation after the First World War and its slump in the thirties; Russia's long history of political brutality and obsession with its enemies). But the practical question is what kind of Europe can best prevent a repetition of history. Germany drew its own conclusion as Giersch [1993] points out "support for European integration became a substitute for patriotism"; the rest of Europe has every reason to accommodate this. Russia after Communism seems to want "normal life", but has difficulty politically to define its relationship with Europe, which in turn should be trying harder to find a properly accommodating formula.

Europe, having maybe purged itself of a fatalistic capacity for mega-conflicts, still shows deep down the most extraordinary capacity for its peoples at the regional level to switch modes between the richest of multi-cultural integration to the most savage of inter-ethnic conflicts, back and forth. Europe harbours over one hundred instances of significant ethnic groups living as minorities in their own countries. The ending of communism has released previously suppressed demands for minority rights. The evidence seems rather persuasive that many of these micro-conflicts can be progressively overcome when the rule-book and institutions of civilised Europe is offered as a credible strategy for modernisation and civilisation. But reminders that these deadly social ailments are an all-European inheritance are still seen, for example in Northern Ireland, the Basque province and Cyprus.

7.3 Eight rules for a European civil society

Integration requires that the rules of the game be clear and enforced. Conflict means that the rule of law has broken down. Rules may to some sound like the tool of the bureaucrat, which they can be, but they are also the guarantee of fundamental freedoms in economic and political domains.

In practical terms eight sets of rules may be identified as the foundations of a European civil society, so vital that they may be compared perhaps to Moses' ten commandments. At least we can ask ourselves if these rules are clear, acceptable and durable enough to deserve to be carved in tablets of stone.

Four are in the political and human sphere:
- rules of democratic institutions,
- rules of individual human rights,
- rules of collective rights of minority groups,
- rules of inter-state behaviour.
Four are in the economic and social sphere:
- rules of open markets,
- rules of macroeconomic stability,
- rules of the social model,
- rules of corporate governance.

There is no shortage of European institutions at work on the setting and implementation of one or more of these sets of rules, even to the point of some competitive overlapping of competences. The question is whether they are defining these rules well enough and whether the membership map of the institutions is well chosen. In fact the system is certainly immature. Some might say somewhat chaotic and dangerously incomplete. Let us review the landscape, with a bird's eye view.

Given the bequest of ancient Greece, one would have thought that the rules of democracy would by now be well carved in stone. Curiously this is far from the case, despite that both the EU and NATO make this the first and foremost qualification for new members, given also that political scientists have offered useable definitions. Also the Council of Europe has the specific task now of monitoring democratic practice, but its work here still lacks transparency. This is a pity since the weakly empowered Council of Europe can now be leveraged up into great influence, as and when its work is taken as the reference for the more powerful EU and NATO.

By contrast the rules of human rights are well carved in stone, in the form of the European Convention on Human Rights and Fundamental Freedoms. Enforcement through judgements of the European Court of Human Rights of Strasbourg is also one of the most remarkable achievements of European civil society. Its soberingly rich case law, until now mostly from the old democracies of western Europe, is now about to be further enriched, if not overwhelmed, as Russia and the other new democracies accede by virtue of their membership of the Council of Europe.

Of the 100 instances in Europe of significant ethnic minority groups, some 20 of them represent around 10% or more of the nation's population. With the dissolution of ideological confrontation, the suppressed ethnic tensions scattered all around Europe's map are tempted to explode, and in several cases have done so. Rules to protect national minorities have been drawn up by the OSCE and the Council of Europe, and good work is done by the OSCE High Commissioner for National Minorities. The rules themselves seem worthy of carving in stone. Again these weak institutions can be empowered indirectly in countries seeking accession to the EU and NATO, but that leaves other important countries less influenced.

The rules of non-coercive interstate behaviour, especially regarding frontiers, have been well drawn up by the OSCE, deserve to be carved in stone, and are supported by NATO's credibility. The OSCE's so-called "Moscow mechanism" effectively declares that disregard for the first three sets of rules so far mentioned shall not be considered as just an internal affair; this principle is a most useful component for the European civil society. But the EU, or more strictly its virtual subsidiary the WEU, lack operational credibility in the military domain, which is a glaring weakness.

Overall the political and human dimension to the new Europe is rather well specified, and the competent organisations have suitably inclusive membership maps, but their powers of enforcement are limited. Still this is a promising framework within which to work. However in the economic sphere we find that the rules have more weaknesses, and the problems of exclusion are also more serious.

The rules of the EU single market, certainly at the level of the four freedoms of movement of goods, services, labour and capital, can be considered carved in stone. The associated legislation becomes the reference for the whole of Europe. But the economic frontiers between the enlarging EU and the CIS are not yet on the way out, and the mix of preferential and bilateral trade arrangements between the EU and the rest of Europe and among these non-EU countries is a mess.

The rules of central banking for price stability in the euro area are quite suitably set in stone, but the Stability Pact rules of budgetary policy are controversial, untested and likely to be unenforceable. They should better be in plastic for the time being, since if carved in stone the tablet could break.

Even worse are the social model rules. The Council of Europe's Social Charter mimics the Convention on Human Rights in its form, but is mistaken in supposing that a form suitable for individual human rights might also work for general social and labour market policy. To make matters worse, the EU's Social Charter in turn mimicked that of the Council of Europe. However before this caused too much damage the EU Commission had a rethink, and in a policy statement in 1997 on the "Modernisation of Social Policy" proposes that these policy variables be made employment-friendly. But still the idea of the European social model deserves a better fate; for example, the principle of universal basic health care is so important, surely when compared to the American nightmare of an elderly person forced to sell the family home to pay for hospital care for catastrophic illness. The social policy rules should also be made of plastic rather than stone, at least beyond some first principles of universality of social security and a framework for labour law, and until solutions are found for high unemployment. The detailed rules of the social model need remoulding in much of Europe

The last, youngest but not least set of rules are those of corporate governance. They are discussed intensely in western Europe, for example on the finer points of shareholder and stakeholder values. But much more important and urgent is the need for basic standards of corporate ethics in the Wild East, mired by bribery and mafia violence. The EBRD has come up with a valuable set of guidelines, which are worthy of being carved in stone and deserve to be boosted in practice through the conditional lending policies of major financial institutions.

Overall, therefore, six and a half out of eight of the rule sets seem quite well specified. The rules of budget deficits and the social model need more testing and refinement, and maybe less detailed specification at the supranational level.

7.4 Three paradigms

These rules for a peaceful, prospering, integrating Europe have to be organised under jurisdictions and supported by institutions. How should this be done? In practice the institutions of contemporary Europe are highly complex, if not confusing. But deep down is it just a mess, or rather a set of trends heading towards a subtle optimum, evolving under some kind of Darwinian theory of institutional survival? Three paradigms are relevant in shaping the emerging map of a Europe:

the federal paradigm
> *- in which the focus is on a given territory. The issue then is the allocation of competences for the rules of policy between the several tiers of government.*

cosmopolitan democracy
> *- in which the focus is on the rules of policy that are needed internationally, and on how best to organise their application, allowing for different possible membership maps of the relevant institutions.*

the management paradigm
> *- this does not pretend to be political theory, but takes the rules and the institutions as given and focuses on getting the given tasks managed as efficiently as possible.*

The *federation* is one form of the *modern state*, characterised by a bunching of vital functions at the level of one national jurisdiction - say macro- and micro-economic policies, internal and external security. The US remains the archetypal modern, federal state. The nation, whether federal or unitary, is the main focus of loyalty of the population, and the main locus of democratic legitimacy.

The EU has often had in mind the federal model, although it would be better to call it a *sub-federal* model, since there is no serious support even in Germany and France for their states to become constitutionally like Texas and California. A sub-federal EU none the less means aiming at an important coincidence of competences at the level of the same jurisdictional map - money, market, external security and elements of internal security. The point would be to create a single power structure with advantages of synergies through coordinated deployment of several functions together. But the role of the member states of the EU would remain still for decades, if not indefinitely, categorically different to that of the state representatives in a typical federal upper chamber, because the European nation is not the same as a state in the US melting pot, and so would remain *sub-federal*.

Cosmopolitan democracy is, for Europe, the main alternative paradigm to federation, leaving aside old-fashioned nationalism which is obsolete. Both cosmopolitan democracy and federation are based on the pervasive internationalisation and integration under way in Europe and the world. However cosmopolitan democracy is structured in a much looser, differentiated and flexible way. It is recognized that many rules of politics and economics require international jurisdiction and supporting institutions (as illustrated above in Table 6.4 and Map 17). However the membership maps of these institutions may be overlapping rather than coincidental. The institutions will be more specialised.

It is evident that both paradigms represent an important part of the contemporary European scene. The issue is what the mix of the two is to become and why.

Federation has the quality of maximising synergies between its functions and acquiring greater power. Cosmopolitan democracy, however, is less interested in power. It belongs to the *post-modern* idea, rejecting that great centres of state power have to be concentrated at the level of a unified jurisdiction. The idea rather is that a set of rules and codes, defined and enforced at a variety of supra- and multi-national levels, largely displace the need for superpowers. Or at least the big stick of the global policeman (US) is normally kept out of sight, at least in a community of nations committed seriously to the rules of civil society such as in Europe. The post-modern state marks the obsolescence of the old moral frontiers - between the *internal* governance of morality through law and democracy on the one hand, and the *external* governance by *Realpolitik on the other.* It is no coincidence that this goes with the world-wide obsolescence of physical frontiers in the increasingly weightless economy.

Finally we also need the *management paradigm.* This complicated European and international system is a management challenge of a very high order. It is not easy to create multinational structures that work efficiently and avoid various hazards such as insufficient room for managerial manoeuvre, or excessive bureaucratic heaviness or insufficient internal cohesion. However there are successes as well as failures in the myriad system, the successes usually reflecting a combination of wisdom on the part of founding fathers with the subsequent build-up of high quality professionalism. Thus fine specialisations and favourable reputations develop associating the institutions with the policy rules in question, and these qualities once established should be recognised.

The national nominees on the boards and councils of the institutions can be viewed as if voting shareholders on the board of multinational corporations. Their votes can be cast in the pursuit of cost-effectiveness, through concentration on core functions and through being open to strategic alliances, and even out-sourcing and leasing of services. The evolving relationships between the EU, WEU, NATO, the Council of Europe, the OSCE, OECD and other organisations suggest such parallels. The map of Europe becomes composed of the overlapping maps of different multinational corporate structures.

Also with the aid of new communication technologies the nation's nominees become more adept at handling particular issues in a multi-institutional environment. One can foresee the increasing use of multimedia video-conferencing of many a multilateral meeting, with greater ease of switching issues onto the agenda of different institutions in search of resolution.

The *management paradigm* may be brought in to help either the emerging federation or the cosmopolitan democracy. It can be used to lessen the hazards of monopolistic bureaucratic structures. It can allow for some restrained competition between jurisdictions, which proves its worth at all levels of government. It also can suggest how some international institutions which are in principle weak in their own powers can be leveraged up in effectiveness by strategic alliances with other more powerful organisations.

Neither the federal (or sub-federal) paradigm, nor the less structured cosmopolitan democracy, are going to make a clean take-over of the future map of Europe. Both will have weight in the complex reality. The main point is that there are two interesting models at play in the field of European integration doctrine. Gone are the days when the federalist was the only alternative to the nationalist. The unreconstructed Euro-federalist is as obsolete as the neo-nationalist.

7.5 Four maps

These ideas help us return to the question what map of Europe is likely to emerge, or which is the most commendable, and whether the foregoing paradigms can help us sort things out. By way of strategic maps of Europe, we can discern four tendencies jockeying for position:

Two-block Europe
> *- with a European Union and associates on the one hand, and a Russian-led CIS on the other.*

Brussels Europe
> *- beyond the EU there is no other, wider European map. Non-EU countries have diverse geopolitical inclinations and the EU itself becomes rather introverted.*

Security Europe
> *- with the all-inclusive map of the OSCE, including the US and all the former USSR, and with a strong NATO core and a weak WEU.*

Civil Europe
> *- with the pan-European map of the Council of Europe, without the US or Central Asia, and with a strong EU core.*

Map 18: Two-block Europe

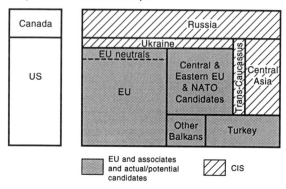

Map 19: Security Europe

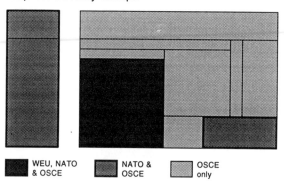

Map 20: Civil Europe

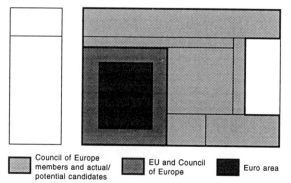

The *Two-block Europe*, with its two cores in the EU and Russia, sees the rest of Europe gravitating towards the one or the other. This map has a lot of history behind it and might be a natural evolution. However it has a serious drawback. It recreates the Europe of division and opposition. And the Russian-led block, the Commonwealth of Independent States (CIS), risks being disconnected from the rules of the European civil society and being tempting for old-style hegemonic behaviour by its leader.

Brussels Europe is a variant, in which the rest of Europe has no structure. This map is more than a possibility, since Ukraine resists Russian domination and the EU's policies towards eastern Europe beyond the enlargement candidates carry little weight so far. In this case Russia, Ukraine and Turkey are left to the hazards of choosing their national destinies without participating in an effective common structure. Russia develops its Asian connections, Turkey its Islamic and Central Asian connections, Ukraine plays in-between games; relations around this triangle could go from the tense to the conflictual. Resentment over exclusion from Europe and regime instability are the risks, which unsurprisingly becomes *Brussels Europe's* major security worry.

Security Europe brings together in the OSCE the participants of the old Cold War with the US, Canada and the former Soviet Union as well as all the rest of Europe. From its beginnings this organisation aimed at comprehensive confidence building activity with its three baskets - military, human and economic. However security Europe's most powerful mechanism, NATO, is divisive. The attempts by NATO to match its eastern enlargement with enhanced cooperation with Russia have not been totally convincing. The WEU inner group is only weakly operational. Moreover as a comprehensive integration club the OSCE has the disadvantage of over-extended membership to become seriously operational. The US presence excludes that this map becomes a main European structure. The EBRD has almost exactly the OSCE membership map, as would have been the case also for the European Energy Charter, had not the US dropped out just before signature of the treaty in 1995. These examples reflect the ambivalence of the US presence in Europe.

Civil Europe is based on the potential membership of the Council of Europe, and includes all of Europe up to its two Euro-Asian powers, Russia and Turkey, but excluding North America and Central Asia. It has the EU at its core. But the mechanisms of this wider European map are so far weak, with problems of the eastern enlargements of the EU and NATO being perceived as divisive in the rest of Europe, unless this Civil Europe were given more substance. We propose that this be done by founding a new structure, which will need and deserve a name: we call it the *"European Civil Society"*.

The critical reinforcement of the functions of this wider Europe would come from establishing an All-European Free Trade Area between the EU and all the rest of Europe, coupled to extended investments in Trans-European Networks for transport and enhanced cooperation in combatting crime and common educational programmes. The synergetic value of these initiatives, combined with a strengthening of the work of the Council of Europe on the monitoring of democratic institutions, would lie in the participating nations coming to feel included in the European project, rather than fester with resentment at exclusion. Maybe this is along the lines that the late President Mitterrand had in mind in calling for a pan-European confederation. But in this context the term is confusing, given that even the EU cannot yet identify itself as either a federation or confederation, but it fits still with the idea of a substantial coincidence of rules and mechanisms at the level of the same, inclusive European territory. The new Europe could be built on not only a *sub-federal EU*, but also the specific notion of an inclusive *European Civil Society*. This would have the ultimate objective to get all the identified, eight sets of rules working at the level of the whole of Europe. The EU would be doing this most intensely, but it would also give priority in its external relations to promote the same rules at the all-European level too. It would leave open the question of how the EU and wider *European Civil Society* might relate to each other in several decades.

Which of the maps is the most likely, which the most desirable? All four are surely going to stay alive in some degree. But the first three - Two-block Europe, Brussels Europe and Security Europe - seem the most likely to remain significant, with the fourth - Civil Europe and the specific *European Civil Society* proposal - the least likely at the time of writing. This is unfortunate, to say the least, since the fourth map seems the most badly needed as the millennium closes.

7.6 A new European golden age

It is, however, quite plausible to make concrete proposals for this fourth map, not just to avoid the hazards of the other three maps, but for the wider Civil Europe to become an outstanding success. The prerequisites for this are double:
- achieve reforms within the European Union, notably for the euro currency area to overcome the initial problems of the "inconsistent quartet" in the policy mix, especially in core countries such as France and Germany; and then by completing the linked institutional reform and enlargement of the EU;
- launch a specific political initiative to give shape and substance to the wider Europe, which we call the "European Civil Society".
   The euro will almost certainly be a success as a stable store of value. Three factors will combine to guarantee this: the virtual price stability in the EU at the outset, the institutional independence of the European Central Bank and its primary statutory duty to maintain price stability. However the overall monetary-economic policy mix at the heart of the euro area is likely to be troublesome, with a real danger of a new "inconsistent quartet" as between monetary, budgetary, social/labour market and regional redistribution policies. With the euro bringing greater rigidity of monetary and budget balance policies, there is a categorical need for greater adjustment capacity in social and labour market policies. This seems to be understood in principle by the leaderships of most countries, but the therapeutic action proves still elusive in some of them. There is encouragement on offer from the experience of some EU countries which have reduced unemployment while reforming their versions of the European social model (Ireland, Netherlands, UK). In addition the EU's regional funds could be turned more towards responding to the new needs of the euro area, like helping regions hit badly in the processes of competitive rationalisation

in the economic and monetary union, which the Commission unfortunately failed to address explicitly in its *Agenda 2000* proposals [Commission of the EU, 1997].

The social and labour market reforms may amount to tough political assignments, but it is clear that they are needed in any case to ease high unemployment and restore sustainability to social security finances. If the euro serves as the spur to get this done faster, so much the better. The prospect of the euro has already had a powerful effect in achieving the impressive convergence on low inflation and the budget policy norms of the Maastricht Treaty. There is every reason to build on these successes with serious social and labour market reform, and the EU's "jobs summit" of November 1997 shows that this point has been taken in principle.

The forthcoming institutional reforms and enlargement of the EU boil down to a few numbers: how many Commissioners? What set of voting weights in the Council? How many new member states in, say, 2002 and again maybe in 2006 and 2010? For the fuzzier questions of improving efficiency of the institutions, a strong dose of the management paradigm is called for. The enlargement negotiations will predictably conclude with a phased accession to the internal market, long transition arrangements for the freedom of movement of persons and some environmental standards, and no hurry at all over joining the euro.

The EU and NATO will enter the 21st century both widening their membership. The advent of the euro would also see a strong deepening of the EU. These are the main prospects. But they do not amount to a well balanced strategy, since they will be deepening the divide with the wider Europe.

Adequate initiatives for the wider Europe are not yet seriously on the political agenda, but instead just the subject of speeches and tokenism. The wider Europes exist in the Council of Europe and OSCE, but they are only shallow institutions. Yet Europe's biggest economic and security issues are, as of today, all about the shallowness of the wider Europe. These issues are about whether the transition countries get on to a durable economic growth path, and about whether they also achieve political stability and civility. These two issues would best be addressed by both a rapid widening of the EU and a deepening of the wider Europe. The EU's official priorities are to deepen and widen at the same time over the next decade. But to deepen the wider Europe is manifestly not its priority. However a convenient opportunity presents itself, on the occasion of the 50th anniversary of the Council of Europe in 1999, to launch something like the *European Civil Society* here proposed, to enter into effect on 1st January 2000. The *European Civil Society* deepens the wider Europe, balancing the widening of the already deep (EU) Europe.

The *European Civil Society* fixes as its substantive objective a single and whole Europe which respects all the eight sets of rules identified above. Some of these rules, notably all the four political ones, can apply identically to EU and non-EU countries. In the economic domain a more specific approach is required. The crucial initiative, as mentioned, would be creation of the All-European Free Trade Area, with the objective of leading on later to expansion of the European Economic Area (i.e. extension of the EU internal market to non-EU countries). This would assemble the critical mass of both political and economic content for the *European Civil Society,* creating a framework for synergies between these different fields. The political leadership of the *European Civil Society* would ultimately rest with the plenary assembly of governments of all the 40 or so member states. By analogue with the UN Security Council or the G7/8 Summit group, the *European Civil Society* would also establish a restricted G-9 group for more frequent deliberations (the 9 countries with populations over 40 million plus the EU institutions).

This Europe would have good chances to embark upon a new golden age. It would assemble unique qualifications: an awareness of a deep common culture, comparable educational standards throughout, and willingness to subscribe to the same basic political and economic values. A robust and balanced structure, consisting of both the EU and the *European Civil Society,* could well protect this whole Europe from the kind of *domino disasters* experienced in Asia in 1997, which resulted from a lack of a balanced set of economic and political rules and institutions. The stage would be set for western Europe to serve as the role model for the east, not just economically but also in the art of political integration. Meanwhile eastern Europe enters a long cycle of fast growth and economic catch-up, thus adding economic buoyancy to the whole region.

As the first decades of the 21st century roll by, the widening of the deep Europe and the deepening of the wider Europe would tend to converge. Whether the two would ultimately merge together into one Europe would remain a mystery for the future to reveal. But at least those who want to go in that direction would have a structure to work with.

---

1. We, the Heads of State or Government of the Member States of the Council of Europe, meeting on .. ..1999 at .... on the occasion of the fiftieth anniversary of the Council of Europe have decided to constitute the European Civil Society.

2. The European Civil Society embraces the work of the Council of Europe, but builds also on the achievements of the European Union and other European organisations to secure an integrated European space of political and economic freedoms and security.

3. In particular the European Civil Society commits itself to a European political, economic and social model, based on a set of common rules:
   in the political domain for
    i) democracy,
    ii) individual human rights,
    iii) collective rights of national minorities,
    iv) inter-state behaviour, and
   in the economic and social domain for
    v) open markets,
    vi) macroeconomic stability,
    vii) a social model,
    vii) sound corporate governance.

4. We welcome the work of the Council of Europe to strengthen the monitoring of democracy in its Member States. To reinforce this work, we invite the Council of Europe to adopt a working definition of democratic standards. We invite the Secretary General of the Council of Europe to publish on his responsibility an annual report on European democracy.

5. We salute the work of the European Court for Human Rights in enforcement of the European Convention for the Protection of Human Rights and Fundamental Freedoms, and underline our commitment to its noble mission.

6. We welcome the entry into force of the Framework Convention of the Council of Europe for the Protection of National Minorities. We welcome the work of the OSCE's High Commissioner for National Minorities, and invite the OSCE to facilitate the closest cooperation of the High Commissioner with the Council of Europe. We invite the Secretary General of the Council of Europe to publish on his own responsibility an annual report on the respect in Member States for the Framework Convention.

7. We reaffirm our commitment to the basic principles governing the behaviour of states and governments enshrined in the Helsinki Final Act of the OSCE and other fundamental texts of this organisation. We welcome the decision by NATO to open its Combined Joint Task Forces to non-NATO countries of the European Civil Society, and similarly for WEU actions under its Petersberg tasks. We invite the WEU to explore with Russia and the Ukraine means of intensifying their cooperation.

8. We decide today to embark on a fundamental action to unify the European market, complementing the enlargement of the European Union. For a first stage we decide to create an All-European Free Trade Area, unifying the European Union and all other economies of our Member States, pledging to eliminate all tariffs between us by 2010. For a second stage we envisage expansion of the single market of the European Union in the manner of the existing European Economic Area, to be opened progressively to all our Member States, in order to create an All-European Economic Area. This second stage may for advanced economies run concurrently with the first stage, and should be completed by 2020.

9. We all express our commitment to the same objectives of macroeconomic stability, central bank independence and sound public finance, as reflected in the priorities of the European Central Bank for its management of the euro and in the Stability and Growth Pact for budgetary policy of the European Union. We invite the European Union to open the European Monetary System, in its new form since introduction of the euro, to all our currencies, with appropriate institutional arrangements for non-EU Member States.

10. We all express our commitment to a European social model, aimed at reconciling high employment with social solidarity and justice. We note with interest developments in the European Union to revise and complement its Social Charter in this sense, and invite the Council of Europe to prepare a reform of its Social Charter with the same objectives.

11. We welcome the Guidelines for Sound Business Standards and Corporate Practices adopted by the European Bank for Reconstruction and Development, and invite the Bank's Board of Governors to give this text official status, thus providing leadership for private financial institutions to require these standards of the business community in its countries of operation.

12. We wish to further broaden and deepen the integration between our economies and societies. To this end:

*i) we welcome the decision of the European Investment Bank of 1999
to open fully its operations in the whole of our space in support of Trans-
European Networks for transport and communications infrastructures;*

*ii)we welcome the decision of the European Union of .. ... 1999 to
reshape the priorities of the Tacis programme in favour of long-run
educational activities, in particular including support of:*

*- the opening of a third campus of the College of Europe in St.
Petersburg, adding to those at Bruges and Warsaw; and of a network of
multilingual European Schools progressively in the main cities of central
and eastern Europe, drawing on the model established already at the
locations of European Union institutions;*

*- the creation of a Foundation of the European Civil Society, which shall
grant scholarships for university studies for students of central and eastern
Europe to study in western Europe and vice-versa.*

*13. The European Civil Society shall be led by ourselves, meeting
normally once each two years, and by our foreign ministers on other
occasions as appropriate. Our presidency shall be chosen by agreement
between us, and shall rotate annually. We delegate work requiring more
intense activity to an Executive Council on which there shall be
representatives of France, Germany, Italy, Poland, Russia, Spain, Turkey,
Ukraine, the United Kingdom and the European Union (who shall also
represent other EU member states) and a constituency member
(representing other member states). The Executive Council shall meet at
Head of State or Government level and in the formations of foreign
ministers and ministers of economy and finance.*

*14. The sets of rules listed in article 3 form an integrated whole. In the
event of serious and persistent breach of these rules by the political
authorities of a Member States, the European Civil Society, meeting in
plenary session of its foreign ministers, may, after a period of dialogue,
decide by ninety percent majority of the Member States and of the
populations they represent (excluding the Member State in question) to
withdraw privileges or participation in other domains, or to suspend
membership. Such sanctions shall be proportional to the breach of rules.*

*15. We note that the end to Europe's post-war divisions has made the
formerly valuable work of the UN's Economic Commission for Europe
superfluous, and suggest to the UN Secretary-General closure of this
agency.*

*16. We note that our initiative today taken largely satisfies the search for
a Charter to represent a "European Security model for the 21st Century",*

upon which the OSCE has been working for some years.

   17. The European Civil Society shall become operational on 1st January 2000. We are pleased to accept the kind offer of France to locate its head-quarters in Strasbourg. Its emblem shall be the flag already identically used by the Council of Europe and the European Union.

Note: The above is not an official text, but part of the present book.

Annexes

A: Membership of European organisations

	C. of Eu.	EU	WEU	NATO	OSCE
EU					
1. Belgium	yes	yes	yes	yes	yes
2. France	yes	yes	yes	yes	yes
3. Germany	yes	yes	yes	yes	yes
4. Italy	yes	yes	yes	yes	yes
5. Luxembourg	yes	yes	yes	yes	yes
6. Netherlands	yes	yes	yes	yes	yes
7. United Kingd.	yes	yes	yes	yes	yes
8. Greece	yes	yes	yes	yes	yes
9. Portugal	yes	yes	yes	yes	yes
10.Spain	yes	yes	yes	yes	yes
11.Denmark	yes	yes	-	yes	yes
12.Austria	yes	yes	-	-	yes
13.Finand	yes	yes	-	-	yes
14.Ireland	yes	yes	-	-	yes
15.Sweden	yes	yes	-	-	yes
Other W.Europe					
16.Iceland	yes	EEA	-	yes	yes
17.Norway	yes	EEA	-	yes	yes
18.Switzerland	yes	EFTA	-	-	yes
19.Andorra	yes	-	-	-	yes
20.Liechtenstein	yes	EEA	-	-	yes
21.Holy See	observ.	-	-	-	yes
22.Monaco	-	-	-	-	yes
23.San Marino	yes	-	-	-	yes
EU applicants					
24.Czech Republic	yes	proposed	-	invited	yes
25.Hungary	yes	proposed	-	invited	yes
26.Poland	yes	proposed	-	invited	yes
27.Slovakia	yes	appl.	-	appl.	yes
28.Slovenia	yes	proposed	-	appl.	yes
29.Bulgaria	yes	appl.	-	appl.	yes
30.Romania	yes	appl.	-	appl.	yes

31.Estonia	yes	proposed	-	appl.	yes
32.Latvia	yes	appl.	-	appl.	yes
33.Lithuania	yes	appl.	-	appl.	yes
34.Turkey	yes	appl.	-	yes	yes
35.Cyprus	yes	appl.	-	-	yes
36.Malta	yes	appl.	suspended	-	yes
Other Balkans					
37.Croatia	yes	-	-	-	yes
38.Macedonia	yes	-	-	appl.	yes
39.Serbia (FYR)	(3)	-	-	-	suspended
40.Bosnia	guest	-	-	-	yes
41.Albania	yes	-	-	appl.	yes
CIS Europe					
42.Russia	yes	-	-	-	yes
43.Ukraine	yes	-	-	-	yes
44.Belarus	(4)	-	-	-	yes
45.Moldova	yes	-	-	-	yes
46.Armenia	guest	-	-	-	yes
47.Georgia	guest	-	-	-	yes
48.Azerbaijan	guest	-	-	-	yes
CIS Central Asia					
49.Kazakhstan	-	-	-	-	yes
50.Kyrgyzstan	-	-	-	-	yes
51.Tajikistan	-	-	-	-	yes
52.Turkmenistan	-	-	-	-	yes
53. Uzbekistan	-	-	-	-	yes
Honorary Europe					
54. Canada	observ.	-	-	yes	yes
55. United States	observ.	-	-	yes	yes

Notes:
1. EU "proposed" refers to the Commission's proposals to the Council for the opening of accession negotiations in the White Paper *"Agenda 2000"* July 1997.
2. NATO: "invited" refers to the invitations to begin accession negotiatioins extended at the Madrid summit of July 1997.
3. The Council of Europe has determined that Yugoslavia has ceased to exist and that Serbia is not recognised as its successor state. Serbia has not applied for membership.
4. Belarus is a candidate for membership of the Council of Europe, but its guest status in the parliamentary assembly has been withdrawn.

B: Demographic and economic indicators of Europe

	Popn. millns.	Life expect- ancy at birth	Adult literacy rate,%	GNP pc p.p.p.	GNP $ billn.
EU	**370.4**				
1. Belgium	10.1	77	99	20 270	227
2. France	57.8	79	99	19 670	1 330
3. Germany	81.3	76	99	19 480	2 050
4. Italy	57.1	78	99	18 460	1 024
5. Luxembourg	0.4	76	99	35 860	16
6. Netherlands	15.3	77	99	18 750	340
7. United Kingdom	57.5	77	99	17 970	1 017
8. Greece	10.3	78	97	10 930	78
9. Portugal	9.9	75	90	11 970	87
10. Spain	39.1	78	97	13 740	482
11. Denmark	5.2	75	99	19 880	146
12. Austria	8.0	77	99	19 560	197
13. Finland	5.1	76	99	16 150	98
14. Ireland	3.6	76	99	13 550	52
15. Sweden	8.7	78	99	17 140	196
Other W.Europe	**12.0**				
16. Iceland	0.3	79	99	19 210	6
17. Norway	4.3	78	99	20 210	110
18. Switzerland	7.0	78	99	25 150	260
19. Andorra	0.06				
20. Holy See	0.001				
21. Liechtenstein	0.03				
22. Monaco	0.03				
23. San Marino	0.02				
EU applicants	**167.0**				
24. Czech Republic	10.3	73	99	8 900	36
25. Hungary	10.3	70	99	6 080	41
26. Poland	38.5	72	99	5 480	96
27. Slovakia	5.3	72	99	6 389	12
28. Slovenia	2.0	74	96	6 230	14
29. Bulgaria	8.4	71	93	4 380	10
30. Romania	22.7	70	97	4 090	30
31. Estonia	1.5	70	99	4 510	5
32. Latvia	2.5	68	99	3 220	6
33. Lithuania	3.7	69	98	3 290	5
34. Turkey	60.8	67	82	14 710	131
35. Cyprus	0.7	77	94	14 800	7
36. Malta	0.3	76	86	13 009	5

Other Balkans	24.6				
37. Croatia	4.8	73	97	3 960	14
38. Macedonia	2.1	73	94	3 965	2
39. Serbia (FYR)	10.5				
40. Bosnia	4.0			814	3
41. Albania	3.2	73	85	2 788	2
CIS Europe	232.5				
42. Russia	148.3	64	99	4 610	376
43. Ukraine	51.9	68	99	2 620	91
44. Belarus	10.4	69	98	4 320	20
45. Moldova	4.3	68	99	3 210	4
46. Armenia	3.7	71	99	2 160	3
47. Georgia	5.4	73	95	1 160	2
48. Azerbaijan	7.5	69	96	1 510	4
CIS Central Asia	53.2				
49. Kazakhstan	17.0	68	98	3 284	20
50. Kyrgyzstan	4.4	68	97	1 930	2
51. Tajikistan	5.7	67	97	1 117	1
52. Turkmenistan	3.9	65	98	3 469	2
53. Uzbekistan	22.2	68	97	2 438	8
Honorary Europe	292.9				
54. Canada	25.0	79	99	21 459	542
55. United States	267.9	76	99	26 397	6 648

Sources: World Bank [1996]; EBRD [1997].

C: National minorities in central and eastern Europe

	Minority	Number	% of Nation's Population
EU Applicants			
Czech Republic (1991)	**Moravian**	1 356 000	**13.2%**
	Slovak	308 000	3.0%
Hungary (1990)	(Gipsies)		(under 1%)
Poland (1991)	(German, Ukrainian, Belarus)		(under 1%)
Slovakia (1991)	**Hungarian**	567 000	**10.8%**
	Gipsy	81 000	1.5%
	Czech	59 000	1.1%
Slovenia (1991)	Croat	54 000	2.7%
	Serb	47 000	2.4%
	Muslim	27 000	1.4%
Bulgaria (1992)	**Turk**	800 000	**9.4%**
	Gipsy	313 000	3.7%
Romania (1992)	**Hungarian**	1 620 000	**7.1%**
	Gipsy	410 000	1.8%
	(German)		(under 1%)
Estonia (1989)	**Russian**	475 000	**30.3%**
	Ukrainian	48 000	3.1%
	Belarus	28 000	1.8%
	Finnish	17 000	1.1%
Latvia (1989)	**Russian**	906 000	**34.0%**
	Belarussian	120 000	4.5%
	Ukrainian	92 000	3.5%
	Polish	60 000	2.3%
	Lithuanian	35 000	1.3%
Lithuania (1989)	**Russian**	344 000	**9.4%**
	Polish	258 000	**7.0%**
	Belarussian	63 000	1.7%
	Ukrainian	45 000	1.2%

Other Balkans

Croatia (1991)	**Serb**	582 000	**12.2%**
	Yugoslav (unspecified)	106 000	2.2%
	Muslim	43 000	0.9%
Macedonia (1994)	**Albanian**	479 000	**23.1%**
	Turk	82 000	3.9%
	Gipsy	47 000	2.3%
	Muslim	23 000	1.2%
	Serb	40 000	1.9%
Serbia-Montenegro (1991)	**Albanian**	1 687 000	**17.2%**
	Hungarian	345 000	3.5%
	Yugoslav (unspecified)	318 000	3.2%
	Muslim	237 000	2.4%
	Croat	140 000	1.4%
Bosnia-Hertzgovena (1991)	**Muslim**	1 906 000	**43.7%**
	Serb	1 369 000	**31.4%**
	Croat	756 000	**17.3%**
	Yugoslav (unspecified)	240 000	**5.0%**
Albania (1991)	Greek	59 000	1.8%
	Gipsy	60 000	1.8%

CIS Europe

Russia (1989)	Tatar	5 543 000	3.8%
	Ukrainian	4 363 000	3.0%
	Chuvash	1 774 000	1.2%
	Baskir	1 345 000	0.9%
	Belarussian	1 206 000	0.8%
	Mordvin	1 073 000	0.7%
	Chechen	899 000	0.6%
	German	842 000	0.6%
	Udmurt	715 000	0.5%
	(160 other minorities)		
Ukraine (1989)	**Russian**	11 356 000	**22.1%**
	Jewish	487 000	0.9%
	Belarussian	440 000	0.7%
Belarus (1989)	**Russian**	1 342 000	**13.3%**
	Polish	418 000	4.1%
	Ukrainian	291 000	2.9%
	Jewish	112 000	1.1%
Moldova (1989)	**Ukrainian**	600 000	**13.8%**
	Russian	562 000	**12.9%**
	Gagauzian	153 000	3.5%

	Bulgarian	88 000	2.0%
	Jewish	66 000	1.5%
Armenia (1989)	Azerbaijan	85 000	2.6%
	Kurd	56 000	1.7%
	Russian	28 000	0.8%
Georgia (1989)	**Armenian**	437 000	**8.1%**
	Russian	341 000	**6.3%**
	Azerbaijan	308 000	**5.7%**
	Ossetian	164 000	3.0%
	Greek	100 000	1.9%
	Abkhaz	96 000	1.8%
Azerbaijan (1989)	**Russian**	392 000	**5.6%**
	Armenian	391 000	**5.6%**
	Lezghin	171 000	2.4%

Source: G. Brunner [1996].

Note: Highlighted minorities are those representing over 5% of the state's population.

D: Wars and War-Related Deaths in Europe, 1990-1995

Identification and location of conflict	civilian	Number of deaths military	total
Albania			
1914-18 WW I	10 000	20 000	30 000
Austria			
1914-18 WW I	300 000	2 300 000	2 600 000
1934 Social. v. Fasc.	1 000	1 000	2 000
1939-45 WW II	125 000	280 000	405 000
Belgium			
1914-18 WW I	30 000	88 000	118 000
1940 WW II	90 000	110 000	200 000
Bulgaria			
1915-18 WW I	275 000	28 000	303 000
1841-44 WW II	14 000	20 000	34 000
Czechoslovakia			
1939-45 WW II	250 000	30 000	280 000
Finland			
1918 Comm. v. Govt.	..	..	20 000
1939-40 v. USSR	..	90 000	90 000
1941-44 WW II	15 000	45 000	60 000
France			
1914-18 WW II	40 000	1 630 000	1 670 000
1939-45 WW II	450 000	200 000	650 000
Germany			
1914-18 WW I	760 000	2 400 000	3 160 000
1934 Soc. v. Fasc.	1 000	..	1 000
1939-45 WW II	1 471 000	4 750 000	6 221 000
Greece			
1917-18 WW I	132 000	5 000	137 000
1940-41 WW II	54 000	10 000	64 000
1945-49 civil war	..	..	160 000
Hungary			
1919-20 Anti-comm. v. Govt.	..	..	4 000
1919 v. Czechs and Roman.	..	11 000	11 000
1941-45 WW II	450 000	400 000	850 000
1956 USSR intervt.	10 000	10 000	20 000

Italy
1915-18 WW I	..	950 000	950 000
1940-45 WW II	70 000	150 000	220 000

Lithuania
1920 v. Lithuania	..	10 000	1 000
1941 WW II v. Germany	200 000	..	200 000
1944 WW II v. USSR	2 000	..	2 000

Netherlands
1940-45 WW II	200 000	6 000	206 000

Norway
1940 WW II	7 000	2 000	9 000

Poland
1914-18 WW I	500 000	..	500 000
1919-20 v USSR	..	100 000	100 000
1939-45 WW II	6 000 000	600 000	6 600 000

Portugal
1916-18 WW II	..	13 000	13 000

Romania
1907 govt. v. peasants	..	..	2 000
1916-17 WW I	275 000	375 000	650 000
1941-45 WW II	300 000	340 000	640 000
1989 govt. v. demonst.	1 000	..	1 000

Spain
1934-36 govt. v. miners	3 000	..	3 000
1936-39 civil war	600 000	600 000	1 000 000

Turkey
1909-10 massac.(Armenia)	6 000	..	6 000
1911-12 v. Italy	..	20 000	20 000
1912-13 Balkan war	..	82 000	82 000
1914-18 WW I	1 000 000	450 000	1 450 000
1915-16 deport. (Armenians)	1 000 000	..	1 000 000
1919-20 v. France	..	..	40 000
1919-22 v. Greece	50 000	50 000	100 000
1977-80 terrorism, coup	..	..	5 000
1984-95 Kurds	4 000	14 000	18 000

United Kingdom
1914-18 WW I	31 000	1 000 000	1 031 000
1939-45 WW II	100 000	350 000	450 000

246   *Annexes*

USSR, former
1904-05 v. Japan	..	130 000	130 000
1905-06 peasant uprising	1 000	..	1 000
1905 pogroms v. Jews	2 000	..	2 000
1914-17 WW I	3 0 00 000	2 950 000	5 950 000
1916 Kyrgyz. mass.	..	..	9 000
1917 revolution	1 000	1 000	2 000
1918-20 civil war	500 000	300 000	800 000
1939 v. Japan	..	13 000	13 000
1941-45 WW II	8 500 000	8 500 000	17 000 000
1969 v. China	..	1 000	1 000
1989-95 Armen.v. Azerb.	..	..	20 000
1992-95 Georg./Abkhaz.	..	..	3 000
1992-95 Georg./Ossetia	..	..	3 000
1992 Moldova/Transdniest.	..	..	1 000
1992-95 Tajikist., civil war	..	..	50 000
1994-95 Checnen secession	24 000	6 000	30 000

Yugoslavia, former
1903 Macedonia v. Turks	2 000	2 000	4 000
1913 Balkan war v. Bulgaria	..	61 000	61 000
1914-18 WW I	650 000	128 000	778 000
1941-45 WW II	1 000 000	400 000	1 400 000
1991-92 Croatia, civil war	..	..	25 000
1992-95 Bosnia, civil war	..	..	263 000

Europe (area wide)
1914-18 WW I	5 982 0 00	401 000	6 383 000
1939-45 WW II	8 723 000	985 000	9 708 000

Europe total	**43 212 000**	**31 409 000**	**75 226 000**
World total	**62 194 000**	**43 920 000**	**109 745 000**

Source: Sivard [1996]

References

Alogoskoufis G., R. Portes and H. Rey [1997], *"The Emergence of the Euro as an International Currency"*, CEPR Discussion Papers No 1741.

Ambrus-Lakatos L. and M. Schaffer eds. [1997], *"Fiscal Policy in the Transition"*, CEPR and Institute for East-West Studies.

Anderson J. [1997], *"The Limits of Sino-Russian Strategic Partnership"*, Adelphi Papers, IISS, London.

Anderson K., B. Dimaranan, T. Hertel and W. Martin [1997], *"Economic Growth and Policy Reform in the APEC Region: Trade and Welfare Implications by 2005"*, CEPR Working Paper Series No 1605, May.

Artis M. and B. Winkler [1997], *"The Stability Pact: Safeguarding the Credibility of the European Central Bank"*, CEPR Discussion Paper Series, N0 1688, August.

Artis M. and W. Zhang [1997], *"On Identifying the Core of the EMU: an Exploration of Some Empirical Criteria"*, CEPR Discussion Paper Series No 1689, August.

Augstein R. [1987], *"Historikerstreit: die Dokumention der Kontroverse um die Einzigartigkeit der Judenvernichtung"*, Piper Verlag.

Baldwin R. [1994], *"Towards an Integrated Europe"*, CEPR, London.

Baldwin R. [1997], *"The Causes of Regionalism"*, CEPR Discussion Paper Series No 1599, March.

Baldwin R., J. Francois and R. Portes [1997], *"Costs and Benefits of Eastern Enlargement"*, Economic Policy, Blackwell, April.

Baranovsky V. ed. [1997], *"Russia and Europe - The Emerging Security Agenda"*, SIPRI, Oxford University Press.

Bayoumi T. And B. Eichengreen [1996], *"Operationalizing the Theory of Optimal Currency Areas"*, CEPR.

Beddard R. [1993], *"Human Rights in Europe"*, Gortius.

Bentolila S. and J. Jimeno [1995], *"Regional Unemployment Persistance, Spain 1976-94"*, CEPR Discussion Paper No 1259, October.

Bloed A. et al, eds. [1993], *"Monitoring Human Rights"*, Martinus Nijhoff Publishers.

Borko Y. [1997], *"Economic transformation in Russia and political partnership with Europe"*, in Baranovsky [1997].

Breton A. [1995], *" Nationalism and Rationality"*, Cambridge.

Brok E. [1997], *"Notes on the results of the Amsterdam Treaty"*, mimeo.

Brunner G. [1996], *"Nationality Problems and Minority Conflicts in Eastern Europe"*, Bertelsmann Foundation Publishers.

Bryce J. [1996], *"Using ISDN"*, Que Corporation, Indianapolis.

Bugajski J. [1995], *"Nations in Turmoil - Conflict and Cooperation in Eastern Europe"*, Westview Press.

Bullock A., O. Stallybrass and S. Trombley, eds. [1997], *"The Fontana Dictionary of Modern Thought"*, Fontana Press.

Chand S. and A. Jaeger [1996], *"Ageing Populations and Public Pension Schemes"*, Occasional Paper no 146, International Monetary Fund.

Cohen D. [1997], *"How will the Euro Behave?"*, CEPR Discussion Paper Series No 1673, July.

Cohen J and A. Arato [1995], *"Civil Society and Political Theory"*, MIT Press.

Coker C. [1992], "Post-modernity and the end of the Cold War: has war been disinvented?", *Review of International Studies*.

Commission of the EU [1996], *"Economic Evaluation of the Internal Market"*, European Economy No 4.

Commission of the EU [1997], *"Agenda 2000: For a Stronger and Wider European Union"*, Brussels, July. *(http/europa.eu.int/comm/dgia/ agenda 2000).*

Commission of the EU [1997a], *"Eurobarometer - Public Opinion in the European Union"*, Report No 46, May.

Commission of the EU [1997b], *"Central and Eastern Eurobarometer"*, Report No 7, March.

Commission of the EU [1997c], "1977 Broad Economic Guidelines", *European Economy,* No 64.

Commission of the EU [1997d], *"Guidelines for Member.States Employment Policies"*, Communication to the Council.

Cooper R. [1996], *"The Post-Modern State and the World Order"*, Demos, London.

Council of Europe [1995], *"European Court of Human Rights: Survey of thirty-five years of activity"*, Registry of the Court, Carl Heymans Verlag.

Council of Europe [1995a], *"Framework Convention for the Protection of National Minorities"*, European Treaty Series No 157, Strasbourg.

Council of Europe [1996], *"Survey of Activities of the European Court of Human Rights"*, Strasbourg.

Council of Europe [1997], *"Activities of the Council of Europe - 1996 Report"*, Strasbourg.

Council of Europe [1997a], *"Report on the Obligations and Commitments of the Czech republic as a Member State" (idem Lithuania)*, Parliamentary Assembly, documents 7896, 7898, September.

Council of Europe [1997b], *"Second Summit of the Council of Europe"*, Press Release, 11 October, Strasbourg.

Dahl R. [1989], *"Democracy and its Critics"*, Yale University Press.

Davidson I. [1997], *"Jobs and the Rhineland Model"*, Federal Trust Study Report, Sweet & Maxwell, London.

Davies N. [1997], *"Europe - a History"*, Oxford.

Dehousse R. ed. [1997], *"Europe - The Impossible Status Quo"*, Macmillan.

De Long J. And B. Eichengreen [1993], *"The Marshall Plan: History's Most Successful Structural Adjustment Program"*, in Dornbusch et al., eds. [1993].

Delors J. [1997], *"Foreword"*, contribution to Dehousse ed. [1997].

Denman R. [1996], *"Missed Chances - Britain and Europe in the Twentieth Century"*, Cassel.

Dewatripont M. [1995], *"Flexible Integration: Towards a More Effective and Democratic Europe"*, CEPR, London.

Dornbusch R., W. Nolling and R. Layard eds. [1993], *" Postwar Economic Reconstruction and Lessons for the East Today"*, MIT Press.

Duff A. [1997], *"Reforming the European Union"*, Federal Trust and Sweet & Maxwell.

Duff A. [1998], *"The Treaty of Amsterdam: Text and Commentary"*, Federal Trust and Sweet & Maxwell.

Dyker D. [1997], *"International Economic Integration for Central Asia"*, Royal Institute of International Affairs, FSS Briefing No 11,.January.

Eichengreen B. and F. Ghironi [1997], *"How Will Transatlantic Policy Interactions Change with the Advent of the Euro?"*, CEPR Discussion Paper Series No 1643, May.

Emerson M. [1988], *"What Model for Europe?"*, MIT Press.

Emerson M., with M. Aujean, M. Catinat, P. Goybet and A. Jacquemin [1988], *"The Economics of 1992"*, Oxford University Press.

Emerson M., with D. Gros, A. Italianer, J. Pisani-Ferry and H. Reichenbach [1990], *"One Market, One Money"*, Oxford University Press.

European Bank for Reconstruction and Development (EBRD)[1997], *"Transition Report 1997"*, London.

European Bank for Reconstruction and Development (EBRD) [1997a], *"Sound Business Standards and Corporate Practices - A Set of Guidelines"*, September, London.

European Monetary Institute (EMI) [1997], *"Annual Report 1996"*, Frankfurt.

European Monetary Institute (EMI) [1997a], *"The Single Monetary Policy in Stage Three: General Documentation on ECSB Monetary policy, Instruments and Procedures"*, Frankfurt.

European Policy Centre (EPC) [1997], *"Making Sense of the Amsterdam Treaty"*, Brussels.

Fernandez R. [1997], *"Returns to Regionalism: an Evaluation of Non-Traditional Gains from RTAS"*, CEPR Discussion Paper Series No 1634, April.

Francois J., B. Macdonald and N. Nordstrom [1996], *"A User's Guide to Urugual Round Assessments"*, CEPR Discussion Paper Series No 1410, June.

Frye T. [1996], *"The Invisible Hand and the Grabbing Hand"*, Working Paper Series 5836, NBER, Cambridge, MA.

Galkin A. [1996], *"Russia's National Interests and the Commonwealth of Independent States"*, Gorbachev Foundation, Moscow.

Gellner E. [1994], *"Conditions of Liberty - Civil Society and its Rivals"*, Hamish Hamilton.

Getty J. [1993], *"The Politics of Stalinism"*, in Nove ed. [1993].

Giddens A. [1993], *"Sociology"*, Polity Press.

Giersch H. et al [1993], *"Openness, Wage Restraint and Macroeconomic Stability: West Germany's road to prosperity 1948-1959"*, in Dornbusch et al., ed. [1993].

Goldhagen D. [1996], *"Hitler's Willing Executioners - Ordinary Germans and the Holocaust"*, Abacus.

Gros D. and A. Steinherr [1995], *"Winds of Change: Economic Transition in Central and Eastern Europe"*, Longman.

Gros D. and N. Thygesen [1992], *"European Monetary Integration - from the European Monetary System to European Monetary Union"*, Longman.

Hall J. ed. [1995], *"Civil Society - Theory, History , Comparison"*, Polity Press.

Halpern L. and C. Wypolsz [1997], "Equilibrium Exchange Rates in Transition Economies", *IMF Staff Papers*, forthcoming.

Harada C. [1997], *"Russia and North-East Asia"*, Adelphi papers No 310, International Institute for Strategic Studies.

Held D. [1995], *"Democracy and the Global Order"*, Polity Press.

Howen N. [1996], *"From Nurenburg to the Balkans: The International War Crimes Tribunal for the Former Yugoslavia"*, in Bloed et al. [1993].

International Institute for Strategic Studies - IISS [1997], *"Annual Report"*, Oxford.

International Institute for Strategic Studies - IISS [1997a], "Bosnia after SFOR", *Survival*, Winter 1997-98, Oxford.

Jacobs F. and R. White [1996], *"The European Convention on Human Rights"*, Clarendon Press.

Kaldor M. and I. Vejvoda [1996], *"Democratisation in Central and Eastern Europe"*, mimeo., Sussex European Institute.

Kant I. [1784], *"Perpetual Peace and Other Essays"*, NYC Hackett.

Kaufman D. [1996], *"The Missing pillar of a Growth Strategy for the Ukraine: Institutional and Policy Reforms for Private Sector Development"*, Harvard Institute for International Development, mimeo.

Kay J. [1993], *"The Foundations of Corporate Success"*, Oxford.

Keane J. [1996], *"Reflections on Violence"*, Virago Press.

Klemperer V. [1995], *"Tagesbuecher, 1933-41, 1942-45"*, Aufbau Verlag.

Kluger R. [1992], *" Weiter leben - Eine Jugend"*, Wallstein Verlag.

Kramer H. [1996], "The Cyprus Problem and European Security", *Survival*, Autumn.

Layard R. and J. Parker [1996], *"The Coming Russian Boom: A Guide to New Markets and Politics"*, Free Press.

Leonard M. [1997], *"Politics without Frontiers"*, Demos, London.

Ludlow P. [1997], *"Preparing Europe for the 21st Century: the Amsterdam Council and Beyond"*, Centre for European Policy Studies, 3rd IAC Annual Report, Brussels.

Macdougall Sir D. [1977], *"Report of the Study Group on The Role of Public Finance in European Integration"*, Economic and Financial Series, Commission of the EC, Brussels.

Mayhew A. [1998], *"Recreating Europe: the European Union's Relations with Central and Eastern Europe"*, Cambridge University Press (forthcoming).

McGarry, J. and B. O'Leary [1995], *"Explaining Northern Ireland"*, Blackwell.

McGrew A. [1997], *"The Transformation of Democracy? Globalization and Territorial Democracy"*, Polity Press.

Meny Y., P. Muller and J.-L. Quermonne [1996], *"Adjusting to Europe - The Impact of the European Union on National Institutions and Policies"*, Routledge.

Minority Rights Group (MRG) [1994], *"The North Caucasus: Minorities at a Crossroads"*, MRG.

Minority Rights Group (MRG) (1991), *"Minorities and Autonomy in Western Europe"*, MRG.

Minority Rights Group (MRG) [1997], *"Central Asia: conflict of stability and development ?"*, MRG.

Minority Rights Group (MRG) [1996], *"Protection of Minority Rights in Europe: policy recommendations based on case studies of Eastern and Central Europe and the Former Soviet Union"*, paper commissioned and published by the Advisory Committee on Human Rights and Foreign Policy of the Netherlands.

Molle W. [1990], *"The Economics of European Integration"*, Dartmouth.

Mundell R. [1961], "A Theory of Optimal Currency Area", *American Economic Review,* September.

North Atlantic Treaty Organisation (NATO) [1997], *"NATO Review-Summit Edition"*, July-August, Brussels.

Neumann I. [1996], *"Russia and the Idea of Europe"*, Routledge.

North Atlantic Treaty Organisation (NATO) [1995], *"NATO Handbook"*, Brussels.

Nove A. [1993], *"The Stalin Phenomenum"*, Weidenfeld and Nicholson.

Oates W. [1972], *"Fiscal Federalism"*, Brace Hartcourt, New York.

Obstfeld M. and G. Peri [1998], "Regional Nonadjustment and Fiscal Policy", *Economic Policy*, Basil Blackwell, forthcoming.

Olsen M. [1982], *"The Rise and Decline of Nations"*, Yale University Press.

O'Hanlon M. [1997], "Transforming NATO: The Role of European Forces", *Survival*, IISS, Autumn.

O'Neill M. [1996], *"The Politics of European Integration"*, Routledge, London.

Organization for Security and Cooperation in Europe (OSCE) [1996], *"OSCE Handbook"*, second edition, Vienna.

Padoa Schioppa T. et al. [1987], *"Efficiency, Stability and Equity - A Strategy for the Evolution of the Economic System of the European Community"*, Oxford University Press.

Padoa-Schioppa T. [1994], *"The Road to Monetary Union in Europe - The Emperor, the Kings and the Genies"*, Oxford.

Paunio J. [1993], *"A Perspective on Postwar Reconstruction in Finland"*, in Dornbusch et al ed. [1993].

Pisani-Ferry J. [1997], *"Monetary Union with Variable Geometry"*, CEPS Paper no 70, Centre for European Policy Studies, Brussels.

Quah D. [1997],"Increasingly weightless economies", *Bank of England Quarterly Bulletin*, February 37:1.

Robinson P. [1996], *"The Labour Market in the United Kingdom"*, Labour Market Studies No 1, Commission of the EU, DGV, Brussels.

Rosamond B. [1995], "Mapping the European Condition: The theory of integration and the integration of theory", *European Journal of International Relations*, vol 1, no 3, September.

Rummel R. [1997], *"Power Kills - Democracy as a Method of Non-Violence"*, Transaction Publishers.

Sachs J. and A. Warner [1996], *"Achieving Rapid Growth in the Transition Economies of Central Europe"*, Development Discussion Paper No 544, Harvard Institute for International Development, Cambridge.

Saint-Paul G. [1993], *"Economic Reconstruction in France: 1945-1951"*, in Dornbusch et al ed. [1993].

Sapir A. [1997], *"Domino Effects in West European Trade, 1960-92"*, CEPR Discussion Paper Series No 1576, February.

Schmitter P. [1996], *"Some Alternative Futures for the European Polity and their Implications for European Public Policy"*, in Meny et al.[1996]

Schulte P. [1996], *"A Framework for Thinking about Political Violence in the European Union up to 2025"*, Royal College of Defence Studies, mimeo.

Sherr J. [1997], "Russia-Ukraine Rapprochement - The Black Sea Fleet Accords", *Survival*, Autumn.

Sivard R. [1996], *"World Military and Social Expenditures, 1996"*, World Priorities Inc., Washington.

Smith G. [1966], *"The Nationalities Question in the Post-Soviet States"*, 2nd edition, Longman, London.

Smith A. [1991], *"National Identity"*, Penguin.

State Department (US) [1997], *"Country Reports on Human Rights Practices for 1996"*, Report submitted to the US Congress, US Government Printing Office *(www.state.gov/www/global/human rights/1996.)*

Times, The [1978], *"Atlas of World History"*, Times Books.

Times, The [1994], *"Atlas of European History"*, Times Books.

Transparency International [1996, 97], *"Annual Report, Sharpening the Responses against Global Corruption"*, Berlin.

Volkogonov D. [1991], *"Stalin"*, Weidenfeld and Nicholson.

Tolstoy L. [1982], *"War and Peace"*, Penguin Books.

Waltz K. [1959], *"Man, State and War"*, Columbia University Press.

Western European Union (WEU) [1997], *"WEU's Operational Role"*, Report to the Assembly of the WEU, Document 1567, Paris.

Wohlfeld M. [1997], *"The Effects of Enlargement on Bilateral Relations in Central and Eastern Europe,"* Chaillot Papers No 26, Institute for Strategic Studies, Paris.

Wolf H. [1993], *"The Lucky Miracle: Germany 1945-1951"*, in Dornbusch et al., ed. [1993].

World Bank [1996], *"World Development Report 1996"*, Oxford University Press.

Index